Walking t

Walking the Edge

A spirited trek the length of the English coastline

Rev'd Graham F Jones

GODALMING, SURREY

First published in 2001 by Highland Books, Two High Pines, Knoll Road, Godalming, Surrey GU7 2EP. Reprinted 2003.

ISBN: 1-897913-62-1

Printed in Finland by WS Bookwell

CONTENTS

DEDICATION

To my fellow travellers
Heather and Sallyanne

Charities supported by *Walk 2000*

THE BARNABAS FUND
BARNADO'S
CARE FOR LIFE Crisis Pregancy Clinics
CHILDRENS SOCIETY
CARE FOR THE FAMILY
THE COMPASSIONATE FRIENDS SIBBS
CYSTIC FIBROSIS RESEARCH TRUST
GLOBAL CARE Homes for Hope
HELEN HOUSE
JAMES HOPKINS TRUST
PHOENIX LODGE
TEAR FUND
BISHOP SIMEON and LIVING SOUTH AFRICA MEMORIAL TRUST
CHELTENHAM COMMUNITY PROJECTS for young and homeless

Acknowledgements

I want to record my huge gratitude to all those who believed in me throughout this mad-cap venture and those who with countless gifts of generosity have seen me through to the end of both Walk and Book. Many are those who faithfully loved, prayed and cared as I travelled the coast, amongst whom I specially wish to convey my appreciation to Audrey Milner-Schofield, Brian Field, and Christine Belsey, along with the wonderful people I met in churches like those at Hartland, Thanet and Skegness. The enthusiasm of Geoff Crago in Gloucester Diocese can only be bettered by the astonishing practical commitment of Tim Watson and the congregations at Cheltenham Parish Church, of which I am honoured to be a member. A big shove came through TEARFUND and Pauline Grainger at the local Childrens Society Office. Sallyanne my daughter and WALK 2000 Administrator held things together while I was away; and Heather my wife trekked in her Polo to find and support me on three truly memorable occasions. Inspiration for the book first came from the community at Lee Abbey and ultimate fulfilment through the valiant efforts of my long-standing friend and journalist, Wallace Boulton. I am also indebted to the patience and flair of my proof-reading colleagues: Christopher Bishop, Sylvia Charlewood and Richard Tweedy. Not least do I mention the gift of a mobile phone from Barclaycard and the eminently successful Mark I and Mark II of nearly-my-closest ally, *Leki* the lightweight walking stick. G.F.J.

Introduction

Two Journeys

I LOVE THE SEA. WE HAVE BEEN LIVING TOGETHER FOR QUITE A while. Whether tranquil or boisterous I have come to admire her changing face: grey, green and moody first thing in the morning, sparkling with vitality at noon and glittering in gold as the sun goes down with the day. For five months, round every headland and into every estuary she has been my companion skirting the coast of England, from Wales all the way to Scotland. Along the Bristol Channel, the English Channel, and all the inshore waters – Thames, Humber, Tyne and Dogger – she has faithfully been on my right hand, always there; and now I have become attached to her presence. I grieve when away and rejoice on return.

Nearing the end of my long walk, on Friday 12th September 1997, I reach the Scottish border and seek, briefly, the atmospherics of Holy Island, 'my final resting place', after 2,035 miles. The sea is coming in and I struggle across from the mainland in the fiercest storm of this entire venture. On Saturday, I am almost numb in heart and foot as I wander around the ancient isle, mostly gazing at the seascapes. Today, it is Sunday. It is time to catch the train home and I am reluctant to leave my partner in clime. Sensing the occasion, she has retreated to a respectful distance. I climb up through Beal to the main road and can no longer see the watery horizon. I stand, really sad to be hitching a lift on tarmac, the main A1 north, to the Berwick train station and then home.

A Range Rover stops and blocks my view. It crowds me and dwarfs me. Almost reluctantly I haul on the heavy, near-side door and clamber up, with boots and bag, on to a vast, stiff, expanse of leather. I perch in silence on the forward edge of the rear seat. In front are the Captain and First Mate of the *Starship Enterprise,* their heads locked to massive, upholstered head-rests. Nothing is said. I feel miserable. I am missing the windy, wild edge of England, disappearing fast behind me. Filled with memories, I am miles away, when a voice brings me back with a jolt. I hear a clipped, classy accent, polite but sarcastic. The voice says, "And how far *have* you walked?" (It is after all only 11.30 in the morning.) I wonder whether to play dead. A suitable pause follows, to gain maximum effect, "Will 2,000 miles do?" I say. Another silence. Then two heads appear, the vehicle narrowly misses the hard shoulder and Tony and Stephanie stare at their hitch-hiking guest. I say, simply, "I have just finished 2,035 miles".

The Chapmans prove to be lovely and generous people and we enjoy each other's company, exploring a little of Berwick. I head for the train and within a few hours am standing on the Cheltenham railway station platform, held in a timeless lock with my daughter. Then plucked from under media microphones, I am propelled into St Matthew's Church, where the people have waited to give me the most thunderous reception of my life.

It had all begun five years before in Lyme Regis. My mother had been sliding into dementia. Her key-worker Daphne from the social services had worked marvels to engage Mum's interest and keep her trust during the cruel onset of Alzheimer's disease. Now we collapsed tearfully into each other's arms after a particularly violent episode. A quick conference and my mother was taken at last 'into care'. We stood talking. "Have you dreams? What would you really like to do if you had the chance?" "Well", I said, "I'd quite like to walk along the coast of Devon and Cornwall". Later with the map of England spread out on the table, Sallyanne said to me,

"Dad, why don't you do the lot?" What a thought! I measured the distance rather diffidently with my milometer. I found it measured two thousand and thirty-five miles. "And that", I murmured, "feels like my contribution to the Millennium". So the die was cast and an adventure born.

The sheer scale, the physicality, the challenge and the crazy scent of danger appealed. I had always loved risk. "Graham!" I could hear my father's imperative voice, "Graham! Will you come away from the edge!" he would shout in exasperation, as I played provocatively with oblivion. My mother used to say to me, "Curiosity killed the cat!" which only sharpened my nose for peril. I have always wanted to know what was behind the door, round the corner, over the fence and beyond the next hill. I never wanted to holiday somewhere I had been before and on the first morning, I was usually first up and off, before breakfast, to explore the environs. Combine that with the lure of the sea and you have a heady mix. Here was a chance to stay with the sea, stick to the edge, and examine every cliff, cave and cove that came my way.

Then I realised that along with the fascinating geomorphology of the coastline there lay, compressed beneath, a slice of the geological time-scale, unequalled in any other part of the world. I would be travelling from the very earliest Pre-Cambrian lava in Cornwall, magma from the earth's centre, all the way through geological history, to the fossil clays of Dorset, the white chalk of the Seven Sisters, the Jurassic limestones beyond Whitby, the coal of the Northeast beaches and, from Cromer to Holderness, the boulder clays of the last Ice Age.

Next it dawned on me that this natural barrier was also a very particular border. I was English and this stubborn edge had been endlessly fought over. It mattered. Returning from the Continent I would marvel at our green fields and immediately ingest marmalade and custard. Later as a clergyman with a family, we lived several years in New Zealand and there I was regarded as just European. I was "*Pakeha*" (paleface) to the Maoris with whom I worked. They drew no dividing lines between the countries of Western Europe. In 1987 the white cliffs of Dover welcomed me back and just asked to be explored. The Walk was to be something tangible to mark and celebrate my Englishness and indeed I felt really Anglicized at last as I completed my journey and entered a Scottish pub. Strangely portentous, this Scottish fellow took me on and soon a bit of a furore developed. And the very next morning, the people of Scotland voted for devolution.

I knew that the Irish missionary, Columba, had arrived in a coracle to civilise the English from the north. I knew that St Augustine had arrived in Kent, with a clerical splash from Italy, and I knew that both were being celebrated across the nation, fourteen hundred years later, this very year. However, and even more heart-warming, I did not find out, until everything was in place, that a vast pilgrimage across the United Kingdom was due to leave the South East on the very same day, 18th May, that I was due to leave Cheltenham, to connect them, as it were, round the edge. So emerged a sense of pilgrimage, and I went to Lee Abbey to be more prepared over a period of several days. I was soon to speak in churches at most weekends along the journey. Forty people at St Matthew's offered daily to pray with me, and nearly forty homes on the route offered to welcome me overnight. It is not surprising that the Walk became a mosaic of meaningful encounters with people and occurrences of remarkable timing.

There was also celebration and joy as cards began to arrive from all over the world. After all, Sallyanne my daughter was 21 a week before I left. A month later I was 60 at my father's home in Lyme Regis. He was 95 three weeks before and Heather and I were in our 30th year of marriage. Most significantly, it dawned on us, seated one day at the kitchen table, that this was truly our family anniversary year. 1997 would mark simultaneously the demise of our first three children, ten, twenty and thirty years before. It was in earnest, then, that we invited sponsorship for children in trouble and were later privileged to distribute cheques, totalling £20,500 all but a fraction from the generosity of friends and family. I had now a twin spur, an invisible contract with my whole six-strong family and a financial contract with innumerable friends, to walk 2,000 miles at £10 per mile.

"Walk 2000" was divided into three sections. The first, from Gloucester down the Severn, took in the South West and the Dorset coast to Southampton. The second stretched round Kent and the creeks of Essex to Cromer. The third spanned the Wash, the Humber and the Northeast coast up to Berwick and the Scottish border. Roughly similar in length, these sections came to represent the three 'thirties' of life, commonly seen as the growing and single years, the partnership and parenting years and, for me, the years in retirement, our future.

There is a wider sense, therefore, in which I invite the reader to travel with me through these three stretches of coastline and also accompany me as I recapitulate the course of my life, as it were from womb to tomb. The walk then becomes a paradigm of life – quite a roller coaster, like the coastal path round parts of Devon. It will be difficult to capture, in the network of words, the immense significance for me, of moving symbolically through my life in the space of five months. Connections were made and the clues are there. My parents and grandparents lived in the first section, and in the second, Heather and I with the family have lived, worked and caravanned. Certainly, it is the very ordinary progress of just one more human being along the cliff tops of England, not really so different from the myriad journeys taken by our forebears 8,000 years ago after the ice retreated, across the land bridge into Britain on the Crete Way, the same path that today still winds its way west over the Seven Sisters to Hengistbury Head and Bournemouth. But more, this book is a journey through life as well as a travelogue round the Edge of England.

Just one additional thought – this book unwraps a mystery: my survival. My ankle turned over umpteen times and often I went sprawling. My personal odyssey through life has been no less incident-free and I expect you have had your moments. Walk with me as we stumble together. Join with me as we get up and go on. Reflect with me on the experiences that mould and make us. My modest claim is that I finished and am still finishing with a lot of help. I refused to take out an insurance policy on my life or property, because life is not like that. I learnt later that my wife did, expecting the worst. It has been said there is no such thing as failure; that we only fail when, knowing we could do something, we do not try.

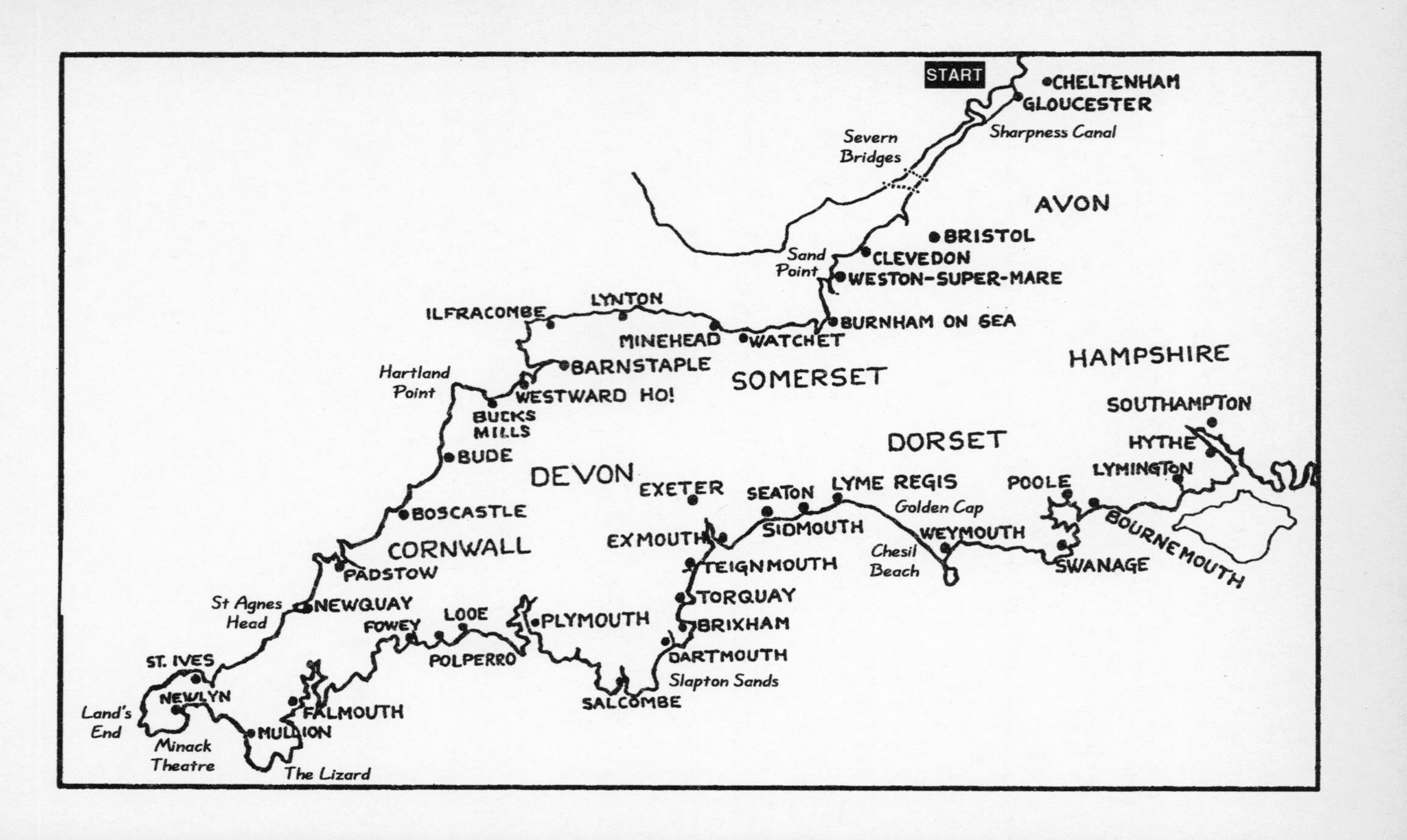
START
CHELTENHAM
GLOUCESTER
Sharpness Canal
Severn Bridges
AVON
BRISTOL
CLEVEDON
Sand Point
WESTON-SUPER-MARE
ILFRACOMBE
LYNTON
BURNHAM ON SEA
MINEHEAD
WATCHET
HAMPSHIRE
BARNSTAPLE
SOMERSET
Hartland Point
WESTWARD HO!
SOUTHAMPTON
BUCKS MILLS
DORSET
HYTHE
BUDE
DEVON
LYMINGTON
EXETER
SEATON
LYME REGIS
POOLE
Golden Cap
BOSCASTLE
SIDMOUTH
WEYMOUTH
BOURNEMOUTH
EXMOUTH
CORNWALL
Chesil Beach
PADSTOW
TEIGNMOUTH
SWANAGE
TORQUAY
St Agnes Head
NEWQUAY
FOWEY
LOOE
PLYMOUTH
BRIXHAM
ST. IVES
POLPERRO
DARTMOUTH
Slapton Sands
NEWLYN
SALCOMBE
Land's End
FALMOUTH
MULLION
Minack Theatre
The Lizard

FIRST LEG

Thirty difficult years
— the long trek begins

Chapter 1

Gloucester to The Severn Bridge

A POSITIVE BEGINNING

IT IS RAINING ON HEMPSTED BRIDGE, GLOUCESTER. I START down the Sharpness Canal on a flat unending asphalt track. I am tired with the stress of last minute preparation. I can hardly believe what I am doing, walking 2,000 miles. I find myself tentative, unsure and strangely unfocused. This stretch is intended to ensure that I feel good and that my kit is right, absolutely right. I fidget with straps and buckles and retie my boot laces. I adjust my binoculars and take a picture of the sun in a puddle. I meet no one. After a while I stop off for a cream tea and snap a rainbow, which seems to hold out some promise. Little do I know that this experimental section to Minehead will soon lead me into mud, flood and fire, into acute danger and an ignominious return to my doctor in Cheltenham.

You expect of any grand venture that the first day will be a good day, even if it only starts after lunch. It is Sunday and it seems a good finale at eight o'clock to see ripples on the water flushing pink as the clouds on the sky-line. At Shepherds' Patch I find the youth hostel full. Feeling the anti-climax and slightly dejected at the set-back, I walk another mile to the *Tudor Caravan Park.* It is dark by now and I strain under the light of a 40-watt bulb. The man takes £5.60p and writes out a receipt. "For a few feet of grass?" I murmur, "I don't want to buy the grass just lie on it." Without looking up, he gestures towards a black hole in the shadows and I just know that I am in for trouble. Perhaps there is a password like "Volvo" or "motor-home". Swallowed up in the darkness, I set off on a compass bearing through hedges, gaps and ditches, triggering irritable curses whenever I hook someone's guy-ropes, and eventually settle down for the night at the far end of a field.

The next day, breakfasted, packed and ready for off, I pause mesmerised before the entrance by the office. Everywhere there are notices, signs and boards. Everywhere there are rules, directions and prohibitions. "ONLY ENVIRONMENTALLY-FRIENDLY GROUND SHEETS MAY BE USED", it says, "NO BALL GAMES", "NO CYCLING", "NO DOGS OFF LEADS" and absolutely forbidden it is for children to climb trees. Earlier I had memorised a four-foot square notice telling me how and how not to use the toilet facilities and then failed to coax any water out of the chosen shower unit. Now in front of me is this huge gate. It is capped with the word 'PRIVATE' and covered with a selection of anti-personnel warnings like "CAUTION – DOGS RUNNING FREE" and "BEWARE OF THE DOG" repeated several times for effect.

I stand back to focus my camera and instinctively turn, aware that a man is looking at me. Yes, *that* man. Suspicion hangs over him like a dark cloud as he advances towards me, face intent, jaw set, and eyes like lasers. His fears are not to be allayed nor his spirit humoured. "Bloody journalist! I know your sort," he begins. "We only allow photographs by us not of us. Get out!" His complexion changes from sallow to ashen. Nothing seems to uncoil his spiralling paranoia. His face comes to within fifteen inches of mine and a long and bony finger within tempting range of my teeth. Then, claiming every fraction of his full height, he drills me again with his eyes and banishes me from his property. "Don't you *ever...*" he shouts. Just then the frightened face of his wife bobs mercifully behind the fence. I seize the distraction and escape, wishing him well. I haven't the nerve to suggest another notice: "BEWARE OF THE OWNER".

Back on the track, I am feeling the benefit of fitness training. The sun is shining and I am striding along at a good four miles an hour. There are mile markers by the canal. I admire several neo-classical lock keepers' cottages, their Doric columns bursting with nineteenth century pride, and then find the tow-path petering out in the tidal basin at Sharpness. The canal has been a happy lead-up to my published starting point, the Welsh border. Skirting two power stations my eye is glued to the distant outline of the mighty Severn Bridge. I am in good spirits, almost exuberant. Having met no one all day I joke with three thirty-something fossil-hunting females and two things follow which take me by pleasant surprise. The girls are lovely free spirits and the largest suddenly plants a daring kiss smack on my lips. I climb up the hill, choose a place to camp, have a café meal and return to find my second surprise. The Severn Bridge has been lit up. With the Welsh hills behind, it is the centrepiece of a magnificent overview of the Bristol Channel at night.

I lie gazing out of my tent at the soaring white towers of the Bridge. Its two slender legs at each end grip the banks and spawn a stream of flowing light north and south. Illuminated as if magically from the sky and shimmering in the inky reflections below, ropes of pearlescent beauty are strung across the waters of the estuary. I think of my parents, united in procreative intent. I think of God giving them the surge of my life and I am in awe. Suddenly I realise something very, very special. I was a twinkle in my Heavenly Father's eye *before* I twinkled in that of my dad. I am excited. It dawns on me that I was His before I was anyone else's. It was from His arms that I was released into those of my earthly parents. I began as a deep pulse of heaven's joy, in a chuckle of His delight. I believe God smiled.

It is said that the most dangerous journey of our lives is that through the womb. It may also be true that the journey before that is possibly the happiest, travelling unimpeded down the fallopian canal. Smaller than a grain of sugar the multiplying embryo has received its genetic instructions and is enjoying every moment of its new life. Wrapped in the ecstasy of love-making, fused if you like out of a mix of divine and human intent and shaped as a perfect sphere, it has at least a week to be swept exultantly along the waiting canal through a waving procession of tiny hairs, before it finds its rest in the wall of the womb. It is a profound discovery to realise myself truly loved before I began my life and at the very beginning of my journey along the Sharpness Canal, to be able to relish something of the freedom and exuberance I would have experienced on the first expedition I ever made within this world. But my revelling was not to last.

Chapter 2

New Severn Bridge to Lynton

BIRTH WAS INDEPENDENCE

STARRY-EYED MY PARENTS MAY HAVE BEEN, BUT INVASION from Europe was on the horizon. My father was in the oil business. With special authorisation from the War Department he was frequently absent, travelling the airfields of the north to ensure adequate fuel supplies for allied aircraft. For her son's birth, my mother had no escape but to return to *her* mother who lived in Birmingham. It was stress upon stress, for they had always been at loggerheads.

On several fronts my mother's dread and general distress deepened. She was full of fear and it seems her apprehensions steadily trickled through to invade the frail life within. While my father was ensuring life-giving fuel to feed the airways of his world, my mother was contaminating the fuel line to her little world, that of her son entombed within. Beryl Bainbridge writes that "nothing is ever so strong again as that which happens to us in childhood" and the earlier this is, the more terrifyingly true. Forty years later, with the help of Dr Frank Lake, I discovered those feelings I had when helpless in the placental wall of her womb. Her bleak interior dread had become mine. It was hopeless to resist. Her channels of nurture only conveyed a seeping death to my spirit. I felt as chained to the wall as Terry Waite to his radiator. As if helplessly enmeshed in a grip of unlove I was receiving stones for eggs, scorpions for fish and no bread that wasn't bitter. The tape-recorded experiences of my journey, re-activated those years later, put these things beyond the scope of this book. They do illustrate, however, that I became disassociated from my mother and my own 'worthless' body and that I lifted my threatened self into the observatory tower of my head from which I dreamed, I think, of freedom.

Thus I missed the necessary bonding and dependency essential for my body to have a healthy start. I suppose I renounced what was never really on offer: a resting in my mother's embrace. I never saw my parents hold each other or even touch in a loving way. So I learnt to do without being needy. How needy I really was has since become plain: to be secure and safe in her arms, to be stroked with affection and gentleness, to be handled, held tight (occasionally) and hugged enough, until healed. But it was not to be. Instead I took up an independent spirit and trusted in my own strength 'alone'. The loneliness that grew within has never quite left me to this day.

The very next morning at Redwick I discover, marooned on the beach, flung there by some Atlantic storm or tide, the stumpy roots of a huge tree, battered and bleached by its travels. Trimmed by a chain saw, it now has centre place in my Cheltenham back garden. It sits over a huge Victorian manhole cover, which seals the entrance to a network of old underground sewers. I have an intuitive and visual way of thinking and I 'knew' by analogy that I had been revisiting important aspects of my own genesis.

Back on the coast, I admire the imaginative masts and sails of the latest, *new* Severn Bridge. It is raining hard this afternoon. I resolve to cut out the long gorge into Clifton and Bristol, and in the teeth of driving rain launch myself over the M5 at Avonmouth. I am duly rescued by Kath at the Gordano Service Station and next day, at last, find myself in more settled weather, emerging from the Poets' Walk in Clevedon. I am lulled into thinking that I have a straight and steady course to Sand Point in the far and hazy distance. If I had had a larger-scale map I would have clearly seen in bold, red capital letters, the words 'DANGER AREA'. Here was the second highest tidal variation in the world, up to fifty feet, and presumably also the fastest.

In dreamy self-confidence I follow the low embankment, specially built to keep out the sea. It shrinks to nothing eventually and, heedless, I plough on, squelching underfoot. I mutter something about Weston-Super-Mud and find myself jumping little gullies of water. By now, I am faced with a landscape of high, spiky, marsh grass to challenge my naïve intention to follow the edge of England. There was no going back and, worse, the grass hides a sinister reality. Hidden from view the area was criss-crossed with a maze of treacherous, sea-water ditches. Exhausted after hours of detour and sheer effort to straddle them without falling in, I face my final obstacle to safety, a tidal creek, the Congresbury Yeo. I gaze in dismay at the vast uncrossable expanse of shiny mud. I test it. My boots behave like banana skins on jelly. I skid quite a distance . Unable to turn round I feel helpless, scared to move. Of unknown depth, this greeny-black primeval ooze, packed with deadly globigerina seemed to mock my high resolve. Just then my world stops. Only yards away, I am shocked to see the white, foaming edge of the tide slither into view. Gathering speed up the creek, this tongue of marine appetite seems set on one more luckless victim. Recalling stories of men disappearing without trace and others rescued by rope and tractor in the nick of time, I scramble back on to firmer ground. Slipping and sliding and my heart pounding, I work up-creek as fast as I can, perhaps half a mile, to outpace the advance of the sea. Already my boots, plastered with this evil-smelling paste, are in a real mess. There could be no delay and I was miles from anywhere.

I hover again on the brink of the glinting morass, reluctant to ruin my brand new rucksack and all my clean clothes. I pause and decide. In a trice I am down to jock-strap and boots only, and everything else, hat, clothes, camera, specs and binoculars are inside the rucksack and the rucksack tied safely inside my cape. There is no one to help and no one to see. I stand up momentarily and manfully to look Mother Nature square in the face, when, simply, my feet come up in front of me. All dignity gone and helpless, as on countless ball bearings, I skim effortlessly down a thirty foot slope into the silent sludge. There is no time to feel my fear. I had noticed some boulders and managed to heave and drop three into the odious depths. They begin to sink but there were no others. Time has gone and the sea is up. I hurl my bundle as hard and as far as I can and step on the first of the rocks. The second is just visible. It holds, but I am twisting. I lurch badly askew and throw myself the final six feet. Spread-eagled in the sticky gel, I lie prostrate, as the incoming water seals all behind me. Breathless but thankful, one limb at a time, I suck myself up and out of the slime. Like a creature from the depths, I emerge, inky-green but triumphant, on the edge of the creek of death.

Feeling a curious mix of Sambo and Rambo, I hoist aloft my oozing bundle and, magnificently well camouflaged from head to foot, I set out to bluff it round the headland to clean water and a wash. But it was not to be. One trickling tap makes everything ten times worse. So just as I am, in the late afternoon sun, I don the cape and like a mobile, khaki traffic cone, slice through the woods and crowds at Weston, across the golf course at Uphill, and, finish it being now dark, straight into the sea.

That night I sleep fitfully in the dunes. Joy-riders, yards from my tent, rip up sand in endless contortions of fume and noise. Next day, the River Axe, another uncrossable creek, forces me six miles inland. I return to the beach and its donkeys. But not for long. At Burnham-on-Sea I leave the sand to go inland to friends. Just as I am skirting commercial properties, behind a perimeter fence, minding my own business, a terrific explosion, just yards away, immerses me in dust and dense blue smoke. I grope my way round and emerge to see a roaring inferno. The building is a mass of flames from end to end. So this is 'Burn'em at Sea'.

If this is what life is like at the beginning of a journey, I muse, whatever was in store for me, yet to come? For most folks life is complicated and often gets worse. So it certainly seems for clergy too. Perhaps "out of strength came forth sweetness": a verse of Scripture mocks me on a tin of treacle. Looking back, real challenges have wrought real changes in me, with and often without my co-operation. Maybe, as for Samson, there will come the strength to make a difference in the end. We shall see.

That night I see heroism. Lil at 90 is violently sick and her daughter Pat shows me the strength that comes in weakness. Feeling more relaxed after breakfast I am taxied to the Edge, ready for my first close-up of a kestrel, the beauty of the Quantock coast, the fascinating ironwork in Watchet and the Kilve oil retort. But nothing could have prepared me for my encounter with Chris. He is dressed entirely in black, with silken trousers and a velvet shirt. His dark and greasy hair only emphasises his ashen face, thin and tight. He says nothing and we part. Two hours later, after dark, I am walking down a narrow footpath from Minehead Parish Church. It is growing steeper and drops beneath bushes into total blackness. Suddenly, there he is in front of me. "Hi, fella!" I said, "Surely, this has to be meant." We introduce ourselves. He is a witch. He is a High Priest of witches. He had trained 1,600 witches and proceeds to rain down curses on Christians, responsible for desecrating the Druid altars and destroying their vestments. "No such thing as evil!" he says, "invented by the Bible in AD 300. The goddesses are telling me to wait, but it won't be long before we give the Christians a bloody nose."

My boots are hurting as I climb the steps out of Minehead and up to the top of Selworthy Beacon, 1,000 feet in dripping, driving rain. I marvel to read that the Lynmouth life-boat has been dragged over the cliff tops fourteen miles into Porlock, to save fifteen men stuck in mid-Channel. I then embarrass myself by having a navigational blackout, spiralling down into the Countesbury Estate, instead of Lynton. Wet through and badly blistered, I finally make it through the Valley of the

Rocks into Lee Abbey, a caring Christian community near Lynton.

What a week! Things have definitely not gone according to plan. Abused by “that man”, sensitive about Chris, shaken by my map reading, shocked by mud, tide and fire, battered by a fierce storm and now seriously lame, I need to take stock. I have been de-skilled and need to learn. I have been wounded and need healing. I have walked in my own strength and need His. So I returned to Cheltenham after my ‘trial’ week and took my blisters to the doctor. “At least a fortnight,” he said. I had ten days to go before official departure from St Matthew’s. So I began to reflect on my roller-coaster week. I think my beginnings have often been difficult.

Chapter 3

Lee Abbey to Polzeath

PRE-SCHOOL MEANT BLACK-OUT

SALLYANNE IS DRIVING THE CAR. I WOULD LIKE TO DRIVE, BUT as she instructs for the Institute of Advanced Motorists, I defer to her skills rather than court her comment. Heather and I are sitting meekly on the back seat. We are strangely silent. Heather is feeling the strain of imminent departure. I have a mobile phone, donated by Barclaycard, and I promise to ring home from call boxes along the way, but that does not ease the pain of parting, nor the worry over my months away on the edge of England.

Soon, I am alone, but among friends. Lee Abbey Community and Conference centre is familiar to me and, being fully booked, they give me the privilege of an empty bed in the staff quarters. To help the healing, I walk around in bare feet. Kindness overflows. Good cooking, friendship, music and laughter all embrace my shrunken senses. For me it is like a homecoming, after the ambivalent start down the Severn Estuary.

Home is where you are loved. My sisters and I had a caring, reliable and well appointed home in Leeds, where I lived for twenty-one years. Mum was very hard working and I was 'not an easy child'. I knocked things over and dropped them. I was thoughtless and barged in and out on impulse. I preferred to be off bird-watching or looking for golf balls on the links behind our house. For me to come home was not a homecoming, usually because I was late. But where could I rest the weariness in my spirit? If I hurt myself, I was scolded: "It's your own fault. You should have taken more care." If I cried, I was a sissy. If I tripped I was a blasted fool. If I didn't get things right, I was a blithering idiot. Otherwise it was "Sunny Jim". I needed a place to hide and so began a passion for making dens out of turf on the allotment or with branches in the woods. My very earliest memory of childhood is making tunnels into dead grass and under rose bay willowherb. It was somewhere to feel safe. In bed I would bore into large pillows or bolsters to find a sense of security. I well remember tricking my younger sister, in another room to come and see my excavation. I had slipped under the bed to simulate a breathing motion. She crept in and duly pounced on empty bed clothes. We were good friends and later had a secret society. We made badges to compete for success in a range of dares, designed to outwit the grown-ups.

No blame is attached to my mother's best efforts, as I look back. She did her dutiful best with her difficult son. But we disaffiliated from each other at the beginning. Both of us had a huge investment in independence. It suited her and I was proud at the age of five to walk nearly three-quarters of a mile to school on my first day, by myself. The tragedy, of course, was that I failed to establish the first inter-personal bridge into life. The bonding with my mother was conveniently skipped by tacit agreement, or just by default, and so I missed the enjoyment of natural dependency, of resting in another's strength. I was only dimly aware of my need of her love, of approval in her eyes and tenderness in her voice. But in the inchoate recesses of our hearts, we had distanced ourselves from each other and I never found myself at home in that primary relationship of trust. My memory is blank, a bit like the black-out and I can find no light in those years of the War.

Thus it was that I set off into life secreting a tough, exterior shell. Often when there was a disagreement I would say I was leaving and just set off up the road, distraught parents trailing behind. Once I tied all my belongings in a red-spotted handkerchief, at the end of a stick, and announced, head up and shoulders back, "I'm off to seek my fortune." It was too late to know my mother's love; besides she had wanted a girl. In those crucial early years, it was my dad who stood in magnificently as a source of inspiration and encouragement.

My journey down the Severn had ended at the doctor's, in a climax of stress. Not only would my feet be required to rest for at least a fortnight, but then I suffered a mild stroke. Answering the backlog of mail and media enquiries, my right hand suddenly trailed off out of control. My forefinger simply would not hold the pen. A scan was duly arranged for June. "In your dreams," I said, with only a few days left before my May departure date. But the message was clear. Thus Sallyanne took over as administrator for Walk 2000 and I found myself ready for a fundamental change of heart at Lee Abbey. I relaxed my steely resolve. I read a few books, shed a few tears, sang a few songs and slept. I was prayed for, cooked for and counselled, until His love seeped back into my soul. It seems we are not born with the ability to love. We have to learn that first, by letting ourselves *be loved*. So I had to rest and trust and believe in the love God has for me and had for me from before my beginning. I arrived blistered and unbowed. I left unblistered and bowed in a quiet spirit of worship.

Recuperating at Lee Abbey took four days out of my planned schedule. To catch up I had to skip over 70 miles of Devonshire coastline and hitch-hike to Bucks Mills near Clovelly. So this next stretch, between Lee Abbey and Bucks Mills, I am walking later on in November 1997, after the main Walk is over. The Conference Centre drops out of view and new-found friends, Joe and Phil, go with me as far as Woody Bay, leafless now in the autumn.

My eye is searching for the Little Hangman and beyond it the Great Hangman at 1,000 feet, except that I cannot find the trig. point for mist. Rainy gusts of wind buffet me into Ilfracombe. This is Tarka the Otter country, and very wet. I toil up the cliffs towards the Eastacott trig. point, like countless donkeys before me, which had taken coal and limestone up to the kilns and precious lime up to the acid moors above, for growing things and burning things, like bodies that couldn't be buried in the granite. Close-cropped deep green swathes of grass bear mute testimony to their labour. That night the only flat bit I find is on the path, where I am spot-lit three times every ten seconds by the automated Bull Point lighthouse.

Morte Point is a spectacular dinosaurial back-bone of vertical rocks whose tail drops into a veritable cauldron of boiling water and periodic explosions of spray. Desperate for a pee and a wash I approach a residential home in Woolacombe and offer my services as part-time temporary chaplain. Fortified by coffee and good company I set out on a long trek across Saunton Sands, the scene of hectic D-Day preparations among the dunes. Still militarised, there are unusual and I think amphibious vehicles patrolling the beach. I slog the estuary into Barnstaple and am lucky to find a B&B still open at "The Crossways". Following the other side of the Taw Estuary, I meet Arthur on the Tarka Trail. He shows me a cairn-shaped memorial to his brother Dingle Bowser, who had fallen off the bridge while fishing at Fremington. Arthur's daily visit is a nod to God.

Tonight, in mid-November, this is my very last night of all. Tomorrow therefore, is my very last day tramping on the Edge of England. It completes Walk 2,000. I leave the Torridge bridge in blinding rain and slump for a lunch-time snack into a house porch-way named Withacot. With or without a cot moments later I am evicted by a scowling old lady. Thoroughly soaked I plod through the shipbuilding sheds of Appledore and pray, as I had done on only two occasions before, for a *Christian* home. I knock beside the only B&B sign I can find.

I am in Westward Ho!, with an exclamation mark unique in the world. It fits 'Lower Villa' perfectly. My jaw drops as I am swept upstairs into the most lavishly appointed bedroom of 'Lower Villa'. Above the bed, a gentle crown canopy hangs above laced pillows and on the duvet is a silken cushion.

Recessed washing facilities lead to an endless fascination of knicknacks. Gold fittings everywhere puncture matching curtains and wallpaper. The TV sits astride a crocheted padded tablecloth and at a lower level a tray of tea-making items invite my indulgence. Everywhere are special plants, even in the bathroom. A burgundy panelled area encompasses the bath itself, resplendent in gold coloured Neo-Victorian plumbing. I lie back in the bath, with a dwarf conifer behind my head and a cascade of greenery from the window-sill. A ceramic clown smiles down on my recumbent figure, largely cocooned in swathes of rising foam, piling up like summer clouds on my horizon. At my elbow are two chocolate biscuits and a cup of tea. Charm itself, the proprietor, Pamela, had lost her husband and is still grieving. Her answer, unique in my experience, is to try to persuade the children not to leave but to have mobile homes in the garden. Her love and her faith are undoubtedly her best hope for the future.

Tonight I have salmon and champagne in town. Tomorrow my mighty trek is actually complete at Buck's Mills. I traverse an ancient wood and come upon a signpost to Clovelly, labelled clearly "Coastal Path" - yet somehow lose my way. I find myself climbing away from the edge and up towards the main road and home. I pause breathless to look back. I am stunned to see a brilliant half rainbow stabbed into the headland beyond. No more, Graham! It is done.

So after hitch-hiking from Lee Abbey, earlier in the year, still very sore round my heels I reconnect with my Walk schedule at Buck's Mills near Clovelly. It is Friday 23rd of May. The atmosphere of square-jawed buildings fits the overcast sky. The Braunds colonised and have fiercely defended this valley through at least four centuries. The last Braund clan survivor died a few weeks ago. His grandfather, James Braund, piloted the Clovelly lifeboat and "never lost a single vessel nor a single soul". With some relief I climb out and up through graceful, overhanging branches that, suddenly bathed in sunshine, are fit for the noblest bridal party. These beechwoods, like resident solicitors, are called The Steart,

Hoggins and Welland Woods, well managed by The Woodland Trust.

Clovelly to Hartland is graded by The South West Coast Path Association, as "moderate to strenuous". It is largely owned by The National Trust under their Neptune Scheme and rated perhaps their finest section. It is dramatic stuff followed south by 'The Iron Coast' of Hartland. At 5am in Clovelly, I awake sweating with a fear that I simply cannot walk another day on my painful feet and would have to abort the whole project. I sit up and read Psalm 132:- "Direct me in the way I should go" - and straightaway fall into a deep and trusting sleep. After breakfast, I dig out a new invention, a packet of blister patches with a difference. These dome-shaped cushions thin to nothing at their edge and underneath, instead of prolonging the problem, they foster a culture of healing. At last, with at least six blisters in place, I have a working arrangement with my feet. The problem had been new boots. Now I have my preferred pair of Scarpas and within a week or so with blister pads my feet are back to normal. I just make sure the laces are really tight so that there is no movement at all in the boot.

I pause at an ornate wooden structure with carved angel wings for its roof. It has been built to remember three little children lost in the woods and never found, probably murdered. Then I find a plaque to five crewmen of a Wellington bomber doomed and destroyed on these cliffs. At one point the path disappears at a cliff collapse and my thoughts return to a conversation I had with Sallyanne in our kitchen. I looked her in the eye and said, "What if I don't come back?" Her other eye misted and we talked. The risks are real. Mine shafts, holes and unstable edges; tides, high winds and shifting sand; and, not least, the risk of personal assault.

Constantly before my departure, people's final injunction was to "Take care!" It was well-meant advice, but not for me. Frankly, taking chances is part of what I am and part of what this is all about. I feel it is His solemn responsibility 'to take care' and mine 'to take risks', though taking care when I take risks is reasonable enough. My parents only encouraged my fascination with danger when constantly urging me away from the edge, for only on the *very* edge was that frisson of excitement. There grew in me a sort of lust for the edge, the edge of comfort, the edge of safety, the edge of life. But risk-taking is more than a rogue aspect to my personality. It is one way of spelling faith. As disciples, faith is the air we breathe. It is a call to go, even if others dare not. I knew I would be out of my own control sometimes, but always then, and especially then, within His. I was never disappointed. I reach Hartland and post back my canister of CS gas, given by a thoughtful friend. After all I have my stick and each morning I use the prayer of St Columba, "Alone with none but Thee My God I journey on my way. What need I fear, when Thou art near, O King of night and day? More safe am I within Thy hand than if a host did round me stand."

The churches of St Nectan in Stoke and Welcombe are part of the Hartland benefice. David and Sheila at the Vicarage scoop me up and drop me off over several days, to benefit from the hospitality of their home and congregations. Their cards and gifts light up every corner of my heart. As I leave them I am facing the longest section continually under canvas, the hardest stretch of roller coaster climbing and the heaviest rucksack to carry. With a week's worth of stores, it weighs about 35 pounds. My calf muscles ache less but my knees have become sore. I doff my hat to the eccentric Vicar of Morwenstow, Richard Hawker, who built a wooden hut on a headland from which to preside in peace over the wheeling fulmars and gulls. Determined not to buckle, I do not sit there long but recall the words I saw on a plaque in the entrance hall to the Eskdale Outward-Bound Mountain Centre, attributed to Sir John Hunt: "We all live far below our capability. If we realise this, we shall never settle for less".

Into Bude and in blisteringly hot weather, I tramp across the beach, skirting English seaside families, with hankies on head, skirts in knickers and children excavating moats for castles that would soon be challenging the tide. I toss a rubber ball to a family, playing cricket with a bit of foam. I inspect Bude canal and climb up to Compass Point. Now, if you know where you are going and from where you have come, you should know where you are from this eight-sided Temple to the Winds. Not so! Moved twice, it still does not correspond exactly to true or magnetic north.

Crackington Haven is full of geological interest, but my attention is on the local bakery van and lunch. Climbing out of another sensational headland I come across Black Hole Café, run by an ex-Prudential salesman. He shares his story. I say "Trust in the Lord!" Quick as a flash, he replies "with all your heart and lean not on your own understanding. In all your ways acknowledge him and he will direct your paths" (*Proverbs* 3:5-6). Shortly after, I drop into Boscastle and find *The Harbour Light*, run by Trixie and Sue selling Christian books, crafts, tapes and cards. Its theme had been pixies until ten years ago, when Trixie had been 'born again on the Torridge Bridge.' Now she finds herself sitting squarely in front of the Witches Museum, run by Graham King. Inside are chilling exhibits, dark and dreadful, frankly calculated to bleach out any enthusiasm for sorcery and broomsticks. Graham is a Wicca and lives by the Wiccan creed: "Do what you will each to his or her own and harm no one." His desire is to re-enchant England with fairy tales, animal sacrifices and relics of Druidity. The circle is their church and the planetary rhythms their calendar.

On the cliff edge I sit and drink cocoa with some folks, enjoying the proximity of puffins, guillemots and razorbills, looking forward to a ringside ledge view for the rest of my stay. Until, that is, I decide to turn in. I find my sleeping bag sodden from the rain. Sleepless and cold I am up before the birds. Possessed with a fresh urgency, I literally steam through Tintagel, Port Isaac and Polzeath until met and rescued by Audrey Milner-Schofield. Audrey is a magnificent mixture of practical good humour and happiness. After my wet week under canvas, her first task is to cut off my socks with scissors, a pair of which was to be found in every room of the house - clearly Audrey's answer to any crisis. A bath and bliss soon follow.

Chapter 4

Padstow to Polperro

ON AUTO-PILOT AT SCHOOL

CORNISH CELTS, THOUGH ARTISTIC AND IMAGINATIVE, HAVE always been tough, learning how to survive from Roman times. Likewise the coastal edge of this famous Duchy is more than a little tough on one pair of English knees. For miles after Padstow I am on auto-pilot, just battling in a lonely and relentless world of physical challenge.

After the War everyone struggled. "Don't step on the lino! I've just polished it," I would hear on arrival home from my new school. Everywhere there were scattered dress-making patterns and half-made lamp-shades. On the table, baked beans, dried egg or bread and dripping. I never went to school with torn pockets or missing buttons and on return there was always a fire in the grate, but within I was struggling. My recurrent dream, which persisted into my thirties, showed me dwarfed at the centre of a vast unfriendly cone-shaped tunnel down which I was always travelling but from which I could never escape. Sleep-walking was a family joke. Thumb-sucking a long-standing source of embarrassment. Day dreaming meant little progress at school.

These were auto-pilot years of which I have no feeling memories. I had to survive. I became ruggedly insensitive and realised I had to succeed, even if no one would clap. I remember hurling myself down a very high and long polished brass children's slide, backwards, upside down and somersaulting in the process, because no one else dared. So Newquay, out on the Edge of England, would have been just my place as a teenager, the waves pounding the harbour, the tide in and the tiny wet-suited surfers risking their lives in dangerous seas. I watch them and leave them, reluctantly, and climb the Huer's Hut instead. It is a primitive stone cottage in which a man was paid to look out for shoals of pilchards in the bay. He would then climb a narrow, external staircase and with a horn summon the villagers to man the boats and encircle the fish with their nets. He raised 'a hue and cry'.

Acutely disappointed I find that the tide has flooded the only bridge over the Gannel Estuary. It means another five miles to bed. I climb up through dense undergrowth on to a flat patch of grass, aware that a while back I saw a large sign "Danger! Adders!" It is too late for cooking and too dark. I have some biscuits and, exhausted, I sleep solidly. In the morning I peel back my groundsheet and underneath, trapped, is a perfect, slightly coiled specimen, dead.

St Agnes is a barren, deserted headland of high vertical cliffs. On this edge of Cornwall I find Wheal-Coates, a surviving remnant of tin mining, several stacks and an empty engine-house. What a place to work and then to have to manhandle the proceeds down the precipitous cliff and into sailing ships bucking on the swell!

Perranporth seems closed. I push on to Portreath. Through a snow storm of gulls fighting for someone's lunch I see that the old yellow stone lighthouse has these words: "They shall grow not old as they that are left grow old, age shall not weary them, nor the years condemn. At the going down of the sun and in the morning, we shall remember them", composed on this spot by Lawrence Binyon. I grew up hiding under the stairs from the bombs. After the heavy snows of 1946, I remember the PoWs chipping huge slabs of ice from the road outside the school. We lugged these into the playground and built an enormous igloo. Two thirds completed, half the labour force mutinied and began to demolish it *and* its defenders. I loved the battle. At Primary School I had easily been 'top-dog'. Here at the Leeds Grammar, and only just eight, I was totally out-classed. One day, we were asked who was the King of the Indian Empire. Making a vain lunge at recognition, I answered, "Gandhi". Fame came unexpectedly as, next time we met, the teacher called me "Gandhi". It stuck so well, my initial being 'G', that I was never called anything else to the day I left. In the early years I was always being assassinated and my behaviour and grades went from bad to worse. Perhaps I was inspired by the great man's words: "They may break my body and my bones. They will have my dead body, but never my obedience."

I need somewhere to sleep. I have had some chips and in my bag there is a pint of milk for breakfast. Perched high and overlooking the bay a small, strange gothic-looking structure invites closer inspection. It is a sort of gazebo. I pull back the blackberry bushes and crawl inside, just as every other form of life simultaneously crawls out. It looks weatherproof, with stone tiles on the cupola-shaped roof, covered by at least half a metre of soil and turf contributed by Mother Nature. I spread my gear round its octagonal girth and lie down at the centre of this masterpiece of devotional architecture. I am well into a dream about lofty spires and vaulting, when something clouts my nose and spits into my eye. In minutes a cloud drops its cargo with precision accuracy and funnels on to my face a sluice of rainwater.

Travelling the edge, I often meet substantial lookout buildings and clustered coastguard cottages. At one time stricken ships were the only source of luxuries. Wreckers, to keep their trade alive, actually smashed beyond repair the new Lizard Lighthouse, in ruins for twenty-eight years. I can see that the coastal path is certainly not about retired people with dogs and pushchairs. All round the south west peninsular, coast guards were paid to be on their toes against smuggling. Daily they would inspect every cliff and cove. Traffic inland was negligible. Trade round the coast and from the coast was England's life-blood, and out of the coastguard cottages went a daily stream of men to their boats, children to school and wives to the market, all along this highway. So this spectacular path hugs the very edge all round the perimeter. And below it today, through Dorset, Devon and Cornwall, the smuggling of drugs yet continues, flaunting the efforts of Customs and Excise.

An arc of unstable duneland borders St Ives Bay. These moving monsters swallowed Upton Barton Farm in one night and then St Gothian's Chapel later and are only tamed these days by marram grass. Threading my way along I have not seen a soul all day. To my joy, nearing the Hayle estuary a couple appears in front. Keen to know if the ferry is working and even keener to have a civilised conversation with someone, I blurt out several enquiries. He just looks at me, long and hard and says very slowly, "My English is very, very bad". I look at him impotent and mimic, "My German is very, very bad too."

Feeling slightly rebellious, I clear the harbour and decide that the quickest way across the water is by the railway viaduct. Two or three miles and several trains later, I am met by a stream of threats and questions that pour out of a signal box window. I just nod, smile and walk straight through St Erths station and into the Wyevale Garden Centre Restaurant, where a bloke recognises me, slaps a twenty-pound note on the table and leaves with hardly a word. I decided that at no time on the trip would I importune anyone for a charity donation. In fact my tee shirt says it all and this leaves me free to talk about other things, like sugar, milk and bread! Also just a walker, without rank or clout, I can listen.

St Ives stimulates all my senses, serving up a homely diet for families, *a la carte* for the artistic and pick-and-mix for clumps of pierced females and their shaven headed guys. All is well up the little narrow back streets, spiced with a rich diet of 'cheeky' post-cards. I sit on the pavement and very carefully lace up my boots for a section that is designated 'severe'. It is over twenty-two miles and described, by the S.W.Coast Path Association, "as the longest and most deserted stretch of the Devon and Cornwall coastline". The struggle continues.

By diverting inland, about lunch time, I find Zennor, its telephone box, a legendary mermaid, and home for a while for D. H. Lawrence. On display is the plague stone, over which money was exchanged through a pool of vinegar, only 150 years ago. I find it hard to read in the cemetery about the ravages of cholera. A cuckoo keeps me company until Pendeen Watch. By now the landscape is coppery, and glowing in the last rays of the sun. I phone Heather on the mobile and tell her I am sleeping down a tin mine, not good timing. Thirty thousand men once worked in Cornwall's tin and copper mines, seven hundred in the Geever complex alone, travelling down shafts 2,800 feet, along tunnels a mile out to sea.

Walking to Cape Cornwall I join up with a radiographer, her face hard and flinty, despite a practised smile. She lives with her mother and maybe has developed a career in which she can avoid feelings and be detached, watching people on the slab and taking pictures. There on the headland a little buff-coloured bird is doggedly taking off into the wind, as though attached by elastic to the twelve-foot pencil monument that marks the cliff end. And so via Sennen Cove is Land's End. It is iconic. It is the farthest west England gets, or the proud start of Europe, if you are coming from Nova Scotia. Conservation and information along with the multi-media and mass catering efforts absorb my interest. However, top of the bill for me is a close-up of the kittiwake colony. I buy a Celtic brooch for Heather and a little lighthouse for Sallyanne and post them. I sign the *Land's End Hotel* ledger intended for Scotland-bound travellers and set my face to the East.

Within a few hours I am stumbling, no less, into live theatre. A production of *Whistle down the Wind* is due to start in a drama-filled stage set into the very granite cliffs themselves. The creator of *The Minack*, Rowena Cade, came from Cheltenham. At the interval and rigid with cold, I hear someone say, "Graham!" Peering into my unshaven face are Jim and Claire, fresh from their engagement, who know me from St Matthew's. We embrace and I am soon installed at the nearest hotel in Porthcurno. After breakfast I explore the underground tunnels of Cable and Wireless, the birthplace of submarine communication. Before 1970 a maximum of 30 'bits per second' could travel to America. Now, with fibre optics, 5,000 million 'bits' can travel instantaneously to Gibraltar in both directions at once. Machine-guns, flame-throwers and hand grenades stayed poised outside throughout the long years of the War.

After Lamorna Cove the path abandons the cliffs and disappears into a confusion of smooth, pillow-shaped boulders, the oldest rocks in the British Isles, heaved up from the earth's core when 'England' collided with 'France' 290 million years ago. England then straddled the Tropic of Cancer as part of one enormous disintegrating continent, Pangaea.

Forget Penzance! Newlyn is far more interesting with its modern art gallery, pilchards' factory and, not least, the National Centre for lighthouses, featuring life inside one. Automated, few can now be scaled to inspect the Fresnel reflector rings, see the 1250-watt bulb and feel the atmosphere, as I did at Hartland. Newlyn is also home to *The Dockers' Rest.* I sink beside my rucksack into a quiet corner of this café bistro, perfectly placed for the fishermen around. Marion, the genial matriarch of this refuge, knew Vincent Marshall, one of four lads recently lost at sea. Another a boy was Scot Roby, whose body was trawled up in nets later. I am reminded that the average life expectancy of fishermen today is only 32 years of age, and twenty such men die every year in the hazards. I order a "tremendous piece of fish please!" and tuck in with one eye on the four-foot mermaid, painted by Marion's daughter, Mandy. Replete I sleep well on the sandy beach with Mount St Michael over the water.

It is heart-breaking to read a plaque about the eight crew lives torn from their families before Christmas in the Penlee Lifeboat disaster of 1981. I learn about the 22 Porthleven fishermen, five ships and crew lost last century and about the 100 officers and men drowned on the Loe Bar in *HMS Anson*. So I am quite moved to meet Tom Henderson, the inspiration behind the Wreck and Rescue Centre in Porthleven.

From my earliest years I had been practical, not emotional, and taught not to be scared or hurt. I first remember feeling joy, and experiencing tears to go with it, when I came to experience the love God had for me, on Palm Sunday, April 1954, in the evening service. Slowly, since then, I have melted and been able to explore a full set of vibrant feelings, as an important part of my physiology and as an essential part of my response to life. These days I know my emotions to be my friends, threads of my history, ties to my loved ones and links to a real world that needs human empathy. I have also come to know there are no emotions that I should reject as intrinsically bad, like jealousy, anger, or disgust. I realise that essentially all emotions are natural, valid and important as precious gifts from God. They are gifts of Himself to be honoured as indicators and motivators for change. My chin does not jut out quite so far.

The Lizard was soon to be my test. My score this day is going to be "satisfactory, but could do better". I arrive at Mullion pretty raw and vulnerable. I have failed to ring through to the Vicar all day, so I just knock on his door at about ten o'clock at night. It is the Archbishop's Sunday for Pilgrimage intended to support all those *en route* across or round the nation. But there is no solace to be had and certainly no shelter, just hot water for my flask and half an inch of coffee in my capsule. I am unfeelingly dismissed in the direction of the village cricket pitch. I tip up the prow of an old rowing boat, whip the grass for vipers, decapitate an area of nettles and settle down for the night, hungry.

Next day in church there is no mention of my presence and the congregation just goes. I retreat to a café, feeling abandoned. I order a *large* helping of steak and kidney pie and am promptly charged double for their inconvenience. Worse is to come in the shape of a 'real, live reptile' on the Lizard, everything I dread in a woman. She is lurking behind the cash machine, cold and contained until, that is, our eyes meet. Her tongue lashes out with a venomous spurt of hot disdain. "Oh no!" she says, "we don't do *that* sort of thing here". I had only asked for the filling of my miserably small sugar container. I am caught helpless and vulnerable on this craggy elbow of England. It is late and I am hungry. I am in no shape to handle the coiled reflex of undisguised superiority, some people's reaction to a rucksack. I notice the pale and anxious young waitresses, flitting like moths from table to table, and learnt later that she had routed the local Roberts family, won control of the village store, and by fair means and foul had come to impose her will on neighbour and visitor alike. Making a mild protest, I notice that she picks up the cup of coffee for which I am about to pay and throws it straight yes! into the sink. However, I see her turn a deep pink when I catch her eye and the ears of those within range and say ever so slowly, "I hope, before this night is out, I meet a human being." I do, Tom and his sister Lisa Roberts, who have just opened their own tea-room nearby. They cannot be more helpful.

I phone Heather for consolation and now it's getting later still. The woman in the most southerly house in England advises against further progress. I manage about five hundred yards in the dark and sleep on the path. In the morning I find, a few metres away, a bottomless hole the size of a house. In squally rain I slog round the lighthouse and the Lloyds Signal Station and look up to see a window quickly open and close. A voice roars, "Come on up! The door's open!" It is John Palmer, a retired clergyman from Mullion, taking shift in the lookout for the National Coast Watch Institution. Our conversation, laced with cappuchino coffee, includes the recent loss of the *Maria Assumpta*. I gaze through huge conical binoculars bolted to the sill, watch the radar and listen to the crackle of VHF emergency channel 16 with snippets of distant conversations, and I'm thankful for the likes of John.

It rains for almost three days and I duck from one youth hostel to another. After Pendennis Castle, with its mock defence of the estuary, complete with the smell and smoke of burning cordite, I take two ferries to St Anthony's just in time to spend fifteen minutes watching and waiting for a merlin to dive from its nest. And now I have two heart-warming encounters that remind me of my praying partners back in Cheltenham. The first is with Ron and Mary Hayward, amazing people, who have set out to find me and return my first section map-case and all its contents, left the other side of the Falmouth ferry.

The second is with Derek Hawkins. He tells me he met God. In a valley where everything suddenly began to grow, where pebbles became rocks, rocks became boulders and boulders became cliffs, he perceived himself only an inch tall, blocked and unable to move among the rushing trees, the cliffs and clouds. Then a voice said, "I've stopped you to look and think. You are that small. Stand up and be counted." Derek continued, "though so small, he saw me. I've never looked back. I have become aware of people and able to love."

I reach the stark stone cross on Deadman's Point ('Dodman'on the map) and am feeling pretty low. Wet for days on end, I pause and breathe a prayer (or does *He* breathe the prayer into me?) "Lord, *please* give me a Christian home tonight." I stop a man in Gorran Haven. He points to friends across the road at *Seaview*. There is a little discreet notice: "You will find a warm welcome in our Christian home". Richard and Jayne Holmes with Daniel and Sarah give me just that and more besides cheese on toast in bed.

Much encouraged, I walk straight through a maritime film set featuring a vast square-rigger in Charlestown, round the huge English China Clay settling pits and across Par village, finely dusted by its windward neighbour. I gaze at the 25 metre day-mark at Gribbin Head and drop down to the ferry. There had been a heavy chain dangled across the Fowey to catch invading Spaniards. Now I wave and pay 30p.

Polperro is Cornwall's answer to Clovelly. The village is first chimed into my dulled and dampened brain by a bell, a wave-activated chapel bell that clanks me along the cliff top.

Skirting a castle ruin, the village is suddenly spread out below, compact and cared for. Every sign is a masterpiece of discretion and style. Each doorway has a friendly face. The post-master is expecting me. He gives me my parcel and with it a large steaming mug of tea. I sort and re-stock on everything from tea bags to muesli, matches, vaseline, batteries, films, cassettes and loo paper. I stuff my smelly socks in and extract out a mixture of custard and talcum powder. 'Honest John', assistant village postie, has chosen to give himself to the community and to his ailing mother as his service to the Lord. Later he would escort Heather and me into town for the sun's eclipse, about 11am on the 11th of August 1999. We sat at the harbour entrance. The light in the East faded, the seagulls squawked momentarily and the whole company of human beings, spread in clusters across the bay, fell into eerie silence. We shivered and waited. All was still, but for a line of little cygnets that set out for home across the harbour mud. Mum at the front, head up and resolute. Dad at the back, "Come on! Time for bed!" They only managed to get half way when light began to dawn from the west. A growing chorus of cheers and clapping broke the spell. There was laughter, photo calls, champagne corks and rescue, for The Light of our world had returned.

Chapter 5

Looe to Lyme Regis

LEARNING FAST ABOUT LEARNING

MEVA AND GISSY WERE ONCE FIERCELY COMPETITIVE villages, facing each other across the river. East Looe and West Looe were likewise in sparring partnership down through history. As I sloshed appropriately through Looe, negotiating the last difficult cliffs of Cornwall, I was aware that there had always been in me a strident spirit of competitiveness, a constant bid for dominance.

I bravely called it leadership, largely unaware of the hidden exhibitionist lad who would do anything to obtain his parents' acknowledgement. I would push harder on the rugby field, swing higher on the high bar and run faster on the track. I was soon captain of basketball, captain of gymnastics and off to the ground-level Olympic trials in London. I became a PT Instructor and acquired my army cross-swords. I ended my days at school as Flight Sergeant for the air cadets, among many other prefectorial jobs. If you stay at school long enough you can get to do just about everything. I was not content in Scouting unless a patrol leader, nor in the Young Conservatives unless chairman. But I did have three lucky breaks, necessary to make these things possible. First a generous dad paid for me to retake GCEs, though most of my peers had left or been forced out at sixteen. Second a new headmaster gave me and the whole school a clean slate. Third a new hero entered my life and gave me a completely unexpected, brand-new beginning within. At seventeen years of age, Jesus Christ came into my life. At that time, in April 1954, I thought it was to be a powerful endorsement of everything I stood for. In fact, it began a painful and gentle re-education about everything I hardly knew until then. "The longest journey is the journey inward," said Dag Hammaskjöld and, as I was literally soon to prove, it also can be very painful.

At the age of nineteen I had walked and climbed forty-five peaks in the space of three days out on the Cumbrian fells. In Eskdale, over twenty-seven days at an Outward Bound Mountain Centre with minimal safety provisions in place, I was one of a number of guinea pigs from public schools. My parents and I both prayed fervently for safe deliverance. Two others in my patrol had to return home injured with broken bones. We had been out on the last three-day expedition and were returning in the final hours via Wastwater. I suggested, in order to avoid a penalty for lateness, that we travel on the *inside* of the Lake margins. I knew the depth had never been measured, but I did not know that the boulder screes, towering above us, were at the angle of poise. As the captain (of course) I went last. The patrol one by one cleared the dangerous cliff-screes and I was halfway across, when there was a mighty rumble and a crunching slide, and everything in slow motion seemed to be on the move. Jumping from boulder to boulder I stayed upright, until one tilted me off balance. I put out my hand, lightly on a rock and, in that instant, another crashed down from above. Blood spurted everywhere. Tendons and nerves hung down. My left hand was horribly split and hopelessly splintered in many places. I shouted, "Blood!" so hysterically that the quartermaster slapped my face. I failed to get the coveted award for courage and leadership and found myself awaiting amputation, in Whitehaven Hospital.

In fact the doctor saved my hand, but I was a gymnast. I had prayed my best prayers and now faced disaster. Not least, I had miserably failed my 'A' Levels and was too old for school. It was not until two red-hatted military policemen thundered on the front door of our house that I began to realise the extraordinary timing of this accident. I was conscripted, they told me, like it or not, into National Service complete with first week's pay, clothing and travel allowances, due and overdue at Aldershot Barracks. And no argument! Until, that is, I was taken to the local MoH office. It was obvious I could not hold a rifle with my left hand in plaster and I was deferred for a year. I returned to school thankfully, re-took 'O' and 'A' Level exams, was accepted at Leeds and later Manchester, Universities, and emerged a Graduate of the Institute of Personnel Management. Were it not for this crucial change of fortune and a chance to learn again, I could never, ever, have considered a call to Ordination. It is interesting that after all my physical activities I really needed 'a break', to redirect my life. I never once have had a broken bone or a deep cut, before or since that decisive moment on which so much subsequently depended. I can still play the piano. That is credit due to a fine surgeon who later went on to practice in Harley Street. I was learning to trust God's timing in the ordering and disordering of my life.

"In acceptance lieth peace," I remember the words of Amy Carmichael. Joyful acceptance of life on the edge of Cornwall is not changing the terrain, the weather or my need for toughness – just my reactions to them. I am at peace. The weather, great and ghastly, is becoming a daily interface through which I can commune with my Creator. The rain is somehow cleansing and the wind animating, teasing and confronting. I can see the changing fortunes of the weather as a bit like life itself, an unpredictable mix of the gracious, the less-than-gracious and the disastrous. Here on the Edge, life is becoming a seamless act of worship, a membrane blending earth and heaven, sunshine and clouds, my life in His. Conventional wisdom from the past was, "Come inside! You'll catch your death of cold." Now I simply *'welcome the weather, whatever'* and soon dry out.

At Rame Head, Heather has met me in the car and taken my rucksack. I stride across the magnificent Edgecombe Country

Park and drop down to the Cremyll Ferry, the end of Kernow. Above a safe-deposit box on the lodge-keeper's wall I see a clock beautifully inscribed in green, red and gold: "If thou dost love life do not squander time". Then I notice in faint, embossed, background lettering: "Time and tide tarry for no one". I hop on the moving ramp of the ferry just as it is sliding away to Plymouth, to the Post House, to Heather and a breather. 'Remind me that my days are just on loan. Forgive me when I treat them as my own.' I've only got so much time in the deposit box.

The Plymouth Dome is a good place to start learning to learn. For one thing, I have a lot of catching up to do on history. Plymouth was defended against sacking by the French and by siege from the English Crown. I brave the high seas with Drake and the *Armada*, with Cook on the *Endeavour* and with the Pilgrim Fathers away at last on the *Mayflower.* I witness the Luftwaffe's devastation of this great port and the obliteration of its townscape. I sit with a kaleidoscope of characters from Churchill to Chaplin. Out to sea is blinking the Eddystone lighthouse and next day I photograph the sun reflecting in the glass of its predecessor, saved and rebuilt as a monument on the famous Hoe. I had switched on Smeaton's Tower.

Thankfully, I am now free of sore knees and heels and have a balance, dare I say a rhythm, in my walking. Perhaps the body works well if left to itself. But it has taken 400 miles to make the necessary intuitive adjustments. It has become obvious to me, for instance, that arms are not well employed relieving the weight off my straps and that rucksacks are not to be hung from shoulders but clamped to hips and pelvis. This way, I am breathing better with an unconstricted waist and my legs are better with the weight transferred directly into them. The lower the centre of gravity, the more stable I feel and my shoulders are used only to keep the rucksack roughly central on my back. Finally a little mini-strap across the chest just keeps everything tight in place. Quite truthfully I have now forgotten my home is on my back. I have acquired an upright posture and can freely use both hands for camera binoculars and the half-eye specs needed to read the map. I can still hear parental imperatives: 'Head up! Shoulders back!' and 'Chest out!' 'Pull your stomach in! Don't push your bottom out!' and 'Chin up!' 'Best foot forward!', as I jerked my frame obligingly to all points of the compass. Perhaps their advice was not too far out.

Received wisdom also taught that the body needs feeding at certain defined moments in the day, otherwise it would pump unused acid digestive juices into my system and turn on me with a volley of well aimed abdominal ulcers. Well, I have discovered that conventional sandwiches at lunchtime actually ferment in my bread basket and cause cramp because the body cannot be doing strenuous exercise simultaneously while stoking its internal larder. I now have a hearty breakfast each morning. Between seven and nine o' clock I consume a plate of muesli, a tub of porridge, two large eggs, two fried pieces of bread and a doorstep or two of bread and marmalade, accompanied by a pint of milk, two mugs of tea and sometimes an extra cup of coffee while filling my flask. Dates, currants and chocolate keep me duly rewarded, as targets come and go along the way, with sometimes an ice-cream in late afternoon. All day I drink about two litres of water through a tube from my left-hand strap and pocket. But still about four o'clock my legs go wooden. That's when I dig out a special Isotonic booster drink prepared at breakfast. It is high on miraculous energy and with a second helping at about seven I can easily go on walking to darkness and bedtime.

Heather has found her way to Burgh Island and because there are people travelling there and back across the sand at low tide, she believes that is the direction from which I will come and her eyes are glued there. I 'Boo!' her from behind. As if to demonstrate her navigational skills, after such a setback, she executes a polished driving performance across the wet sand, to visit the famed Art Deco hotel of the late twenties, and back before the tide beat us to it. If she can do that, I muse, she will find Cheltenham later on in the day.

Noble thoughts about the raindrops on my cheek being the loving tears of my Heavenly Father are soon justifiably washed away by heavy drizzle, and I fall into step with the Baxters. Joshua is in a plastic bubble on Dad's back and Isaac and Toby dangle from a cheerful but dripping Mum. We take coffee together and I resist a lift to East Prawle. There a robust Christian farming family dries me out and next morning in bright sunshine, Helen and Roger undercharge me for the privilege.

The day starts inspiringly with a profusion of small birds going about their innocent business. At Hallsands herring gulls are wheeling in the thermals only inches above my head, as I look down at the ruins of houses collapsed into the sea. The village lost its protection when shoreline shingle was used to extend the Naval dock facilities. However, in between is Start Bay, and central to that is one terrible, heart-breaking catastrophe. In 1944, 3,000 villagers were asked to evacuate their homes and farms and in just six weeks to leave and take everything with them. This was to assist military preparations for Operation Overlord and it was here in the month of April that three German E Boats (to the Allies: E for Enemy) swept in to wipe out nearly 1,000 US and Canadian personnel. The plan was to use the Slapton Sands to simulate D-Day landings. From Lyme Bay a convoy of five 'Landing Ship Tanks', ships holding hundreds of men and packed with tanks, guns and lorries set out to meet a similar convoy of three from Plymouth. Escorted by only one corvette, the long line of eight crowded vessels advanced in darkness towards the target beaches of Slapton. Minesweepers were out in front and aircraft overhead. All was going to plan. Earlier small-scale beachheads had been successful with live ammunition. But German intelligence had picked up an unusually high level of radio messages and alerted three submarinal captains.

In the dark of April 27/28 three German E Boats slipped into position, discharged their torpoedos and surfaced to straffe the ships with devastating 20mm x 40mm firepower. One after another, many of the convoy blew up and sank.

Hundreds of men died in blazing holds, hundreds on deck and hundreds in the cold waters of the English Channel. 946 servicemen were lost in this terrible debacle, the details of which have been written up in *The Forgotten Dead* by Ken Small. He managed to recover a Sherman tank from several miles out to sea; it now sits astride the foreshore at Torcross. Hiding from the sheeting rain and thinking of the war, I emerge slowly from the *Start Bay Inn* to rejoin the trail across these fateful sands. Poignantly, I photograph a small girl in white before the tank in black on which was a red wreath of poppies, fluttering US and UK flags.

Berry Head has been tough going, an impressive limestone spur occupied in Bronze and Iron Ages and fortified ever since. It was used by Cromwell in the 17th Century, then later, during the American War of Independence and again in the Napoleonic War with France, when over one thousand men and fifty horses were billetted here. Finally two 6-inch Naval guns were installed to defend Dartmouth in the run up to Hitler's aborted Operation Sealion. In Brixham I see the replica of Drake's *Golden Hind* and Battery Gardens, where there are two 4.7 inch gun emplacements and the mountings for searchlights and anti-aircraft guns that raked the night sky during Hitler's bombing campaigns. I sometimes wonder and rehearse on some lonely windswept stretches of the southwest coast what I would do if someone pulled a gun on me and threatened to shoot. "I can't see that's very sensible," I would begin, calming him down, "If you were to pull the trigger, it would only send me to heaven and you to hell. Why don't you wait until I have shown you how to get to heaven, then we can both get there together." Of course I might just have shouted, "Blood!" hysterically.

David Cawrse, a Bodmin farmer, gave me a handsome hazel thumbstick, which I still have and treasure, but which did seem to have a mind of its own. When bored with poking out people's eyes it would trip me up and otherwise just chew my thumb to bits. A *Leki* Lightweight, a telescopic stick with a rounded wooden handle, proved to be the answer to my needs for defence and attack. It probably deterred a bunch of overly wild youngsters in Leigh-on-Sea and enabled me to deal with umpteen hostile nettles and brambles along the way. More importantly, I would shorten it to maintain pace going steeply uphill. I find it helps me to transfer strength from my upper torso into my legs. It also helps to correct balance negotiating stiles, uneven ground and muddy corners. Though I much pooh-poohed a stick earlier on, I would not be without it now. We have travelled together 500 miles, *Leki* and I. "Indestructible!" I was told by the makers. " Titanium steel!"

However, neither science nor prophecy could have saved us from the red, slippery mud of Babbacombe cliffs. We pass a memorial tribute on a bench: "What is this life if full of care, we have no time to stand and stare". Chance would be a fine thing, I think, as we gingerly start down a narrow path. Too late, the slope is convex and gravity takes control. Devoid of style we lurch, then over-correct in several contrary directions and plunge some twenty feet, cartwheeling together through wet fern to land spread-eagled at the bottom like a flattened Sputnik. Bent, buckled and breathless we lie in dismal silence. The makers bluster a bit about a replacement until I threaten to wave my curved and crippled friend in front of the next television camera.

I am much heartened later, when I stop for water. A golden-haired, fresh-cheeked young lady positively bounces out with eagerness to serve me, filling my bottles with milk, sugar and cooking oil and finally stuffing my pockets with cake. She is breathless with excitement on meeting her first Long Distance Walker, and so am I.

That night, a little furtively, I slip into the Dawlish Warren RSPB hide just as it is dark. I make two unexpected discoveries. First, I am impressed with just how light a moonless night sky really is, compared to the blackness in a human dwelling and second, how noisy it is inside a nature reserve. Periodically the Paddington to Penzance Express roars round the edge of the estuary and every rattle and clink conveys itself faithfully across the water. And behind me, until the early hours of the morning, still echo the shrill music and screams of a visiting fun fair. I am glad early morning to watch the birds feeding, curlews, redshanks and knots, and then gently to stroll towards Starcross. There I learn of Brunel's answer to the horse and carriage, an 'atmospheric railway'. Between Exeter and Newton Abbot he established 12 stations linked by a long tube down the centre of the railway. Suction was provided by a pumping-house, and leather valves provided the air. Speeds of up to 70 miles an hour were achieved. The only problem was, the rats enjoyed tannin and relished the leather.

I have long since had a passion for driving things and once managed to get myself into the driving seat of a fully laden diesel train and drove it with its passengers from Rugby to Bletchley. I can still feel the thrill of a hands-on experience, bridges zipping continually over my head, and being told to tuck down a bit when I went through minor stations. I piloted a Centurian paddle steamer in Finland, a dual-control Tiger Moth in Yorkshire, and a hearse in Staffordshire down the Motorway with full clerical gear flapping out of the window. The closest I got to disaster was operating a digger in the grounds of our brand-new vicarage in Newcastle-under-Lyme. The machine so whizzed round and round and up and down in mindless insensitivity to my instructions and perilously near to our french windows that my wife had a succession of apolplectic fits.

Prior to our retirement in the Cotswolds, I bought a gleaming new Rover 214, to cheer me up a bit. On my birthday that year, Heather consulted Elite Registrations with the same object in mind. She wanted to find a suitable personal number plate. All efforts to combine my name with clerical titles, VIC, REV or PADRE failed to find anything even remotely suitable. About to give up, the woman asked Heather to wait. She explained that, every day, a new random combination of first-time letters is released by the computer and offered to the general public, a combination that no one could anticipate beforehand, nor, of course, replicate later.

"Quite amazing!" she exclaimed after some time away. "You're not going to believe this. Today, this morning, the initials released by the computer are in fact *your husband's*, "GFJ", and in that order. What's more," she continued, nothing has yet gone from the screen. You can have any number you like from A1 to A20." Here in Exmouth I am encouraged by the occasional 'GFJ' and everywhere are 'FJ' number plates because that is the area code in South Devon. At the time, three years ago, I was feeling Z52 and right off the charts. Now, I reaffirm to myself, if He says that's the case, I am both 'GFJ' *and* 'A1'. I just have to believe it. Loved unconditionally, as we all are in Christ, I marvel at such extraordinary precision timing. I am hushed in spirit as I prepare for my visit to the Baptist congregation in Exmouth.

Stoked up with fish and chips and accompanied by beautiful deep pink cloud formations I climb Salcombe Hill two days later and sleep on the edge overlooking Lyme Bay. It is an area dedicated by the owner as 'permanent open space'. An inscription reads: "no sounds of worldly toil ascending there, bar the full burst of prayer". From within my sleeping bag, I phone my ageing father and cease the struggle.

Sallyanne and her friend, Sue, have joined me to walk this day into Lyme Regis. Heather has taken the rucksack and we have delicious weather to skirt the bays of Branscombe and Seaton. Finally, we venture into a long, five-mile wonderland, the Dowlands under-cliffs, knowing that there is no way out, only forward or back. The Great Bindon Slip happened here on Christmas Day 1839. The middle section of long ridges parallel to the sea suddenly slumped rotationally, leaving a deep chasm, 200 feet deep and nearly a mile long, on the landward side. Goat Island, untouched since, dangerous and inaccessible is stranded seawards beyond deep, black crevasses in the ground. Overhung by lianas and overgrown by tall ferns, the path is profoundly scary.

On the eve of my sixtieth birthday the sun is beaming happily out of a clear blue sky. Behind me are five hundred miles and a lot of learning. With me is my precious daughter, walking the last few miles into Lyme Regis. Ahead of me, my faithful wife is cooking and preparing for a family feast and celebrations, which include my father's ninety-fifth birthday. Lyme feels like an old shoe, ageless and always there, stuffed with story, fossils and families. The Cobb and old codgers, contentedly sit with the sand and slot machines along the sea front.

At last I take my boots off. The neighbours come round to toast my father, who has just received the Eagle Star's gold award for sixty years of claim-free motoring, and with it a free subscription for the rest of his life. With my cards I open a large bottle of champagne and Sallyanne announces a birthday surprise, a balloon ride for us all. The weather on my birthday is perfect. The Walk has lift-off. I just know I'm going to make it. At twenty-one, Sallyanne has lift-off. She'll make it too. My life-journey has lift-off after four varsity years of my father's patience with his late-developing son; and now we all have lift-off, drifting above the Devon countryside together, all except Grandad who cannot get his leg over the basket.

Chapter 6

Lyme Bay to The Solent

WORK WAS NOT WORKING

I FIND MYSELF MAKING SMALL TALK AND TAKING unnecessary photos, unwilling to part from the family. My enthusiasm returns as I climb above the town, sorry to leave but also glad to go. I approach a stile-gate on a rise and at that very instant a buzzard comes in to land, its huge wings outstretched and talons about to grip. Yes! I focus on the last stretch of the first major section, one third of the Walk which ends in Southampton. I take a grip on myself as I survey the fractured edge of the Black Venn landslips. This is the Lyme Regis Marine Wild Life Area, an experiment in coastal management. It extends four and a half miles along the cliffs and one and a half miles out into Lyme Bay to include the steamship *Baygitano* sunk in 1918. The Warden, Adrian Brokenshire, gives me fossils, an ammonite in fool's gold and a belemnite snout. His inspiring manner reminds me of my 'A' Level teacher, Mr Grange, who first quickened my interest in geomorphology. This area was once a vast sub-tropical sea. Had I been a bit younger, a hundred and fifty million years ago I could have swum in a direct line through 'the Cotswolds' from Lyme Regis to Whitby, or perhaps hitched a lift off-shore on a willing plesiosaur. As it is, the final ascent to the summit of Golden Cap, the highest point on the South Coast at 618 feet, is quite an effort and I promptly slip fifteen feet on my *derrière* down some wet grass the other side. The South West Coast Path Association proudly informs its clientele that along its 613 mile length walkers will climb the height of three Mount Everests from sea level and for me that's only as far as Poole.

I had peaked in my first job and then came a cropper. I was far too confident as a young man, ambitious and driven. In my earliest years I had exiled tender feelings towards myself and others and substituted a tough but deceptively friendly exterior laced with suitable propaganda I myself believed. I had developed labyrinthine ways to re-interpret failure and a phenomenal ability to escape self-reproach at any price. The dogs of self-discovery were kept firmly at bay. Fresh from Manchester and now a Member of the Institute of Personnel Management, I could talk myself in and out of anything. So it was that, against stiff opposition from twenty-five other interviewees, I landed a job in the Central Personnel Department of Albright and Wilson Mfg Ltd, in Oldbury, manufacturers of phosphorus. Blind to my life-long aversion to chemistry, I was impressed by the Company's image and landed the big fish. I was taken up a long corridor to an office beside the Personnel Director. I believed I deserved it and yet had walked up a cul-de-sac of self-belief and self-delusion and within six months was feeling isolated, confused and dysfunctional. I was enjoying the job, responsible for recruiting school leavers from public schools. I had career exhibitions in different places, took candidates to expensive hotels and ferried them into the factory for lectures on a whole range of household products. I would wear the Company tie, and speak to the Company motto: "For the peace and enlightenment of mankind". But within me were angst and greyness. The Personnel Director said, off-handedly, "Are you happy here?" I fudged and dodged the issue but within nine months, I was on my way. As I said to the girls in the office, some of whom had tried to seduce me, "I'm sorry to leave but glad to go."

I went to Joseph Lucas and began piece work on the night shift to get experience of the shop floor. It was mind-wracking tedium, stamping out coils for alternators. I was working with lantern-jawed, sunken-eyed, ashen-faced escapees from society, marriage or the Law. During the day I was interior decorating for my grandma in Harborne and, with insufficient sleep one night, dozed off on the job. No quarter given or received, I was sacked on the spot. Self-questioning was not my forte and I obtained offers of work as a labour officer with the MoD and as an assistant warden at Bristol YMCA. These I turned down, to their annoyance and my own further embarrassment. Truth was still a stranger, but I was learning. However, the one thing I simply refused to consider was the Church. I had three excellent reasons – women, committees and bishops. So that was that!

The rain blots out most things. I am trudging head down along the front, unaware that my camera has been picked up in Burton Bradstock. It fell through my over-trousers. Underfoot the sand becomes pea gravel and I begin the long assault on twenty-four miles of shifting shingle past the brackish waters of the Fleet and a thousand swans at Abbotsbury towards Weymouth on the infamous Chesil beach. I am tempted up to the ruins of St Catherine's Chapel and find a prayer on a slip of paper: "A husband, St Catherine, a handsome one, a rich one, a nice one, and soon!" I'm sure she managed it. I clamber over shooting ranges and Colin and Margaret lift me out of numb and sodden tiredness into the friendly ambience of St Aldhelm's Anglican Church in Radipole next day.

Over three centuries from The Great Fire of London to Post-War redevelopment, millions of tons of Portland stone have been poured into London. 'Any ol' iron' formed ballast for the sailing ships on their return journey and, not surprisingly, along the promenades and high streets of South Dorset can still be found bollards, stumps and decorations, bearing capital motifs. Gazing seawards, from the back of crouching Portland, the sea is both maternal and maleficent. To the east is the protective harboured bay and to the west the destructive power of Chesil Beach. Ocean waters dispense or dispose at will. From outer space, 'the most beautiful face on earth' is marred when seen from a floating piece of wreckage. A stormy sea is a wilful and pitiless scourge. Such is the undertow on Chesil Beach that human life cannot survive the drag and repetition of endlessly revolving breakers. 140 passengers and crew of the *Alexandra*, March 1815, 300 people on the *Abergavenny*, 1805, and over 1,000 soldiers on three military vessels in 1795, are witness to the contemptuous indifference of the sea on this beach. Not far away, as undertaker and gravedigger, she disposed of nearly 2,000 triumphant fighting men returning from action as they tangled with the Isles of Scilly one foggy October night, in 1707.

However, over the millennia this 'beautiful face' has a creative edge carved by demolition, deposition and the forces of subduction. Again it is a ceaseless blessing that the North Atlantic Conveyor, as oceanographers call it, pushes the Gulf Stream to caress our shores, sending palms into Penzance and plankton onto the continental shelf, at a latitude exactly that of Labrador on the edge of Eskimoland. Moreover day and night the sun adds its power and the moon its pull so that the beach is renewed twice a day for the delight of trippers, bathers and surfers. Pumped with adrenaline, wind-surfers skim the rippled surface into the setting sun, or scythe between breakers at break-neck speeds. Fishermen, seamen and smugglers fear the stormy tiger in her moods, but thankfully stash away their bounty on return. No one in England lives more than sixty-five miles away, and all owe their survival to the natural block and barrier that is the sea. Those who live on the edge come to respect their landlady, knowing that overnight she can snatch away their dreams and dissolve their grand designs. For me, travelling light, she is fascinating company, a ready conversant always at my right hand.

On the quayside a local reporter scribbles "Making Waves" to catch his readers. Indeed, I'm outside the Childrens Society Centre in Weymouth called *Waves* and Jonathan organises a boisterous and kindly coffee stop, before I have to buy myself another camera nearby. The journey to Poole was dotted with interest. I find a metal plough-tip from horse-drawn days in the hillside above Durdle Door and, in the cliffs below Lulworth firing range, fossil tree stumps, a fascinating string of round stone orifices near the beach. Mike, a geography professor, has joined me through this military leg of the walk and we see an impressive display of massed tanks, the village of Tynham, commandeered for the SAS, and endless warnings about unexploded shells. A few coves on and enjoying a quiet lunch, the Royal Marines invade our bay in high-speed landing craft and we seem to be escorted off by a very noisy helicopter.

Time now to bid farewell to the luxury of a marked path. I acknowledge the BP nodding donkey pump at Kimmeridge and doff my hat to the Rev John Clavell's attempt to further his interest in astronomy, the classical 'Clavell Tower'. I sleep on Old Harry's precarious back, sympathising with the loss of his wife and recall the grandeur of The Purbecks and quite breath-taking scenery. I make short work of Swanage and finally with some delicacy step through the long naturist beach on my way to the ferry and Sandbanks crossing Poole Harbour. Now, after 650 miles, at the end of the SW Coast Path, I am to choose my own route, unaware that it will soon lead me into a lot of trouble.

Gone is the happy diversity of the cliff-top footpath. Now, it is the brutality of concrete, tarmac and paving slabs. Six miles to Branksome Vicarage, twelve miles to Hengistbury Head, and in between the promenades, Westbourne, Bournemouth, Boscombe and Southbourne. They all hit me like a wind-surfer colliding with the side of a house. From flexible and elastic my body is now being jarred. I am walking in a sort of robotic submission and not enjoying it.

Being enticed into the Hope-FM Community Christian Radio Station is easy enough because again it is pouring with rain. I hear the discjockey whisper through his mike to the producer, "Scrap the programme," and I am tied into kindly but probing interrogation interspersed with music. All aspects of my life and the walk are irresistibly teased out of me. Over and over again, I put my faith and my foot in it and feel terribly vulnerable over our family experiences. As is so often the case, it seems my glib words and easy assertions are soon to be tested.

Mid-afternoon I come out of the *Russell-Cotes Art Gallery* and find the rain has stopped. I walk the length of Hengistbury Road to my paternal grandparents' home. A knock and a cool reception prompt me to head for the beach and Point Café where Arthur and Hannah Jones are indeed remembered by Raymond and Dorothy. Restocked with the usual basics I set out to explore Hengistbury Head, a little hill continuously defended from the old Stone Age. At one time it had been connected to the Isle of Wight via the Needles. This hill fort once crested a river valley, now the Solent, and before the drowning of the English Channel there were settlements here of hunter-gatherer families 12,500 years ago. Wanting to soak up the atmosphere I decide to pitch in the lee of the Coastguard station, which in the dusk is barely visible. In no time I have more atmospherics than I can handle. I stop bewildered. Dense clouds of swifts, thousands of them, are swooping from all directions mopping up the insects on the heather and heath. Clearly it is a pre-migration inter-galactic convention at its peak, a magnificent display of aerobatics.

I am not sure whether the display of bat-like swoops and dives are intended to stretch all records for speed and tight turns or whether it is actually very personal and I am being mobbed. Thankfully I get my head inside the tent. I am shivering and have some soup first, then the usual colloidal mixture of custard, dates and sliced mango. I clutch a hot mug of tea and finish off some chocolate biscuits, thinking about the day and the children. I had found on a trig. point just yards away, a memorial to Babe Connor McCabe. He had lived just four months, like my baby son, Allister. I sleep restlessly. In the early hours, I awake breathless with pains in my chest. I have a chest infection after the damp misty atmosphere all yesterday and in the tent last night. After breakfast I hoist my rucksack and with the usual prayer take three steps. The first is 'faith' that everything still works. The second is 'hope' that I would get where I was going. The third is 'love' that whoever I meet and in whatever circumstances I meet them it will be a mutual blessing. A sharp pain down the side of my right lower leg draws my attention to a large area of swelling. Today, everything is *not* working. I decide to walk it off and trust and hope…

Stepping off the diddy ferry to Christchurch, I look back on the tranquil scene of mist on the Head, bobbing corks on fishing nets strung to catch the tide across the ubiquitous mud and by my side the huge pile of whelk pots, someone's livelihood. Here at Mudeford quayside, aptly named, mud has become an art form in subtlety and understatement – that is, until another machine, a bright-orange refuse collector roars up and swallows nearly everything in sight, except the mud.

Beach huts are magnificently English. They cluster in ribbons all the way round the South and East, in summer shyly tickling and toying with the sleeping sea, and in the winter barricaded from her tantrums. Difficult to insure, rent or buy they are usually cared for, often lovingly stencilled and frequently decked in frilly curtains. Twice I had tea from a battered aluminium kettle and a crock teapot. Here the Council huts are uniformly green and capped by ochre-red roofs. At Herne Bay they are numbered up to four hundred, chunky and set back to last, except that the sea has evidently acquired a taste for them and large chunks are missing. Wells-on-Sea and Cleethorpes impress, but none are so ingeniously named and decorated as at Southwold – 'CEEZRUF', 'PLAICE AND SHIPS' AND 'MA'S BAR'.

Some places ooze old-world charm but not *The Needle's Eye*, a café on Milford sea front. It is a one-story shoe-box. Massive RSJs, plywood and square panes of glass are given a deafeningly loud colour scheme, bright yellow or blue for everything that doesn't move, and a sea of orange plastic chairs, the only things that do. I choose a corner table, rest my forearms on the blue-check plastic table cover and I'm stuck. I begin to register the amazing frieze of dolphins, octopuses and happy smiling sea horses. In the other corner sits Dave with a big pimply nose and a shock of greyish hair, feeling loved. He is faithful at his office-cleaning job. He just likes to ride around on his bike and then come here to be cared for. Behind the yellow laminated counter is the secret of success. "Hi! I'm Carole Ann Parish. Carole with an 'e', Ann without an 'e' and Parish as in 'Church'. We're all Parishes but now my family are Smiths," she adds with a laugh as riotous as the colours all round her. "I just shout 'em down." I love her style but I have to keep moving and a mile or two further along I do find my old-world counterpart to *The Needle's Eye* at Keyhaven. The *Gun Inn* has "Malt Whisky Galore" advertised among mounds of spilling flowerpots. A gust of belly laughter surges out as I come in. I make for the loos marked 'Buoys' and 'Gulls'. I am told the cellar was used regularly as a temporary dump for the stacking of corpses. I didn't stop.

Like personal friends, my boots and the rucksack both need occasional attention – basically a spot of glue. I hole up until Monday at Portland Lodge. Hal and Eileen Box are family friends near Lymington and I am so glad of a break, still feeling pain in my leg and chest. I could not know how dramatically my next and final day would climax before reaching Southampton. Mended and booted, and feeling cared for, I strike out on the Solent Way for Bucklers' Hard. Hidden in a vast acreage of woodland on the deep and protected River Beaulieu this was Nelson's ideal place to build his fleet. I wander through the authentic buildings and the Agamemnon Boatyard. I can imagine the great English flagship on its first journey to the sea. A very peaceful walk up the river brings me to the village and Lord Montagu's Motor Museum. A chance meeting with His Lordship round the famous *Bluebird* brings back memories of my next job over thirty years ago working for Sir Alfred Owen. He owned the *Bluebird.* He had over fifty companies world-wide and his Central Personnel Department was in Darlaston.

As one of his welfare officers I met him on his return from Australia. He went straight into the factory to talk with his men on night shift. Next morning, he asked me to come through to the Chairman's office to discuss a proposition, which usually meant to accept his instruction. As the Patron of a number of parishes he had responsibility for clergy. One such had fallen sick. This vicar had two churches. Would I take charge of one of them? "What!" said I, "Do everything? Take services?" I sputtered. "But I can't! I'm not licensed!" He picked up the phone. "Stretton..." he said to the Bishop of Lichfield. Next morning, a Lay Reader's licence sat glowing on my desk. "Use the car" (a blue Mini) he said, "and split your time between factory and parish and get on with it." One foggy November evening I groped my way up the drive to St Martin's Vicarage in Bilston. I was introduced to a kindly vicar, a shrunken man, wreathed in a thick black overcoat and Homburg hat. He stood under a forty-watt bulb in the hall. I was shown into a half-empty dining-room and given a half-empty cup of tea with half a tea-cake. As I was only to spend half my time in the parish, perhaps I was destined or doomed to have everything in halves. I went to live in one half of the Vicarage and we were only given half an egg each, the Vicar and I, on which to go to work. I soon lost about half my weight until my emaciated shape became so evident to the good folks in St Francis' Church that I was rescued by a 'Mrs P', who loved to put Nestle's milk in my tea and gravy to the edge of my plate. With Mr and Mrs Enoch Priest I felt halfway there and was ordained four and a half years later.

I have spent far too long in the Motor Museum. I set my sights on Southampton and quicken my pace waggling my butt like a marathon walker round the headwaters of the Beaulieu estuary. Some distance ahead a rather cocky and stoutly built woman sees me coming and mimics my walk, showing off to her friends. I pursue a steady course and relish the encounter. As I come level I use my stick to deliver a carefully timed though friendly wallop on her buttocks. To my satisfaction I just catch sight of her flushed cheeks and the uproarious response of her friends. I enjoy the open heath, the velvet close-cropped contours of the grass, and the ponies of the New Forest, and plunge on through larch and pine woods. I follow the electric pylons towards Fawley Refinery and then leap a stile into a housing estate. With a growing sense of achievement and a one third finale, I rocket through the houses and hitch a lift into Hythe. I just manage a quick telephone call to my overnight hosts and head for the ferry. It is nearly six o'clock, as we had planned. Hythe is all decked out but I am not for stopping. Ticket in hand, I squash some fish and chips on the boardwalk, and spring aboard a marvellous little red and white diesel train. It squeaks and creaks its way across half a mile of rickety pier out into the Solent and in no time I am exploring the Red Funnel passenger ferry on its way to Southampton.

In the well of the lower deck I happen to see the liner listings for 1997. It is the complete visiting schedule for all the great ocean cruise ships in and out of Southampton, over the year. My attention is suddenly riveted on the entry for this particular day. I check and check again. There is no mistake. This day is the departure of the famous P & O Steamship *Canberra.* This journey, of all her journeys, is the penultimate voyage before she is sent to Pakistan for scrap. This ship is close to my heart and filled with memories. In 1983, with forty-three packing cases, three bikes and a little yellow Polo, we set sail for a demanding job in New Zealand as Co-Vicar of Holy Trinity, Tauranga. In 1987, still with our packing cases, we also returned on the *Canberra* but missing our daughter Elizabeth. She had died two months previous. The Captain was under instruction from the churches to look after us on our homeward journey. With maritime pride and precision I know the ship will leave on time and the time listed is 6.20 pm. Twenty minutes to go.

The ferry touches the quayside. I'm first off. There is no time to lose. I embrace my waiting friend and in minutes we are whistling through the complicated maze of wharves and warehouses to the departure terminal. Suddenly, I am there Quay Number 106. The Great White Whale towers above. I remember afresh the vast height of the decks, tier upon tier, our home for six weeks out, going West through the Panama Canal and seven weeks back, coming from the East, through the Suez Canal. I can see the ship in a hurricane clamped by four tugs to the dockside in Los Angeles. I can see the ship smoking after fire caused by a disaffected Goanese steward. I can see the ship riding the blue tranquil waters of the Solomon Islands with little red lifeboats ferrying the passengers ashore. I can see the mountainous buffet meals on deck, the swimming and entertainment below and I can see the deck-chair where I fell asleep sun-bathing. I can see now above the bulk of this mighty boat the distinctive mustard-coloured twin stack, belching exultantly at the prospect, any moment, of freedom.

On this and on every departure, as on her trip to the Falklands War and back, there is the local regimental brass band. The music stirs us to patriotism and nostalgia, celebration and sadness. The balconies are bursting. Everywhere is stacked and packed with people, some shouting out words of affection and life-long loyalty. Cheering breaks out as party poppers burst and shower thin paper ribbons from ship to shore. Thousands of people are clutching lines of love. They will hang on for dear life to harness the ship to shore, until the very last strand is broken. My eyes fill and my heart pumps with agony and ecstasy.

I can see our cabin filled with flowers from the churches and hear the Captain's kindly words of welcome. I can see so many moments of our poignant history writ large in this mighty maternal vessel, straining at the leash, when suddenly the air shakes. A mighty thunderous blast on the ship's hooter drowns all else. Three times and then a fourth and the four-inch thick hawser is lifted free and dropped into the water with a splash. An aching gap begins to open up and with it all our separations. Amid the din and commotion there is a terrible stillness inside me. Choking I cling to my friend. Immobilised by grief I cherish each tiny moment as the countless coloured streamers stretch and snap and quietness falls on all who watch. I am wrapped in wonderment and stare endlessly as the tugs, one by one, leave her and she slips silently away. The *Canberra* heads for the sea and like our three absent children is gone all too soon from our view. I know my Father's hand and recognise the timing of this encounter-beyond-human-contrivance, and my heart is awed with yet another piece in the mosaic of meaning, my journey round the Edge of England.

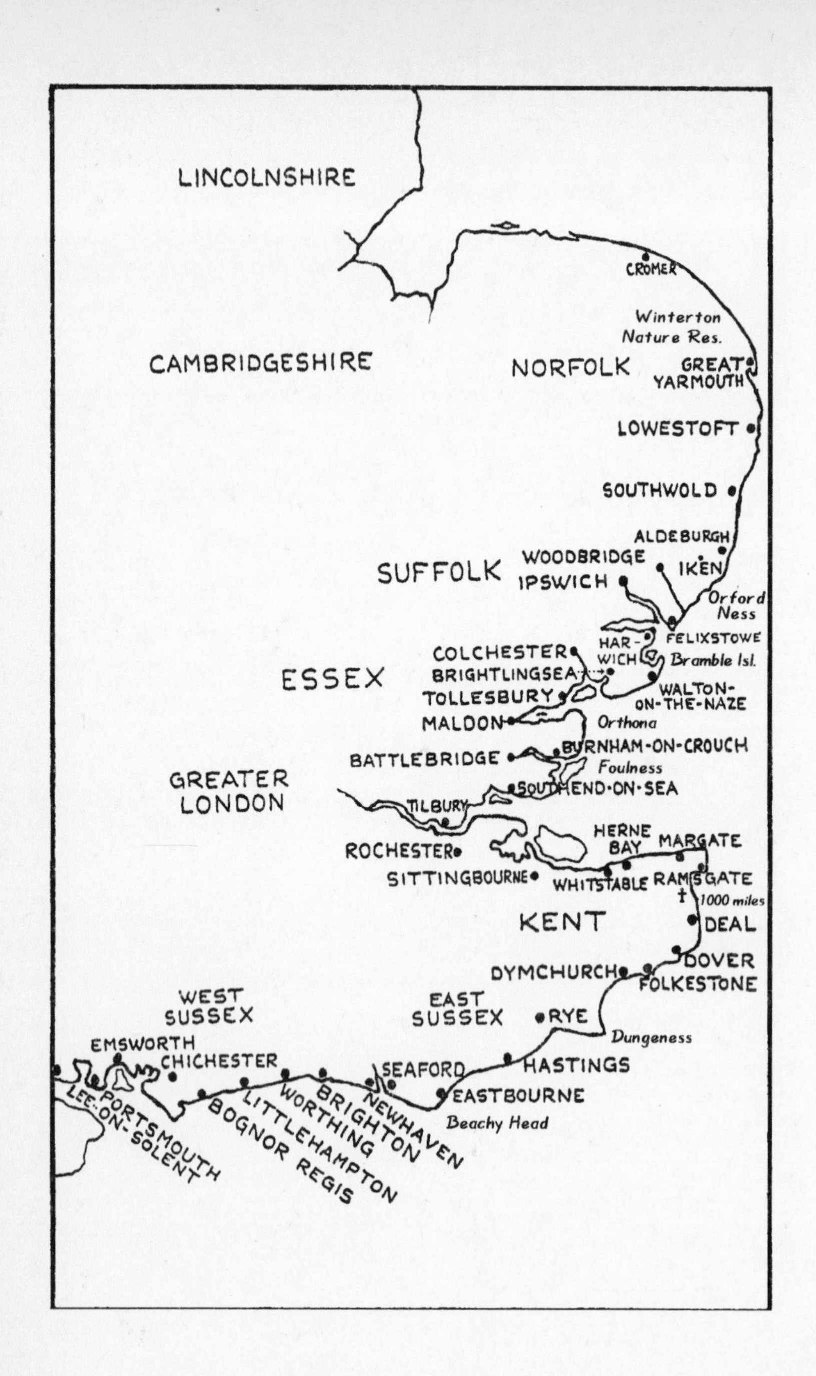
LINCOLNSHIRE
CAMBRIDGESHIRE
NORFOLK
CROMER
Winterton
Nature Res.
GREAT
YARMOUTH
LOWESTOFT
SOUTHWOLD
ALDEBURGH
SUFFOLK
WOODBRIDGE
IKEN
IPSWICH
Orford
Ness
HAR-
WICH
FELIXSTOWE
Bramble Isl.
COLCHESTER
ESSEX
BRIGHTLINGSEA
TOLLESBURY
WALTON-
ON-THE-NAZE
MALDON
Orthona
BATTLEBRIDGE
BURNHAM-ON-CROUCH
Foulness
GREATER
LONDON
SOUTHEND-ON-SEA
TILBURY
HERNE
BAY
MARGATE
ROCHESTER
SITTINGBOURNE
WHITSTABLE
RAMSGATE
1000 miles
KENT
DEAL
DOVER
DYMCHURCH
FOLKESTONE
WEST
SUSSEX
EAST
SUSSEX
RYE
Dungeness
EMSWORTH
CHICHESTER
HASTINGS
SEAFORD
EASTBOURNE
Beachy Head
PORTSMOUTH
LEE-ON-SOLENT
BOGNOR REGIS
LITTLEHAMPTON
WORTHING
BRIGHTON
NEWHAVEN

SECOND LEG

Thirty testing years — partner, parent and pastor

Chapter 7

Southampton to Worthing

LEARNING TO BE LED

MEET TWO MIGHTY MEN, BRIAN AND GERARD. BRIAN Field, several years my senior at school, was the very embodiment of all my boyish hopes. He was a big chap with broad shoulders, huge hands and, on the rugby pitch, a magnificent pair of sweaty heaving thighs. His face, like a crag from Ilkley Moor, had vertical cliffs and overhanging ledges. He had the squarest jaw I had ever seen. But it was his eyes that endeared me to this man. They shone with Christian love. He had time for me. He would look me in the eye and wink. I was a young Christian and Brian inspired me to serve the Lord and speak up for Him in the two years I had left at school. I can still hear his gravelly voice calling me "Gandhi!" I did not see him again, until forty years later, we met on the sea-front near Worthing at the end of this week's walk.

Gerard was a year or two behind me at School. I hardly knew him but he noticed me. I was leading a boys' Bible Study group that met for twenty minutes before school began. Perhaps twenty-five lads would gather especially early to think, read and pray up to the bell for Assembly. Since that time Gerard has been a successful lawyer with a great sense of humour despite working for the Crown Prosecution Service. He loves the Lord, the Gospel, France, prisoners and children. He leads United Beach Missions, which annually staffs about forty holiday activities for children at the sea-side and also Freemantle Evangelical Church. Within a few minutes of arrival I am swept into Gerard and Phillippa Chrispin's lounge to meet fifteen other smiling, laughing and energetic people, aged from three to thirty and am announced as being the one who first inspired Gerard to walk the King's Highway. I sit down wondering if I have craggy features and sweaty thighs.

Drained after seeing the *Canberra* depart, it is wonderful to relax in their Christian home, to pause, rest my legs and relish a third of my journey as now over. I view with an unfocused apprehension the prospect and challenge of walking the next section round the South coast, Kent and the Essex marshes to Cromer. It will also take me in heart and mind through the next thirty years of my life, the privilege of partnership and the parenting of four children. But first I must finish my twenties, a transition, a necessary time of adjustment, painful learning and the joyful discovery of partner and parish.

I limp downstairs on Monday morning and am soon in the doctor's. I tell him I had beaten the worst that Devon and Cornwall could throw at me. How come I was fit there and now on the flat, I'm crippled? It transpires that the rough terrain effectively and continuously massages the feet. The surfaced promenades of recent days have left my feet unexercised and the tendons have now gone into spasm where they connect above the ankle. The sheath that holds and lubricates the movement of my right foot is badly inflamed. "Six weeks, young man", said the doctor patronisingly. I explained my five-month schedule, and an average of nearly twenty miles a day. "It's gristle you see," he explained. "It's inflamed. If you don't rest, it will not go away. You will just have to push through the pain." "What!" I exclaim, "for 1,250 miles?" I wince. He grimaces and gives me a prescription for my wheezing chest and my swollen leg. My left leg is not too bad. Perhaps the stick has helped.

Tony Curtis takes me round Southampton in the car, thankfully. The ancient walls and an empty churchless tower, deprived of its nave and congregation in the war, leads finally to the chemist. With a fresh and delighted smile on her face, the pharmacist hands me my first free NHS prescription, something to swig for my chest and something to swallow for my legs, plus bandages for extra support, my induction to pensioner-hood. I sound and look a sorry sight at sixty. I hobble out of the door and clutching my stick I set off down the Solent, every step a limp. I passed time with some men digging for lug-bait in the mud. A while later a man sinks up to his neck and is only just dragged out in time by the emergency services. I am reminded that one of our New Zealand tea-chests was dropped off the quayside into the Solent mud. Divers retrieved it for us to inspect later in the ship's hold. Apart from toys and a ruined evening dress I recovered a bookmark. It said: "Hold thou me up and I shall be safe". I limp past *Netley Castle Convalescent Home* and am sorely tempted to ask for a bunk and biscuit. I find the Royal Victoria Hospital no help at all a few miles further on. It has been a vast mile-long complex, inspired by Queen Victoria herself to cater for the needs of men in the Crimean War. A solitary tower, now marooned in its park, is all that remains today. I take a lift up to the dome at the top, a sort of defiant cupola, which tops a squat octagon of Victorian brick. There isn't even a chair to sit on.

Leaving the Solent I capture on film the 630-foot Esso refinery tower and turn east. I scramble over the sea-going pipes of a BP oil terminal, skirt a Beaufors anti-aircraft gun, still in its emplacement, and head for the Harbour-master's office at Hamble, set amid a forest of masts and no fewer than five marinas. It is raining hard. All I want is shelter and a forecast. At 7 a.m. every morning he receives the inshore waters weather forecast from the Bracknell Meteorological Office and this applies to anyone up to twelve miles out to sea. I was glued to a chair as well as the script: "thundery showers with gusts up to 25 knots". I strongly connect with the "deepening depression" slowly moving my way. "Hail and heavy showers developing into longer spells of rain" hardly lifts my spirits. "Visibility poor". I wait no longer and stumble down the wooden steps into the boatyard. I had better just 'breeze through' this sodden corner of Hampshire. Reflecting on the penetration of weather into the English language I feel for my imaginary life jacket and, head down, make for the ferry to Warsach.

Somewhat revived at Bill and Joan Loomes' I am dropped off on the jetty path. Reluctant to leave behind the comfort of the car I hang on to the central pillar just a shade too long. "Ouch!" the rear door traps my thumb. Do you know it takes a whole year to grow another nail? At Lee-on-Solent, I pass the Marine Rescue Centre and the Fleet Air Arm base that sports a gigantic hovercraft. About twenty-two large glass panel windows on each side encircle a cavernous area, about twenty by thirty metres, capable of picking up a liner-full of people. The locals of sleepy Lee don't seem the slightest bit impressed. I pass within inches of two old ladies sitting bolt upright together and fast asleep. Further on there is a recumbent lady on a deck-chair snoring soundly under her white floppy hat, from which three or four pink chins ripple down her chest.

This is a busy part of our coastline. Not least it sends fuel along the seabed direct to Heathrow. Palmerston authorised over twenty forts to defend the area. The policy appears to have succeeded, if deterrence is the name of the game, as Fort Gilkicker and Fort Cumberland, to name but two, were never used in anger. First on parade is the Royal Navy Submarine Museum, where visitors can clamber through HMS *Alliance*. The Jolly Roger flags reflect the piratical flavour of the very early submarines, which seemed then a bit un-British. Across the ferry and into Portsmouth I pass HMS *Warrior*, the world's first armoured steam battleship. In 1860 she required 700 officers and men to man her fifteen sails, forty guns, engines and five-ton anchors.

Ray and I meet on the flagship *Victory*. He had walked the South West Coast Path and personally takes me round the ship, the scene of Nelson's victory over Napoleon at Trafalgar. 850 men were needed to fire a withering broadside of cannonballs every eighty seconds. She has been afloat since 1778, and was completely restored this century. But it is the *Mary Rose* that captures and holds my imagination. The 'flower of the English fleet' and Henry VIII's favourite warship, she sank in action, her gun-holes set too low and left open as she turned to face the enemy in 1545. Now she is slowly breathing again and soon to be re-united with her artefacts in an interactive display at Portsmouth. She is rejoicing in an aqueous shower of wax and water, to stabilise her molecular structure. Brendan Ely, Development Officer, tells me that, once housed, it will be an awesome moment to stand beneath 300 tons of this Tudor giant.

I spend the night in a Domesday Book Manor, acquired by King William in 1066 following the Battle of Hastings. The Wymering manor site is stuffed with Roman remains so place and building are of enormous fascination. Alone with my thoughts in the extra-ordinarily ornate dining-room, I am served egg and chips by the warden of the Portsmouth Youth Hostel. In the morning I set out early for town, treat myself to a tray of sea-food and meet 'Bim'.

I have been turned away from the gates of the Naval Dockyard thirty minutes before opening time and am feeling miffed and irritated by the red tape of the po-faced officers and very patronising policemen forcing me to delay on an otherwise very pleasant morning. Nearby is 'Bim'. Just my man! In splendid isolation he has parked his unlikely trailer-cum- fish-store on the common 'hard' where he alone is claiming ancient trading rights. Hard it is and tough he is by name and nature, Bim perseveres. It took him two years to get permission from nine different bodies, surviving a string of less than neighbourly objections. The Council charges him £50 a week rent and un-itemised costs of £200, £300 and now £400 every year. Every conceivable obstacle is being put in Bim's path. No signboard is permitted, no parking is allowed within six feet of the pavement and no platform to keep old ladies from falling down the little steps. Bim was a computer engineer with British Telecom for twenty-one years. He talks of two wives, two kids and two dogs. Though he is amiable, law-abiding and conscientious, the Council continues to harass the man, but fails utterly to dowse his sense of humour. Now he can spend four months of the year in Mexico.

With a nickname like Gandhi I do have strong sympathies with non-violent resistance as a preferable democratic option wherever possible – which does not mean, incidentally, that Christians should just roll over and wave their legs in the air. However there has always been in me a combative instinct that extols the virtues of strength and admires the spirit and courage of the soldier. Outside the D-Day Museum at Southsea are two bronze larger-than-life effigies: a resting soldier with helmet off and a commanding 'Monty' with his beret definitely on. I recall the blue plaque outside *The Rising Sun* at Warsach, which commemorates the departure of 3,000 hand-picked commandos in 36 landing craft, bound for the beaches of Normandy to the inspirational skirl of bagpipes. Operation Overlord is also featured in the marvellous Royal Marines' historical presentation at Eastney.

I walk out of town via the Cockleshell Community Centre which pictures men who bluffed their way through the very gates of hell. I am soon to meet Ray leaning over the railings at Withernsea, looking out to sea, his eyes streaming yet more salt into the ocean. He was one of 27 out of 600 paratroopers to survive the drop at Arnhem. He had bravely crossed the lines several times before being taken and marched to the mines in Poland. He stood up erect, as I left, like the other proud statue of a Marine at Eastney Barracks. 50 million people died in World War II of which 20 million were Russian. Half were not even in uniform. Perhaps, knowing the Human Genome, famine and disease will be no more, but greed will always remain. Maybe "the worst of war *is* behind us," as John Keegan has said. Will death alone be left to challenge our self-confidence? Just then I bump into a MoD man just retired and missing his wife. She has died leaving him to grieve.

The weather lives up to its forecast and I squelch bedraggled round Langstone Harbour. I meet Fred, the last surviving cockle collector in the harbour, tough, tattooed and content. A little later I trip over a family of baby black-tailed godwits and see the shy back of a greenshank, before being hauled, leaking all over, into an English Nature Land Rover. The sky opens yet again and the warden and I sit, thankful to escape the worst of the deluge. Aiming for Emsworth with my eyes closed, I splosh on to Hayling Island, and 'islands' are definitely out for this journey. I return to finish the Solent Way and am soon welcomed by bustling Belinda and sit down before a steaming hot meal in the Thomas' cul-de-sac home.

'Bozzum' is next or Bosham as it is on the map. Roman below, Saxon on top and elsewhere Norman or Early English it is memorable indeed to have Evening Prayer in the chancel. Peeping through my fingers I espy a raven engraving and underneath, a slab of stone. It is the coffin lid of a little girl aged eight, the daughter of King Canute. The latter not only found time to be King of Denmark, Norway and England, but also to sit and defy the sea, from whence his forebears came, threatening the villagers and forcing them into this church tower for safety. The tower is featured in the Bayeux Tapestry with King William at prayer.

West Wittering to Bracklesham takes me from the cosiest to the most chaotic holiday accommodation and into a maze of broken down caravans and a cracked swimming pool. I learn that the next time the sea breaches the shingle, the Council will let it. It will turn the area into an extensive nature reserve and Selsey back into an island, which is its name, Seal Island. Patrick Moore will have more privacy for his telescope and another Patrick I met there will be undisturbed when he finally decides to commit suicide, the wish he expressed to me.

I have been much refreshed at Chris and Anne's in Bognor Regis. With returning vigour I set out to walk a good twenty miles and overly press the pace. Soon I am limping again on the hard unyielding promenades. Middleton-on-Sea is followed by Littlehampton and its rowing boat ferry. I buy a large spiral ice-cream and sit down to enjoy the entertainment. People everywhere are throwing their arms wildly in all directions. A plague of flies has descended from nowhere and some of the children are indulging in a frenzy of murder and mayhem. It reminds me of a sign I saw on a front gate: "Sod the dog: beware of the kids!"

At Goring-by-Sea I am in big trouble. I can hardly walk. Looking ahead I know that there is nothing but tarmac through Lancing, Shoreham, Portslade, Hove, Brighton, Rottingdean and beyond to the Seven Sisters. Both legs are playing up and swelling above my boots. Men are supposed to be tough and uncomplaining. They don't give in and they don't give up. Chin out I walk metronomically all day until suddenly, astride the pavement and true to promise, is Brian Field, his curly grey hair blowing in the wind. A moment to remember after forty years. Soon, boots off, I am resting in the joy of Brian's pale-green Metro, gulping down hot coffee and tasty meat-filled sandwiches. But something has to be done. We decide that the tent, sleeping gear and cooking utensils are not needed, along with food. They will have to be left behind during the trip round Kent, to be collected on my way to Tilbury. Then Heather offers to meet me at St Leonards-on-Sea, to keep my day-pack in the car and arrange accommodation for the next few days. I shift *Leki* from my right to my left hand side, hoping that will even the strain. I think of Jacob who would not be parted from his stick, but used it as an aid to rest and worship.

Something will have to be done about Graham's body. It needs fixing. I enjoy walking. It is earthy and grounding, a rhythm of constant adjustment, but I have to listen to my body more carefully, allow it to speak to me. I know that if I take too much out of my body, it simply refuses to lift its head off the pillow next morning. If it is short of water, it gives me a headache. I consciously unclench my hands, arms and shoulders to relax into a point below my diaphragm, somewhere between bottom and belly. With a rucksack clamped to my pelvis, that is my centre of gravity. It means I am not walking on my legs like stilted appendages, but walking *in* them. They are me.

Also at the age of 25 Graham himself needed fixing. My preferred place to live safely was always in my head, from which vantage point I could re-enforce my notions of superiority. Mentally I would always be well prepared for most situations and talk my way in and out of human encounters. Status and strength were passwords. I kind of liked large institutions, where there was safety in hierarchy. With the best of intentions my father would ritually advise against vulnerability and my mother always counsel independence. However, Christ within, there began a slow melting of inner defences and the emergence of a new way of living. Stridency gave way to gentleness and the path of service instead of the plinth of sainthood. I have never quite conquered my need to impress and propaganda still comes too easily to massage my public persona. I used to call it playing to my strengths and giving a lead, when it really was asking others to keep up with the Joneses.

Jesus, Moses and the Israelites experienced the test of wilderness before enjoying the fruits of ministry. Mid-twenties for me was a wilderness of wandering and doubting and loneliness. I had heard his call: "You are my beloved son". Now he wanted me to be 'his servant'. In 1962 I taught in St John's Harborne Sunday School. On my Sunday off, I sat in church listening to Jim Packer preach from Matthew 28. "Go into the world. Preach, teach and heal. I am with you to the end." Everything receded. I was alone with Him. Suddenly, it was there. A call! Unmistakable! Tears flowed down my face, only the second time since my conversion eight years before in St George's, Leeds. Soon after, I was offered the job at Rubery Owen and then work in St Francis' Church, Bradley. I lived in the most deprived area of the Black Country, and was soon immersed in the good, the bad and the ugly.

Brian takes me home to meet Sheila, all the way to Maidstone (and back on Monday to Worthing). In his office he has a funky telephone - an old-fashioned train that blows recorded steam and rattles recorded wheels when activated. That night I dream of my journey into the ordained ministry from the days of the Mission in Bradley, Bilston. Really a lot of hot air and rattling. On my second application, I was recommended for training and I duly arrived at the London College of Divinity.

I took an instant dislike to Hugh Jordan, the Principal and quintessential headmaster and wondered how on earth I ever landed myself in a theological college after my resolute aversion over several years. I had three great and clinching objections. One, the church seemed full of bossy women with large hats. Two, I disliked bishops. Far too highfalutin', know-all and self important for my liking. Three, I had a congenital loathing of committees ever since "Susan" crossed me, while I was chairman of the local Young Conservatives. In those days *I* had to be boss, so God sent me on a training course, LIFE, to learn how to be bossed and biffed and battered into submission, into accepting His leadership. It took many years to register that ordination is 'stepping down'. One day it dawned on my dim and immature brain that women, bishops and committees reflected exactly my three biggest hang-ups: a distant mother, an authoritarian Dad and the demands of teamwork. Being strong would have to include being vulnerable.

Chapter 8

Brighton to Thanet

HAPPY AND HARNESSED

TO GET MARRIED AND ORDAINED, ALL IN THE SUMMER OF 1966, was a bit intense. Heather and I arrived in Chesterfield to a temporary terraced house and I began to build our bed, yes, in the bedroom. The price for years after was little puffs of sawdust from the mattress whenever we turned over together. There was a single stone sink in the kitchen and no bathroom. The loo was next to the coal-shed outside in the yard and not a blade of grass could be seen. However we enjoyed every micro-moment. We had taken our honeymoon in Ireland in Heather's Mini evocatively registered 374 KOK. We travelled north and south in deserted areas exploring each other and camping. Then back to the parish to begin life in earnest.

The Importance of being Earnest was written in Worthing and that is about the town's best description, deadly earnest. I leave worthy Worthing for brighter Brighton. On the way, Hove seems a bit stuffy, but dropping down into Brighton I feel the easy hedonism of Britain's Queen of southern seaside resorts. The flamboyant fantasy of the Royal Pavilion oozes romance, extravagance and playfulness. The Palace Pier, on its forest of iron legs crawls out to sea like a giant millipede: with a huge domed hump half-way, with stalls and shades along much of its back and on the end the antennae of aerial circus rides. There's cheek and frivolity written across

Brighton, with its rock lollipops, Little Titties and Little Willies, alongside candy, crabs and children. The performing fleas have disappeared along with Brighton's first two pretentious piers, but a freedom to revel is still almost palpable. Mind you, I catch the Theatre Royal with everything hanging out, its doors wide open, disgorging unwanted carpet, plates of spaghetti and empty mugs of tea in a sort of mid-season disembowelling. Electricians and engineers trail wires and cable radially from every exit on to the street, in one mighty intestinal heave. I jump aboard the next train along the beach. *Volk's Electric Railway,* leading to the plush east end of Brighton, is a bit unworthy by comparison, although the earliest electric railway in the world. In keeping with good style the huge marina has been extended into a maritime village. You can ease your cruiser up to the front door, step out and then be served tea in your floating conservatory. It's all a bit tricky if you are given to sleep-walking, but it is for real. There is an *Asda* superstore, bowling alley, eight-screen *MGM* cinema and, of course, a *McDonald's.*

Heading along the beach I am dazzled by huge chalk cliffs. We are now in Cretaceous country, the South Downs of East Sussex and, soon, the North Downs to Dover in Kent. These white cliffs brought a lump to our English throats, as the Canberra on its way to New Zealand turned away from the land of our birth. In tropical seas millions of years ago shrimps lived off the algae and their faecal droppings sank to the sea bottom forming chalk. At one centimetre every thousand years they grew to become 300 metres deep and after a drop in sea level they have emerged as 'the white cliffs', icons of our land, though just a pile of poo. Actually they are being re-digested today by the common limpet. Yet again these voracious gastropods eat the green algae found at the base of the cliffs, re-excrete the chalk out to sea and undermine our efforts to shore it all up. Along these cliffs walked our ancestors also in pursuit of food-mammoths, elk and wolves. I was able to see a variety of such bones among human remains in Britain's earliest site, Kent's Cavern, near Torquay. After the collapse of the land bridge to the continent these animals were hunted to extinction, but The Crete Way survives to tell the tale.

Equally as white is the King George Memorial at Peacehaven, topped with a brass globe of our planet – now thoroughly green. It is the point where zero longitude between South and North poles intersects the coast and eventually leaves to cross the North Sea at Cleethorpes. I sit for a while listening to several garrulous students and think about the distance of just one degree. Sixty miles is due West to Southampton, where I have come from and, strangely, sixty miles, due East, is The Isle of Thanet, where I'm heading next. It is also about mid-day, so judging by the sun's position I have to sit here for only four minutes and I shall have travelled 60 miles. My heart is beating about sixty times each minute. Big Ben moves its finger sixty times each hour. Tick! Tock! Tick! Tock! We breathe in. We breathe out. Time passes by and I am 60. No one can speed it up, nor slow it down, without leaving this terrestrial ball. Time is what prevents everything happening all at once and why sometimes we have to wait years before we see how certain things are allowed, or given. I make a mental note to enjoy time and not just spend it, or pass it, or kill it or fill it. I want to make time for people and use time to love. I want to look on, not back, because our story is unfolding and my story is part of His-story and history is moving on. "When as a child I laughed and wept, Time crept. When as a youth I waxed more bold, Time strolled. When I became a full-grown man, Time ran. When older still I daily grew, Time flew. Soon I shall find, in passing on, Time gone. O Christ, wilt Thou have saved me then? Amen". (Chester Cathedral clock.)

I take a beautiful evening photo of Newhaven, where the gigantic cross-channel ferry dwarfs the little fishing boats. I push on along the railway line to Seaford, which rather lost the plot when the river took itself and the 'old haven' to the other side of the valley. Doctors Christine and Julian Walters are waiting for me in a lay-by. We are soon embedded in a fish and chip shop and talking of our old youth group memories, of

The Magnet coffee bar, of Bill on drugs, of Colin in crisis, of Sue and Jean singing in the Christmas play, *Another King*. The Walters now have their own youth group, five lively teenagers. Trim and a little weary, Christine has the hair of a Mona Lisa, with a much better smile – a sister in Christ. I found a B&B and next morning I set off to find the other Seven Sisters awaiting me beyond Seaford Head. At Hope Gap a fulmar effortlessly planes the edge with hardly a movement of its thin aeronautical wings. Skimming only two or three feet above my head I marvel at its skill and cool daring, the envy, no doubt, of any coast-guard trying to head off smugglers in Cuckmere Haven below.

Cresting the first of the Seven Sisters I meet Anne Chichester, a vicar's wife, and John, a Singapore lay reader. In glorious sunshine, we sit and put the world to rights near Birling Gap. Here there is a little world to put right which has already gone wrong. A seventy metre stretch of the cliff edge is being shaved annually by the sea and with the domino effect only seven coast-guard cottages are now left standing. Jean Fawbert wants action. A few weeks ago a Strategic Defence Option was published 'to do nothing' I quote: "The existing undefended shoreline and undeveloped cliff-top permit short and long term adoption of do nothing. This is the preferred Strategic Option". Can you better that for pomp and piffle? So with no insurance and no market value the residents face the harsh facts of geological life. And just weeks away two hundred yards of cliff were about to fall leaving the Beachy Head lighthouse even further out to sea.

Hastings boasts the largest beach-launched fleet of fishing boats in the UK. Stubby and reliable, they feed the fish market and keep the Stade area alive. There are fifty tall, net-drying, tar-preserved sheds on the shore. Dizzily the East Hill Cliff Railway takes me up and into the Castle. Hastings is now a home for refugees and migrants, though traditionally it has always attracted boarding house custom from London. My wife Heather was a Parish Worker in Hornsey Rise responsible for manning a terraced holiday property near the Castle.

Later on, the children stayed in Coombe Haven Caravan Park, St Leonard's, and we have happy memories.

Heather and I met and first kissed in a ploughed field. We were on a parish mission and part of a small team at Bagnall in Staffordshire. Heather had been a teacher and was training for parish life. It was five years before I left industry, trained for the ordained ministry and we were ready for our first curacy.

Preparations for the Walk have put much strain on us partly because Heather has wanted to come as the support team and provide accommodation, with the very best of intentions. My decision to walk singly means our relationship is on a low-fat diet, no buttering up. It has been hard for Heather not knowing whether I was OK at any particular time. She has met up with me on three occasions, for several days and now to relieve my legs she is taking most of my kit in the car. We are staying with Wallace and Marian Boulton. He was an usher at our wedding. It is our wedding anniversary and we are having a special meal at Fortes in Dover. But it is not working. I simply cannot manage Heather's feelings as well as the daily demands of the walk. The mobile phone helps, but essentially this is a solo event. I cannot handle the difficulties of daily rendezvous with Heather. For me now the journey is somehow interrupted. The pilgrimage is on hold. I am grieving for the immediacy of each day walking with my Father. I am realising that I have to be alone for this walk to succeed. I need to encounter myself interacting with the moods of weather and landscape. Most of all I need to be alone for others. I cannot be tuned into everyday moments of meeting and ministry while I have a three-cornered pre-occupation with the needs of wife and family. In any case, I do need to be alone to unravel the purpose, the subtle threads of this event, right to the end. All the shades of white, black and grey are important and all the consequences of exposure to risk need to be accepted as they happen and woven into the fabric of each day as I am led. I am harsh, too harsh and Heather is miffed and feels rejected. She cannot express to me her deep feelings. She takes my photo outside the Nuclear

Power Station, on the seaward limit of Dungeness and sets off to drive home. Rather woodenly I return to the Edge and hobble my way out of Dover. Emotionally we are both wounded. I make a mental note to return to this compelling desert-like landscape, 'the fifth continent' and not least to its Royal Military Canal.

Red brick Martello Towers look rather like upturned buckets. Roughly five hundred yards apart, the distance needed to cover the beach with protective canonfire, these squat, round gun turrets could house on top a swivel cannon and inside a couple of dozen men. Built to repulse Napoleon in the early nineteenth century, they line the coastal areas between Newhaven and Dover and between Brightlingsea and Aldeburgh. Only forty-three remain out of a hundred and three. They have become homes, gardens, museums and visitor centres. All stand as witness, either to the waste and eccentricity of politicians, or to our recurrent need for strong defences – or both.

The gaunt stone memorial to The Battle of Britain is a seated pilot looking out to sea amid a huge three-bladed propeller at Capel le Ferne. Every concrete bunker I pass, every gun emplacement, every searchlight base, every communications mast, all speak to me of the hardship and toughness required to secure and maintain our freedoms. Operation Dynamo came first when, at the end of May 1940, eight hundred vessels set out again and again to brave Stukas, bombs and torpedoes to rescue the remains of the British Expeditionary Force from the enemy. Over two hundred boats were sunk, but 340,000 British, plus French, Dutch, Belgian, Polish and Norwegian troops were saved, plucked from the jaws of the advancing German armies and berthed within the expansive arms of Dover Harbour. Only sixty years ago, the Battle of Britain came next. The Messerschmidts matched the Spitfires and Hurricanes, so the battle in July and August was between men, their courage and their intentionality. The RAF gained crucial air superiority and stalled Hitler's plans to invade these shores. But in the years that were to follow, the coast round Dover and Folkstone became known as "Hell-Fire Corner". At St Margaret's-at-Cliffe there is a monolith of Winston Churchill and a reminder of that designation in his words: "Never in the field of human conflict has so much been owed by so many to so few." Dr Robert Runcie has said, "At the heart of the Christian faith is a Cross, not an eternal calm. We are called not to avoid conflict but to redeem it."

The Castle and cliffs of Dover are riddled with corridors in a mighty military complex now open to visitors and filled with the sirens, sounds and sights of war. The harbour is a law unto itself with its own life and rules and police. Likewise The Tunnel except that the mole that dug it left not a hill but Samphire Hoe, a flat area extending out to sea, a marine park in the making. Nearby is the biggest fridge in the UK built to process the kinetic energy generated by the trains.

I am glad to be climbing out of the noise and concrete of the busy port. Just about to go into fifth gear at the sight of a straight and beautifully white chalk path my gaze falls on a strange collection of planks and bits of carpet under a tree. All around I can make out bits of human debris. I stop to investigate the heap when from deep within come regular stertorous sounds from a human epiglottis. A tramp's privacy is to be as respected as anyone else's.

I set off for the South Foreland lighthouse and find it private and closed to curiosity. Undeterred I know that the North Foreland lighthouse is soon to be fully automated, the last of three hundred under the care of Trinity House. At Hartland in Devon I was captured first hand by the complexity of the Fresnel lenses, the huge one-and-a-half thousand watt bulbs and the sheer drama and atmosphere which is common to all. Yet each lighthouse is unique, from the Longships at Lands End to the Longstone on the Outer Farne Island. Many now have helipads, some have solar panels and the satellite DGPS has won its place. I look out to sea. Four miles off shore there are, silent, 1,500 vessels scattered over the Goodwin Sands. 15,000 lives have been sucked and swallowed into those depths, including the entire crew of the South Goodwin lightship in the 1950s. Not least one hundred and fifty million pounds worth of gold and silver, it is estimated, have been lost there to King Neptune.

In 55 BC, on his second visit, Julius Caesar sought to extend Rome's boundaries. It is not surprising that his soldiers were defeated, staggering up Deal beach with eighty pounds on the back, plus armour, shield and sword. My rucksack only weighs between 25 and 30lbs. I am 12 stone, clothed, 14 stone with kit and 16 stone fully laden with food and liquid topped up to camp overnight. A few miles later is the successful Roman beach-head and then the fort at Richborough which followed Rome's successful arrival in AD 43.

Deal is unostentatious but interesting. On its seaward side it has a Tudor Rose castle built for the Warden of the Cinque Ports and houses designed by the architect of Portmeirion fame, Clough Williams Ellis. The clinker boats are an impressive sight and so is the bus that has to back into the bus station, otherwise it would never get out. Anyway I jump on but arrive too late for a press and public appointment at the *Viking Ship Hugin and Hengist.* How can anyone celebrate the arrival of the Vikings, I ask, after all that pillage and plunder? And here am I all ready for mass media coverage and not a soul in sight, just two children kicking a ball and a woman walking her dog. Anyway Mr McKenna, packing up his 'TREATS' kiosk, is so moved by the general indifference of the natives that he awards me a *Walls* 'Mountain' ice-cream with his compliments.

A quick call brings Kath Brown from Margate and a ride to a very special place. It is the landing site of a benign immigrant with peaceful intent, an Italian missionary monk called Augustine. A doubtful character in his early years, his heart had been won by love from above and Pope Gregory sent him to win the hearts of the English, or rather the Angles. King Ethelburg was first into the Kingdom and his kingdom followed close behind. It was fourteen hundred years ago that

Christianity came to Kent to re-evangelise the nation after the Romans had left. Coincident in that year was the death of another passionate Christian, Columba, who had been sent from Ireland. From Iona he sent missionaries all over to bring the light of the Gospel from the north. He brought a reverence for the people, the land and community – a spirituality which speaks to our fractured families, barely held together by received values. On the day I left Cheltenham, several hundred Christians left this spot at Pegwell Bay, they to journey inland and I to travel the coast. I sit and pray and give thanks. I am half way.

One thousand miles! I take a day off and plunge indulgently into the sea. Well, it's only about nine inches deep, probably polluted and very weedy but my reward. Staying the weekend with Kath and Tony Brown is a vivid reminder of our call to community. In their tall terraced house I walk from one surprise to another. I must be a little discreet but the strangest of folks emerge and disappear, all in various stages of bewilderment, including me. The Social Services regularly second their 'service users' to this modest little community, over seventy guests so far. The Browns have their own grown-up children and they have buckets of kindness left over.

But more surprises follow. They catch me limping. No messing! In a flash, round comes John Yallop, their vicar, and several pairs of hands anoint my leg with love and faith and prayer. Soon I am on a whirlwind tour, over Saturday, Sunday and Monday round six different groups of people in Holy Trinity, St Mark's, St Paul's, St Phillip's and the Northumberland Gospel Hall, Cliftonville. Much of this is the inspiration of Christine and Randolph Belsey who scoop me up, with a spunky bunch of teenagers, for a regional TEARFUND rally. Then they drop me on to all sorts of unsuspecting folks, most of whom continue the Thanet Christian tradition of praying for everyone and everything in sight, usually starting with my leg. For thirty-six hours I am immersed in wonder, love and praise. There is joy everywhere and on Tuesday morning, yes, healing too. My leg seems fine. I have absolutely no pain at all!

I visit the Shell Grotto, an amazing underground complex of rooms and passages in which all surfaces are completely covered with seashells, conceivably the work of Phoenicians, two thousand years ago. I have a packed lunch on the floor of Margate's empty Victoria Ballroom, do the Gay Gordons, walk the length of the fun and fantasy façade on the prom' and finally imagine Mods and Rockers launching pre-emptive strikes at each other on the beach in the '60s after which the town's reputation sank into permanent decline.

However the Belseys are undeterred by any such nonsense. They currently care for a stream of immigrant people – this time, gypsies from the Czech Republic and Slovakia and refugees from Kosovo. Standing with them at the Benefit office, in the Post Office and at court shames those who would blame. They have, I perceive, the precious gift of empathy, of knowing instinctively what the other person needs, being able to sit where the other person sits and walk in his shoes. They put themselves out accordingly. No study of Scripture, no high philosophy, no coded regulation of church or state, can outshine the simple dictates of empathy. Without it our relationships lack affinity with fellow human-beings. There is no check on our behaviour as Number One. Otherwise individualism and opportunism determine our choices and greed takes the place of self-giving. If we only do what is right in our eyes, then the Sermon on the Mount goes right out of the window. Empathy is the core of morality, the tunnel into our neighbour and the stuff of common decency.

After singing with the radiant Christians from the Isle of Thanet, and after seeing their love in action with strangers, with families, with teenagers and with toddlers, I am dropped off happy on the path west. I think of the Thames estuary and begin the second thousand miles of my walk.

My pockets are stuffed with snacks and in my hand is a banana. On it has been written by Christine, with a felt-tip pen: "Philippians ch.3:12-14" ['One thing I do: forgetting what is behind and straining towards what is ahead, I press on towards the goal to win the prize for which God has called me heavenwards, in Christ Jesus']. My leg feels normal. No pain, the swelling is down and I am not limping at all. So I 'press on', as instructed, past Birchington Beach and Plum Pudding Island to Herne Bay. And there I fall flat on my face.

Chapter 9

The Thames Estuary

GUT-SQUEEZED TWICE

I AM DULY BUOYED UP BY THE WEEKEND IN THE ISLE OF Thanet and truly thankful to be without pain. With my light day-pack I set out on a long sea wall, topped with hard core, and find my patience sorely tested by the time I reach Reculver Towers, what's left of a Saxon church within a Roman fort. I drop into Herne Bay, with its monstrous attempt at pier modernisation – an activity centre looking more like a carpet warehouse – to emerge on the other side utterly dismayed. I am faced to infinity with a four metre wide stretch of concrete. I panic inwardly, my nerve breaks and I catch a bus five miles to Whitstable. I dismiss this faithless breach of honour with a quip, "the Vicar must keep off the hard stuff" and feel ashamed. (It has since been walked).

"I came. I saw. I conquered!" was Caesar's proud boast. Rome had come to conquer and subdue. But she would soon have to accommodate herself to the indigenous people among whom she had come to live, and would have to learn and live and love like anyone else in order to stay here. Force would give way to trade and exploitation to respect with mutually beneficial agreements. In the same way in the late sixties I could easily stand in for any over-confident male in the first heady days of nuptial conquest. Zealous as a new curate, I was also signalling smug and chauvinistic satisfaction to the parish in Chesterfield, confident that I could keep out of sight certain well-contained insecurities. Now before me as a new experience and as a challenge, the Thames basin lies totally unexplored. A succession of adventurers and merchant sailors have left its shelter and travelled to make a fortune and I am travelling into this area on foot and unsuspecting. In the first flush of a new situation in Chesterfield, where I was determined to succeed in life and gather the fruits of my endeavours in both marriage and ministry, I would have to leave my emotional moorings and tackle the sticky slippery path of having disabled children.

Whitstable wins my heart. I can see that it works. A sand and gravel business fits in with twelve fishing trawlers. A marvellous oyster-shed, shop and exhibition centre lead me into the town full of charm. I set out to reach a raised highway, once the tidal wall. Seawards there jostle converted sheds and properties. Landwards are several interesting alleys. To reach the highway I have to manage one of them and choose 'Squeeze Gut Alley'. It has to be the narrowest public throughway in the UK, beating 'Squeezebelly' in Port Isaac, Cornwall. The black painted walls on either side rise up three stories to guttering only six inches apart at a critical point where the path twists. For a broad-shouldered bloke with a rucksack, it is only just possible to proceed without collecting a down-pipe souvenir.

Heather and I had our first squeeze-gut experience when Allister was born in April 1968. We had a beautiful and perfect little boy. A cascade of congratulations tumbled through our letterbox and for a week we were on cloud nine. As I went to and from church I would whistle a coded message of encouragement to my wife opposite in the hospital ward. A week later we were in Sheffield Royal Infirmary facing emergency surgery. The baby's stools were not normal, his stomach was swollen and during an operation his heart had stopped. We were told Allister was now mentally handicapped. We began to feed, care, visit and pray. Then another operation followed and this time Allister's chest was affected physically he would never be able to run, only walk. For three agonising months we lived on the phone and on the ward until the battle was over. Heather could not attend the funeral, stunned and encapsulated with grief. All we had were terrible memories and two contradictory piles of cards, many torn up later in an explosion of Heather's anger. "You'll have another one. You're still young," some said. The Vicar popped caring little notes through the letterbox and for good measure, a few weeks later I was in bed with mumps. "He has not taught us to trust in His Name and then to forsake us and put us to shame." I preached about the Father who gave up His Son and got on with my job. But our world had changed forever. For Heather, whose mother had died when she was four and whose father had left soon after, the skylight had closed on hope. We grieved very differently and apart, neither understanding the other. Time passed by, but on that little hinge swung the door of our future.

I survey the dreary flatlands of the Thames estuary and exchange sand for mud. Ahead is a succession of dismal discoveries on bleak featureless muddy inlets. At Oare, I am so glad to meet a generous couple, Lawrence Brockwell and at home Christina. They talk with me about two special pictures he has painted from intuition. One with a path that turns away from two oast-houses, his parental past. The other, with a path, that leads straight to a church and a leafy future. They are his journey from disappointment to discovery.

Oare villagers are protesting. A rubbish tip? Where vegetables are packaged from all over the Garden of England? Not likely! At Uplees I learn that a hundred people had been killed in an explosives factory. At Conyer I nearly tread on a dead yellowhammer. At the marina pub I have lunch with genial and salty old-age travellers and finished the day struggling through a bunch of hostile New-Age travellers on my way to meet two journalists from *The Star* in Sittingbourne. Lawrence joins me for some of the way, but it is a long and lonely plod round the edge of the Swale and the Medway estuaries, on to the Isle of Grain. Gas storage, refuse dumpage, chemical wastage and abandoned ammunition sheds disfigure the area, though it is still a huge granary. Foam and detritus are marooned on each high tide. "Tax-Free Area" says it all, along with the sharp and haunting call of oyster catchers and a particularly anxious red-shank, flicking and diving at me. I am camping near her nest.

Lawrence has arranged for me to see John Fleetwood, an orthopaedic surgeon. He confirms that my leg does indeed seem all right and, pure joy, he gives me some heel cushions, wedges of foam to put in my boots. To the end of my walk, they are like a dream to my feet. I leave Lawrence just after Upnor Castle and pass a forest of foam-padded boat supports, looking like the backyard of an orthopaedic hospital. Today I have recovered my full pack and no signs of discomfort in my leg. I think of the Southampton doctor's prognosis, rest for six to eight weeks or limp to the end. I think of the prescription of love, faith and prayer given me by the Thanet Christians and joy soaks my soul. Tears of gratitude trickle down my face.

Cystic fibrosis was the problem. One in twenty UK people carries the gene. If two carriers of the dormant gene become parents, statistically they will have one child without, two children as carriers and a fourth with Cystic Fibrosis. In practice therefore, the majority of at-risk couples, will never know that they could have cystic children. The doctor encouraged us to try for another child and Rachel was born in August 1969. We left a year later for Leeds, to work at St George's.

We lived within sight of the Town Hall, in a two-bedroom council maisonette beneath a tower block, Marlborough Grange. Round it were spaced the ambulance, police and fire brigade headquarters along with British Telecom so that at every emergency cacophony would break out as vehicles raced one after the other to the outskirts of the city. Rachel would be tethered to railings below our window playing or wandering at the end of an extended clothesline. Next door lived batty Christine, and overhead, Jimmy Saville's sister.

I was familiar with St George's church for two reasons. I used to give gymnastic displays at their Annual Garden Party.

On one occasion I flew off an over-polished high bar and landed within inches of the crowd, in a perfect tiger balance, on my head. The crowd stood, roared and clapped. Then I crumpled. Second and most significantly, on April 11th 1954 while still at school, I landed on my feet, or rather on my knees, in the Kingdom. The speaker said, from 2 Corinthians ch. 5, "that the love of Christ leaves us no real choice. Because He died for all, those who live can no longer live for themselves but for Him, who died and rose again." I surrendered to that love on Palm Sunday and left the evening service with an abiding joy that only deepened, when I returned, sixteen years later, as a curate.

Back on the Edge and before I leave Kent, I attend St Luke's Church with Lawrence and Chris along with Brian and Sheila. The vicar suddenly leaves to be with a dying member of the congregation. Before departure he announces for sale that day a new video called *Ten Minutes*. It is a joyful explanation by people who have found Christ, a short visual-aid to finding faith. Many have sought my help along the route especially after hearing about our children. I would often distil my thoughts into three or four onomatopoeic words. "Stop! Drop! and Flop!" For instance: "*Stop* in your tracks! Just stop what you're doing! Stop and reflect! Where now?" Then, "*Drop* whatever comes to mind, drop whatever it seems you must! Drop your objection, your grievance, your problem! Drop your sin! Drop your guard?" And then "*Flop!* Let yourself flop into His arms, into His hands and into His Grace. Sink into the mighty sea of His limitless love and forgiveness! Sink into His un-judging acceptance of you-as-you-are, and thank Him for reaching out to you!"

It *has* to be easy for any man or woman, boy or girl. Then '*Pop*!' goes the champagne cork of life, abundant life, fullness of life and in comes the joy that goes with it, though for some the cork does not always come out in one piece. "My joy," said Jesus, "no-one can take from you. My peace I give to you. If anyone believes in me, out of his innermost being will flow rivers of living water." Like the disciples of every generation, in whatever class or culture, we receive the intoxication of His Presence within us and joy just spills out. Sometimes, as in times of trial, it just seeps out gently. At other times it will surge out in worship. Joy is one authentic sign of salvation.

From earliest days and from the times of the low tide 'horse ferry', when London Bridge had sixteen arches and nearly as many terraced homes on its length, the Thames has scoured and deepened its valley. The result has been the Isles of Grain, Sheppey and Thanet. Some think the Goodwins will also emerge to follow suit. Unfortunately the South East is tipping and the sea level rising, so my problems in marsh and bog, as I literally stick to the edge, will be as nothing compared with the struggle of the Thames barrier to stem the rising threat to London. Still, the river breathes again after a century of pollutants. She remains liquid history, full of myths and dreams and a real source of pride and wealth, as I approach the entrance to the Port of London. The offices are closed so I head for the Tilbury ferry. The watermen of the *Martin Chuzzlewit* seem refreshingly in tune with their paymaster, Old Father Thames. I reverently step off on the other side.

But the Thames is also subversive. I know the Tilbury docks from our farewell to Bud and Beattie, cousins returning to Australia. On the same spot, 22nd June 1948, fifty years before, people came to England who were destined to change the face of our nation. Four hundred and ninety-two Jamaican migrants disembarked from the *Empire Windrush* to make a new life for themselves. Innocents abroad, they were Christians, they were patriots and they had British passports. All they wanted to do was to get a job and work. Three hundred had served in the RAF with pride, and wished to return. Others, men and woman, had boarded to make up the numbers. All believed they were coming *home*. This was where they belonged. Their ancestors had come from Africa, India, Asia and Europe. But *they* were British; they loved the Queen and sang the National Anthem. They were bringing their Britishness with them. For most people in this country it

Walk 2000

The author has got the T-shirt!

Family Album

Rachel, aged 8.

Elizabeth, aged 13.

Right, Sallyanne, aged 21;

Below: Heather, my wife, on a low-tide excursion to Burgh Island;

Bottom: a snapshot of myself setting out on the final leg; and later home at last with Sallyanne.

The Severn Bridge: an illuminated start; below, at Burnam, an explosion and fire.

The Canberra leaves on her last voyage: a coincidence, since the same ship took the family to New Zealand and back.

Parched ground – I drank 4 litres of water every day.

Various aspects of the path I trod.
Opposite page–clockwise from bottom left: cabins at Southwold, boulders form the path at Lamorna Cove; steps I needed to climb over at Tintagel; and white cliff path at Dover. This page–clockwise from top: Path through barley (was this right?); the Iron Coast near Hartland; tin mine near St Agnes, Cornwall.

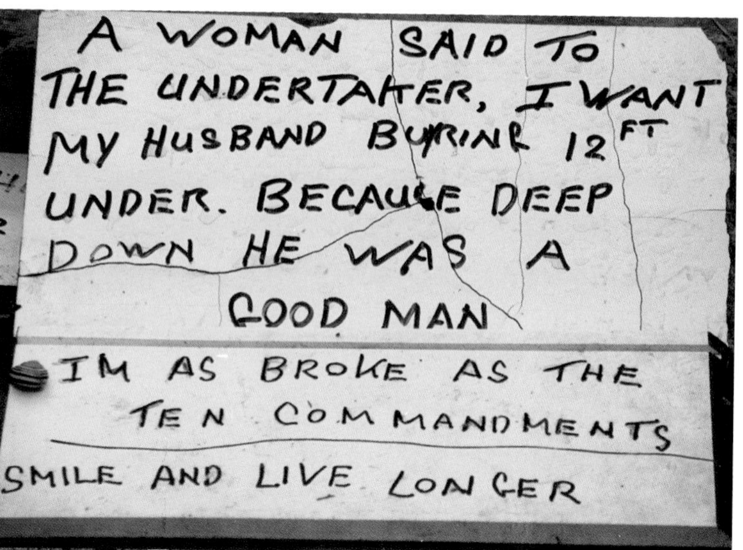

A collection of signs I saw, including, top right, the ugliest one; 'Thisldo' – the most original name for a B&B; danger signs, and my reaction to them! Also the stone memorial over the daughter of King Canute, who died aged 8.

YOU ARE APPROACHING
A RESTRICTED AREA
This is not a public right of way
or footpath. You are strongly
advised to return the way you
came as trespassers caught
anywhere in this area will be
prosecuted under the
Explosives Act of 1875 & 1923.

TO THE GLORY OF GOD
AND IN MEMORY OF
A DAUGHTER OF KING CANUTE
WHO DIED EARLY IN THE 11TH CENTURY
AGED ABOUT 8 YEARS.
WHOSE REMAINS LIE ENCLOSED IN A
STONE COFFIN BENEATH THIS SPOT

PLACED BY THE CHILDREN OF
THE PARISH. AUGUST 1906.

FILL UP ON
FISH

Thank you

I owe thanks to so many, that it is not possible to give all their names: but I hope many will recognise themselves on this spread.

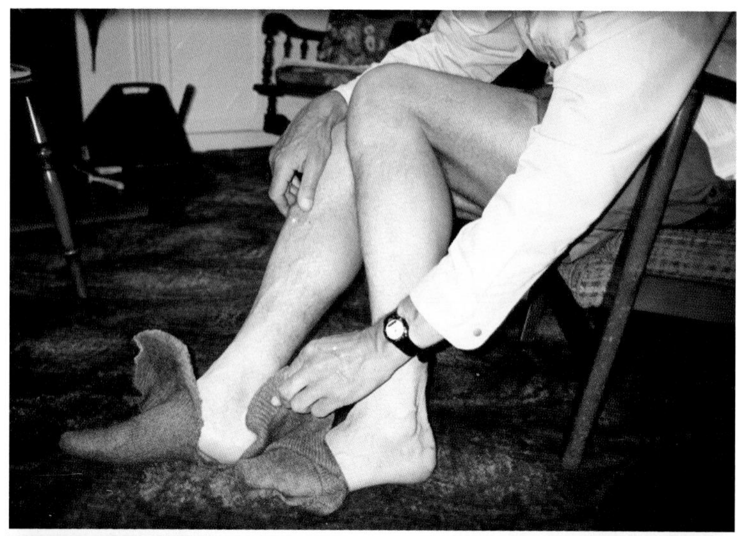

The sport of walking

Opposite – from top: cutting off socks; the boots (and calves) that did the job; under Northumbrian storm clouds, fifty miles to go. This page – from top: a view of London from an estuary bivouac; a damp night in the lee of a coast guard lookout; my wet gear.

I slept on a mud bank in the Blackwater estuary.

Sand sculpture: monster on a Norfolk beach.

Transporter bridge: I found the North East working.

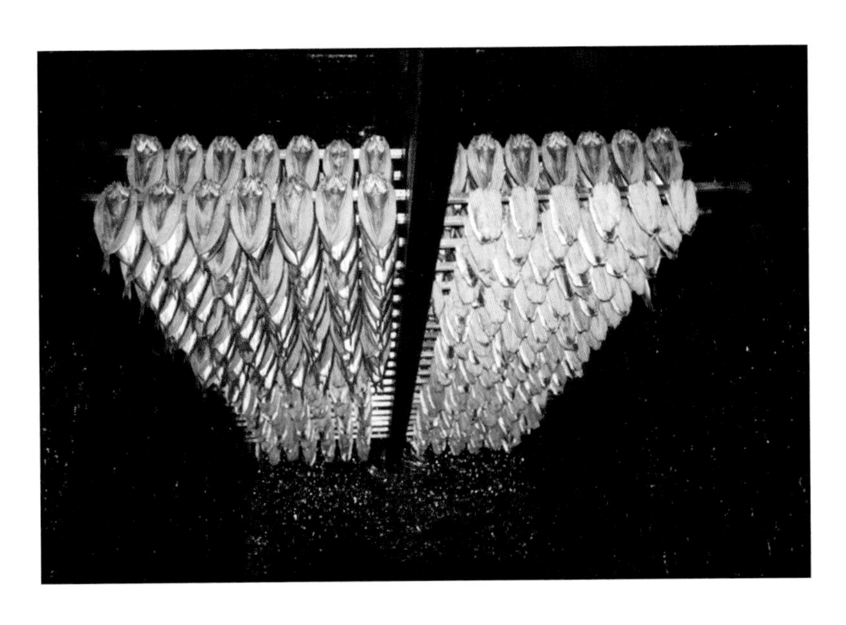

Kippers hanging like bats in Craster.

Morte Point, Devon: the dinosaur lashes her tail

Thank you for the clouds *GFJ*
– even though they're grey;
Thank you for the rain
– even though it drenches.
Thank you for the pathway
– though that too is very dirty;
Thank you, Lord, for the future
– its brightness is yet to be revealed.

Pilgrim poles guide me from one shore to another

seemed a non-event, as long as they kept themselves to themselves. To others they seemed like marauding darkies, descending like locusts on this green and pleasant land. Ignorant and unreflecting at that time, I regarded Caribbeans as subjects of fun or objects of derision. They'll never make good, not if their dress sense and standards of dental care are anything to go by.

I once knew an Indian boy at school and idly wondered what fluke had brought him there. Now I see black faces everywhere, MPs, television presenters, bus drivers and bishops. I am sitting opposite a girl on the other side of a coffee cup. She wears a mass of dreadlocks, is as black as night and talks to me as an equal. She has no chip. She lightly wears a cultured approach to life. She is an English woman and a doctor in Clinical Psychology. To cap it all, she has a better command of educated English than I have. I remember Gandhi (in the film) having a row with his wife. I echo his searching question, "What is the matter with me?" I talk with my daughter. She has no hang-ups about skin colour and I realise that I have had a powerful lens clamped over my eyes. I realise that I too am 'coloured', as we all are, with different shades of grey, pink, red, yellow, brown and black and that the only truly white person I will ever see is in a coffin. It is a shock at first and then a challenge. Nowadays there is in me an excitement that wants to share my passport with anyone who has a deserving right or claim to live here without regard to race, seeing that we all originated from Africa and the Middle East in the first place. Today we have an authentically British, home-grown, black Afro-Caribbean culture, full of smiles and positivity. Britishness is a shared story, an inclusive cross-ethnic and cross-national word that has breadth and vision. I'm proud to be 'a Brit' in a multi-cultural society that happily spreads itself round the world.

Meet Stan Farrow, a Brit from his white wavy hair to his polished black shoes, a modest, stocky, genial faced Eastender, who moved to South Ockendon after the War. In council property he lives a simple lifestyle looking after the interests of his children, Stan, Miriam and Brenda, while they go out to work. Nothing is too much trouble despite heart problems. He takes me to the Belhus Park Chapel, where he is elder statesman, and escorts me through a weekend of celebration. It is their fortieth anniversary. I meet Sarah and Joanne, terrific teenagers, and enjoy their warmth and hospitality. Like the name of the local hairdressing salon, many here forty years ago just wanted to "Curl up and Dye", in a neighbourhood without any community and little infra-structure. But not Stan! He takes me to Somers Heath Primary School where Heather, my wife, taught before I knew her. I go to the church in which Heather worshipped, where she had received the Lord as Saviour under the ministry of Charles Searle-Barnes, with whose widow I will soon stay in Cromer.

Finally Stan drives me round Canvey Island. The high sea defences, which followed the floods and fifty-eight deaths of 1953, have robbed the islanders of their horizon. Now they build upside-down houses, live on top and sleep below. It still feels under siege. Gladys and Alan in their clean and cheerful bungalow seem to exude the spirit of wartime defiance, though now it is all about 'pensioners rights'. I am given a traditional East End welcome with *Rose Cottage* china and a tea dance, from which I only just escape.

Back on the trail Tilbury Fort puffs out its gleaming white chest, a magnificent entrance portal of sculptured marble, deep bas-reliefs, canons, heraldry and Ionic pillars. The inside echoes dismally to my footsteps. A father and son, sole visitors, pay to fire the gun. I leave. The French had sacked Gravesend and the Dutch had just fired several British warships, so Henry VIII built five defensive forts round the Thames estuary, of which this was one.

On the maps of Henry's day, Shell Haven is an inlet, which gave its name to the headquarters of the mighty Oil Company for which my father worked. When he started you could buy a single embossed jerrycan of petrol. When he finished, a merchant tanker could carry 800,000 gallons of crude oil. My parents were given a specially burnished manuscript with a Shell mnemonic to celebrate their 60th wedding anniversary. Shell tanks and power station chimneys recede and soon I am walking through level open ground except for ditches and trenches. It was then that a man's head and perspiring strawberry torso bobbed up from nowhere. He was excavating the waste of the centuries. I pick up an encrusted object, a Bronze-Age artefact or part of a Victorian teacup? "Thanks!" I said, "I've got some bits like that at home." With the antique collector of Thurrock behind me I stretch out into Essex, a long way round Benfleet and on to Leigh. The railway has protected the edge from over-development and I find Leigh-on-Sea unpretentious and unspoilt. I choose my evening meal from some fresh shellfish stalls, down-wind of their acrid aroma and find a stone plaque marking a Thames valley spring, about 1712. It is inscribed: "Thou hast greatly enriched it with the river of God." Psalm 69. It marks the beginning of the East Coast of England. Thankfully it marks the end of the mud and the arrival of sand.

To celebrate the transition, Southend has built the longest pier in the world, one and a third of a mile, down which a tiny red sliver of a train is disappearing seawards. Two little boys with baseball caps and buckets are teasing and torturing some stranded crabs. They are sitting on the sand at the seaside. All seems to be serene and English, until BOOM!

Chapter 10

Southend to Tollesbury

LIVING WITH HOPE AND HEARTBREAK

HAVING, LOVING AND LOSING CHILDREN INVOLVES MANY delayed reactions. The mind and heart cannot process all the data at once. The loss of a little child in particular is a mighty explosion that impacts later. Like a depth charge there is a delay before powerful subterranean energy surges into the heart and home of a family. Sustained by dignity, the support of others and the need to cope with daily tasks, the inner devastation creeps up only gradually but surely. Disease and death cannot easily be faced straight on. It takes time. Our ten years in 'The Potteries' were punctuated by a series of sub-sonic booms as we travelled emotionally through the highs and lows of trying to establish a family and discovering cystic fibrosis in each of our first three children.

A twelve-foot metal spiked fence driven well into the sea brought an end to my dreamy enjoyment of London's play-ground, Southend-on-Sea. I was soon to learn that the MoD has the gateway to Essex. I find Foulness and it is forbidden. I have only travelled a mile or so inland, forced away from the Edge, when a terrific 'BOOM' seems to lift everything in sight about six inches. The people are always making insurance claims for cracked and broken glass. Tantalised by this explosion, I turn and head straight towards the sound. High security bristles down a long and narrow road clearly intended to warn off even the most resolute. I am met by the Rock of Gibraltar.

This encounter rather blows apart my notions of Essex, a quiet and inoffensive backwater of old-world hideaways. Here are strategic defence secrets and at Mistley an underground nuclear bunker. I am also to be tested by a sequence of uncrossable creeks and inlets that will threaten my safety and exasperate my optimism. And now, like the first day of any Army induction course, the sun goes in and the rain comes down in deadly earnest. The Edge has gone and with it my bearings. I am inland and lost. Is this fresh water or salt water in front of me, going east or going west? Everywhere anonymity, flatness and mud.

I trudge past the *Captain Mainwairing* pub, through Little Wakering and Great Wakering not knowing where I am going, until I find a twenty foot aluminium 'bath tub', immobilised by railings and embedded in mud. It is a creek, which will take me to the Roach and then I will have to go twenty miles inland and back, just to get a mere stone's throw to the other side. When I get there, I shall find the Roach leads me into the Crouch and an even further journey of a hundred miles up and back to the far side of *that* estuary and only then to the coast. And that is about *one third* of these benighted contortions. That scenario will then be repeated twice more before I straighten up to go north by Suffolk and Norfolk. I sigh and return to some houses.

I need milk, water and two slices of bread. I cruise a bit not wanting rebuff and meet Pete weeding his front border. His open eyes are sad. He has lost his close friend Cosy in an accident. He had been abandoned by his birth mother, bullied at school and divorced from his wife. He has inspiring memories of a one-legged Eastender, his adoptive mum, who 'had faith to forgive people.' He is really depressed over three recent bereavements and has prayed for someone to help him. "The very next day", he wrote later, "you appeared on my doorstep." He is devoted to his partner Trish, and Morrigan and Miranda, their cats. He has the largest known collection of sleeved vinyl records from the '70s, from which he makes a living. Contentedly I stumbled along the uneven creek wall looking for a dryish hump on which to sleep, and gaze in awe at a celestial duvet of mauve and pink cumulus spreading across the sky.

I awaken this morning about eight-thirty too tired to move, until, that is, I see walking ahead of me Leigh Tanner, a very curvy and unselfconscious platinum blond. She works on a caravan site and has developed powerful bronzed shoulders and arms. She is speed walking into Hullbridge, her pink striped shorts bouncing from side to side. With difficulty and some diffidence I catch up and find an open trusting nature. "I believe," she says, "if you're nice to everybody, they are normally pretty nice back." "Yep!" I say. "Most of the time I get a lot of satisfaction out of being nice. I dunno. I get a lot of, like, sense of achievement." "Yep!" "Because you've, well, helped someone." "Yep!" I say breathlessly. "When you give a little, it's OK, 'cos lots of people want to give a little back." She laughs infectiously. My Rachel would have been just her age and would, I guess, have worn a similar trusting smile, had she lived.

The Right Reverend Richard Chartres, Bishop of London, has a mentally handicapped brother, Stephan, who without any worldly prospects whatsoever is still full of joy. It seemed obvious to Richard Chartres that joy must come from a source beyond this world, from God. To be without the presence of sickness and suffering in one's family may mean that we actually miss the chance of knowing at first-hand the blossom and the fruits of God-given, tear-stained joy. To be spared misfortune, physical, mental or emotional, may itself be a form of deprivation. It may be no blessing at all. It may lead to a selfish life and an arrogant attitude. It could even be, if the truth were known, a sign of weakness not strength in a family, as the parents are really not *able* to bear such a thing. To have a handicapped child is one form of privilege, or as a surgeon said to me after a lifetime's experience, "these children are given to those who can care" and do. Families with disabled members may be necessary, shining beacons within our so-called enlightened society.

Elizabeth was born soon after our arrival in Staffordshire and Sallyanne followed three years later. Rachel for a brief spell was the leader for Elizabeth and Sallyanne. She loved her life and made every moment count. She gradually accepted the deterioration of her breathing and digestion and once said to me that God must have a plan to allow all these problems. And some plan it was, that unfolded partly in the way she died and partly in the way she lived. Newcastle was a splendid place to live and the church a strong community in which to be. Joy and John Caddick-Adams were outstanding leaders and in a fine gesture offered the Jones family a new vicarage site from their land, which was set at the heart of the parish.

We had arrived to live in a rambling, twenty-two-roomed brick Victorian property, with servants' quarters in the basement. One day I discovered there an outbreak of the dreaded dry rot. There pulsating in the middle of a damp flagstone was a fiery red floral shaped fungus pumping out spores to every corner of the house. Our health was affected and most importantly Heather was expecting Sallyanne, our fourth child, a baby that was totally unplanned, except as a twinkle in our Heavenly Father's eye. We moved into a temporary furnished house, which 'suddenly' appeared the day I was searching, and the seven-strong Prof. Graeme Clark family from Australia came on cue to stand in for me that year at the old vicarage. The new vicarage took shape and behind on the lawn was soon a mighty slide and climbing frame to attract our neighbours' children. Below on the full-length patio was a racing track for anything on wheels. Beyond was the old railway cutting and Brampton Park, where, in the snow, I would drag the children in two yellow baby bathtubs, cornering to screams of delight. These years were also scenes of unfolding horror. Over eighteen months each child was tested for cystic fibrosis and each child discovered that their colds wouldn't go away and that coughing became a necessary part of normal behaviour. It was just life.

Gradually streaked through our family life came the dark, marbling affect of fear, guilt and anger about having sick kids. Heather gave herself to the slow demise of Rachel as helplessly we followed the downward spiral. I was having fierce interminable dreams, in which I knew, as a stark incontrovertible fact, that I had killed my children and now was being hunted, harassed, accused, judged and condemned by the police. In the light of day I was scared but couldn't show it and angry but couldn't express it. Until, one day, my wife suddenly picked up a pile of dirty dishes and instead of washing them, hurled them straight through the kitchen window. Heather was suicidally depressed and with the prospect of losing two or three sick children she wanted to take them with her. Several times we wept our way through the night on the lounge settee. We could fill the hole in the window but we could not fix the gaping hole in our hearts. The church folks were wonderful and the verger, Frances, became an indispensable help in the house and a grandma to the children. I sought advice and went to see Dr Frank Lake in Nottingham. Over several years I was helped to face the unfaceable, in myself and in my family. So began in earnest the inner journey towards healing and a life's journey that flowered in ministry to the hurt and bereaved. The former gave me back a full and elastic range of healthy emotions. The latter led us to New Zealand.

I reach Battlebridge and enjoy a good laugh and a warm welcome in the *Barge Inn*. Next door I banter with Joe Pettit who rather dryly comments on my hometown: "Here I lie with my three daughters, all through drinking Cheltenham waters. If I'd stuck to Epsom Salts, I wouldn't be lying in these 'ere vaults."

Now heading east on the north bank of the Crouch I completely fail to see that there is yet another series of creeks and lakes to my left and spend the afternoon trapped on a sea wall, getting back virtually to where I started. Setting off again, there is a spectacular regatta under way with spinnakers billowing before an easterly wind. At last in Burnham-on-Crouch it is way after dark. The receptionist at the *Ship Inn* donates an attic room and with it toasted cheese and *Horlicks*. Their guest was dead to the world by 10 o' clock that night.

The modernistic Corinthian Club is the last building in Burnham. Turn left at the wall and you have seventeen miles, no less, of unmarked embankment. Well, there is a pill box in a wheat field, there is an outflow patch of concrete from which baby swallows learn to fly and there are hundreds of vipers. Otherwise sky meets coast and heaven meets earth, with nothing in the way, except occasionally a distant puff of smoke to the south and 'BOOM'. I leave the starting pads on course for the Orthona Community I am so keen to join overnight. Beyond lies the Blackwater estuary, an ageing Nuclear Power Station, a caravan village called Ramsey Island - and Tony Benn.

Meanwhile I reach a Roman fort already half lost to the sea, and a Saxon church erected on the west-gate foundations about AD 660. St Cedd, the first to come south of four brother missionaries from Lindisfarne, became Bishop to the Anglo-Saxons and this became his 'cathedral'. In course of time it lost its porch, its north and south porticoes, its chancel and apse and became a farmer's barn for hay, though now restored as a chapel for the Christian community nearby. On arrival, I have the feeling I am too early or maybe too late, or am I too tall or too poor, or too dirty, too niffy or too scruffy? Nobody notices me. I am totally ignored, the crashing non-event of the day. Somebody pulls out a piece of wide ribbon and announced it as the smallest armchair in the world. With it, we are to meditate among the dunes. I wake up an hour later, thoroughly refreshed and am soon in conversation with a brainy Christian called Richard, with whom I am to spend the night. He describes his conversion as 'multi-orgasmic' and has just been contesting in *Countdown*.

I learn that a new warden is soon to arrive and take charge. The cocoa is good.

About mid-day and half way up the Blackwater, I am stopped in my tracks by barbed wire. There is a sign, which says "PRIVATE! KEEP OUT!" with an arrow pointing inland. Now, I am not a man to be easily roused. But no one, I say to myself, no one owns the Edge of England. It is not for sale. I had been told that the one-time peer Viscount Stansgate lives along these banks. He had been our MP in Chesterfield and now this, after all Wedgewood-Benn's public denunciations of privatisation. I am straining at the leash. I gingerly negotiate the barrier fence and carry on along the shoreline, to relish the prospect of arguing the toss, whether I am on the edge of the Blackwater or on the edge of his garden. Mentally preparing myself, I rehearse the words of the Queen Mother, if necessary to outflank him. "What you do for others," she said, "is the rent you pay for the room you occupy on earth." I pass his boat. I pass his summerhouse and advance in full view of the windows in front of his house, marshalling those things I shall say should Tony Benn be getting the upper hand. "Look Tony," I shall say, knowing he likes the ordinary man-in-the-street approach, "Look Tony, w*ho* really owns all this? We only have the privilege of using things. We pay money only for the right and responsibility of utilising things, before we pass them on, but not to acquire their deeds of ownership. We all live in this world together. I'm like the birds and the bees and the beetles" (modesty is also a good thing). "I'm just like any other form of life passing through. If it bothers you, close your eyes! Good day!" Sadly no one emerges and, to honour the venerable politician, I edge off his stage facing left, just so he cannot really complain.

I am escorted convincingly off the next section by a determined gaggle of Barnacle geese and so I approach Malden from its back garden. There are lovely views of ochre-coloured sails, mostly furled and topped by pennants fluttering from the masts of a number of Thames barges, their starboards intact from stellar navigation days. Some still carry grain to the city breweries. Many were towed back and forth to Dunkirk and many were lost in the *mêlée* of Operation Dynamo. I cross over the Blackwater Bridge and dive first right. Unfortunately it turns out to be a cul-de-sac. Not for going back, I climb up to a tidal ten foot wall round yet more barbed wire and cling precariously to a chain-link fence, as I edge my way round and back to safety. I am soon to prove the wisdom of my daughter, Sallyanne, that 'success come from good judgements, good judgements come from experience and experience comes from bad judgements.' For now all seems well. I am beginning to appreciate the strange mixture of mingled sea and land, of meadow and marsh and the horizontal landscapes, streaked in olive, apple and khaki green. I stretch into a good pace round a nature reserve and by a converted boathouse. I then pause to collect basics from a caravan park. We play toss and grab with my milk, sugar and water containers, which sail backwards and forwards over yet more chain-link fencing swathed in matted nettles to the general amusement of the donating families and their children.

So it is with an airy disregard for difficulties and a cockiness born of calling Wedgie's bluff, that I come to feel I can handle anything that gets in my way. I determine to push on through deserted natural wetlands. I know my glycogen resources are running low and take out my secret weapon, *Isostar*. I have a good drink of this high-octane fuel, finish it up and am pretty sure that my legs will continue to serve their master until nightfall. With no public enthusiasm for this area, it seems the local authority has not bothered to cap the embankment, except with unwalkably rough crushed concrete. It goes on and on and on. I pass Osea Island, where alcoholics have been marooned to dry out and where dedicated locals have smuggled the means to ensure that this never actually happened. I make many sinewy detours round muddy inlets, all the time aware that my tent cannot be used on this hostile surface. On my left is a flimsy barbed wire fence and behind it high reeds and marsh. On my right is the equally inhospitable black gel of nature, the Blackwater

Estuary, and I know that this mud can swallow a man without trace. I push on without any sign of a space to camp. I am pushing my legs through their weariness and the sun has dropped to the horizon. A sagging balloon, it dips and disappears from sight.

For a while there have been banks of stranded mud in the estuary and now, despite a twice-daily dose of salt water, some have sprouted a bilberry-like covering of vegetation. Another detour, more crunching on the concrete, and I can see some rusty iron scaffolding going out into the estuary. Some iron spikes support a series of flimsy nine-inch planks, which span a distance of perhaps thirty metres to a scrubby island of mud. All are in a poor state, some enough to send any council safety officer into apoplexy. They put my heart into thumping anxiety. I reason that if I can get out and back before the tide turns, I will be all right for the night and it is now nearly dark. I begin the journey and thankfully seize each spike as it comes. Fifteen feet below yawns a shadowland of that dreadful black ooze, from which I can expect no mercy. At last in my tent on the bilbury bank of mud, I press the light on my watch. I calculate seven or eight hours to the next high tide and make careful preparations to escape first thing next morning. Each boot goes into a plastic bag. My rucksack has become my pillow. Everything else in my tent, including my stick, is zipped up eight inches on either side, just in case. My alarm is set for five o clock and I calculate that the sea will be back to claim this space soon after.

The high-pitched bleep of my *Casio* waterproof watch penetrates my brain and quick as a flash, I stare out of the tent. The sky is flushed with a new dawn and to my relief the adjacent mud banks still have an eighteen-inch dark shadow above the rising water. Then I see the wonder of where I am, hidden from view. All around me intent on feeding are curlews, redshanks, lapwings and oystercatchers, whimbrels, sandpipers, dotterel and golden plover. I quietly focus my binoculars and camera. It is breathtaking and I am soon lost in the magic. Two elegant egrets are scooping up slugs and bugs unaware of my presence at their breakfast table. I photograph the scene and the sunrise, entranced by my grandstand view of this quotidian spectacle, and put away my camera. But no one has told me of the containing effect of the mud banks, that the water level rises only slowly as it spreads out across the estuary area, until when duly enclosed there is a high tide surge, up and over these banks of mud.

Suddenly in the scrub around, I see the inky black reflection of water. The banks have gone. My tent is a waterbed and I am afloat. There are only seconds to spare. I pause for clarity and action. There is no time to rummage for my jock strap deep in my sleeping bag. Just as I am, I jam on my hat, spring out of the tent and stab each foot into a boot, already straining to float away. I sling my rucksack strap over one shoulder, grab each end of the bivi-bag tent in my other hand and turn to cross the bridge. But alas, it has gone. The bilberry is awash and I am marooned. I splash nervously towards the edge of the mud-bank my weight on my back foot. If I slip off, I'm gone too. I am feeling for that blessed bit of wood that can take me to safety. I have to be careful. I can see some spikes still visible. It is as if my world is on hold. I am hanging by a thread. Then I touch something hard and inch by inch I begin the tortuous journey through the water and over the menace beneath that seems just waiting for me to slip. I hold down the panic and secure one foothold first, before moving the other. With a rising sense of triumph and relief I finally clamber up on to the wall, throw down my kit and turn rather ridiculously to stand there in my boots, breathing hard and shaken. I see the two plastic bags, printed 'Safeway' not 'Gateway'.

It seemed, however, in August 1977 that rescue for our daughter Rachel was not to be. We had healing prayer and the laying-on of hands. We had endless letters, texts and messages. She had made several marked improvements after special moments of ministry in the hospital, but now Rachel had collapsed into a coma.

Then unexpectedly and quite suddenly rescue came, as, indeed it will, for all who die in the Lord, the Defeater of

Death. The CF demon was not to have the last word. Neither disease nor death could hold her clamped to that hospital bed. She opened her eyes, eyes that had been only slits for days she opened as wide as saucers. She stirred her arms to hug her parents, arms previously too weak to hold a cup of Horlicks. She found her legs and stood to show us she was well and used her lips to describe the things she now could see. She wore a smile that covered her head, and she moved her body, with a health and well-being that was soon the talk of the hospital. She lost her fear and regained her colour and over several hours and with several staff, Rachel got better and better, to the astonishment of us all. Filled with life from another world she was transformed, while still she stayed within the ward. As the sister in charge described to me later "it was as if Rachel was absorbed in the happiest game of her life," and that was her death. There was a sea of uniformed hospital staff at the service, nurses and doctors, physios and radiographers, cleaners and orderlies, and of course, friends and other parents, who had seen something of Rachel's approach to her life and death. The huge church seemed full, not for ten minutes but sixty, as many stood to honour this little girl. At the age of eight, she seemed to stand tall with us all, a beacon of hope after a life of hardship and a death that defies understanding which will be detailed in a later chapter.

This wonderful experience helped us adjust to Elizabeth's dire future, which was not to be the carbon copy we had feared. History does not repeat itself and we were given two other totally unexpected interventions. First Sallyanne was born eighteen months before Rachel died. Unplanned, well and spunky she became an indispensable friend to Elizabeth, her sister of three years senior. Then after ten years in Newcastle we were invited to travel to the Bay of Plenty in New Zealand.

Drowning is not part of the plan. A hearty breakfast and prayer sees me back on the trail to Tollesbury. On the way I meet Jane Culver, all alone on the wall. Her men are in the distance digging in the mud. I think of Heather who had so often uncomplainingly held the fort while I was busy elsewhere. Sister Horan of Abergele wrote these words: "When God created the world, he wished for some plants to grow on the barren mountains. He asked the Oak, but she said she required deep soil for her roots. He asked the Honeysuckle, but she needed something to grow against, a wall or a tree. He asked the Rose, but she said she was too delicate and could not withstand the winds. He asked the Heather. She said she did not consider herself beautiful enough, but if God wished it, she would grow on the mountains – and God wished it. He gave Heather the strength of the Oak, the fragrance of the Honeysuckle and the beauty of the Rose to adorn the beautiful mountains."

The Rt Hon. Tony Benn, interviewed on leaving Westminster, said, "It is inter-connections between individuals that make up human endeavour." I leave the Edge, hungry for humans, to find a real village community. Tollesbury has just that, Vera, Jim and Dianne in the paper shop and Rev. Keith Lovell with Christian folks in the Lighthouse, where the children play and drink squash. Kirstie gives me a large pot of tea over a bar counter and I meet Bob in *Hope Inn.* When we lost Rachel, it was the people at St George's who sustained us with their hope, their love and their prayer. It was the New Zealand High Commission, loud and clear, which then said a definite 'NO!'

Chapter 11

Colchester to Harwich International

WE ENGLISH BECOME "PAKEHAS"

It is raining with a quiet grim persistence. I've had enough. Mercia Island in front of me is not on track anyway and I am in no mood for the unexploded bombs of which I had been warned. The beautifully painted sign for Salcott-cum-Virley shows a wet estuary. I set my sights on Colchester and hitch a lift in a van. It has four lads on a stag party, definitely the worse for wear, but good fun.

Hospitality continues to be unforgettable. One day I am with a bus driver, the next with an 'ex-number two' at the Cabinet Office. It could be a farm, or a bed-sit, a bungalow or a beach hut. I really never know if I am to be treated to the best room or the box room, the lounge carpet or in with the kids. I may be encountering a busy lawyer or a brainy lecturer, a whirlwind of teenagers or the solitary existence of a ninety-plus widower. My journey is one of surprise and unending appreciation. Tonight Janet is expecting me in Colchester. Living by herself and diffident by nature she will probably sacrifice more of her time and personal space than anyone throughout the journey.

Slightly irascible, deeply private but unfailingly hospitable, Janet serves a tasty meal of fish accompanied by a selection of vegetables. Somehow I can imagine her saying to herself, "I have this *man* and he's staying overnight. I've got this house the way I like it. It's organised enough and it's secure, that's the thing." Front and side, the doors are specially fitted with double catches, five lever mortice locks, bolts and a spy-hole. "I chose this house for its position. It has special lattice windows at an angle, so I can see up and down the road. And now I let this man just walk straight into my life. I don't know why. We've nothing in common. I'm androgynous and Cabbalistic. Frankly he's intruding, but I can't really say No!" We crush into Janet's Cinquecento and attend communion at the oldest of the town's churches. Colchester is also Britain's oldest recorded town and after the service I am treated to a tour of the Castle Park and Keep, the ruins of the priory, the *Hole in the Wall*, a pub next to a genuine Roman gateway and the Cromwellian siege house. That night Janet (not her real name) shares terrible memories of being bullied at school and of life through many incarnations. She remembers in the Middle Ages being accused of witchcraft and led to the stake. Dragged through the jeering people she was within reach of the fire when out of the crowd leapt her father. He grabbed a firebrand and killed her stone dead with a lunge to her neck. The weal, which she rarely reveals, is a permanent reminder. Androgyny is the outcome and the Four Trees of Cabbalism part of her self-understanding. Her personal cryptogram is Egyptian and means 'expansion of the heart'. I have the awesome privilege of sharing her home, a little of her heart and her determination to be there for me.

A failed, abandoned hulk of a catamaran and a successful working tide mill preface my call for water at Ralph's. His father left him at five and his elder and only brother was killed at twenty on the Continent. He is still trying to make sense of life but nonetheless ready to serve a ham and cheese sandwich and tea. Bill welcomes me into Brightlingsea Parish Church. Round its walls are featured tiny square ceramic tiles with details of those drowned from the sea-faring community: over two hundred persons, since 1872. In the chancel, Nicholas Magens, co-founder of Lloyds Insurance, takes the prize for the most flamboyant rococo memorial I have ever seen. In defence of the faith and the faithful Bill shows me a twelve-foot, eight by six-inch oak beam, buried in the wall by the door. Giving it a great heave he advances to secure the west entrance against approaching enemy invaders, to my applause. So hospitality does not include the enemy.

At Brightlingsea, John and Hilary Le Seve are preparing to leave on holiday early next morning, yet cook and care and see me snug on their sofa, while the children gambol round our legs. Before I leave very early, I photograph the family, Miriam and Rebecca barely with their eyes open, trying to wave me goodbye. They remind me of Elizabeth and Sallyanne much younger. They told me of a near boating catastrophe, when they only just avoided all being taken out to sea. It reminded me of a day when, I cartwheeled in heavy seas harnessed to a catamaran at the entrance to Lyttleton Harbour in New Zealand.

The New Zealand authorities, under pressure, relented over taking a disabled girl and gave us a two-year visitor's permit which meant officially I was not supposed to work. A new food supplement Pancrease, unavailable in the UK, enabled Elizabeth to put on weight and live a full life, even playing basketball and going off into the bush. I relaxed into an open-necked, short-trousered lifestyle, working in three busy churches. The sea air helped Elizabeth's chest and the harbour enabled me to push off on a windsurfer from the end of our road. For two years it was a memorable and productive period, in which groups flourished and a counselling centre was opened. I worked as an ecumenical contact minister in Welcome Bay, as co-pastor to an English and Maori congregation at Maungatapu and as co-vicar in the parish church with Archdeacon Michael. The uncomplaining love and acceptance offered to this English pastor and his family was far and away the determinative factor behind whatever was achieved. Lasting and genuine friendships grew out of a steady sprinkling of picnics, barbecues and potluck lunches in Tauranga on the Bay of Plenty. Our visas were extended.

In the third year, diabetes and osteoporosis were added to the catalogue of Elizabeth's problems, which included

Crohn's Disease. Her pills grew to ninety-eight a day and there were soon about forty to fifty things we had to remember to do for her as each day passed. I had promised Heather in 1977, that as she had given herself to Rachel, so would I to Elizabeth. Elizabeth's time had come. Stuck on to the window of her bedroom she had completed a collage of her whole life, which included her favourite foods and activities, ending with whitened hair on tissue paper, 'a shawl'. Above were the words, "My Life in Heaven, Rewound and Replayed, E.J." She wrote a book about her brother Allister's bravery, *The Boy who got his Greatest Wish*, typed her Will and completed her diary. The Bishop told me when doing for Elizabeth I was working for the Diocese and to remember – these are wonderful words – 'that when I was with her I was on duty for him.' Elizabeth had decked out her wheelchair with carpet, a klaxon and a special fun numberplate incorporating the initials of her boyfriend Nigel. Sallyanne steered her wherever she needed to be and at the end did things for Elizabeth that showed amazing courage and dedication. Humour and laughter stayed with us at meal times and coming to us daily were her friends from school, church and hospital. Young and old alike just wanted to be with her and love her and listen to 'the wisdom of a sixty-year-old' in the language of a girl of thirteen.

We cried as well together. We visited the school in her wheelchair and seeing her friends on the dance-floor, there came tears of anger to her eyes. Alone among the animals we have tears and smiles, about forty muscles to express our most subtle human feelings of joy and sadness, regret, delight and laughter. These feeling responses are intended to discharge the system and keep us healthy. As a boiler under pressure needs to expel surplus energy, so our feelings need to flow over and out. Otherwise, we have to acquire ironclad resolution to keep ourselves in check – but that way we become uptight within and brittle with others. We lose the precious gift of empathy. We may have tear-stained outbreaks of hysterical laughter, or uncontrollable anger, but such moments do not drain the system. They only leave us still insensitive and inflexible. In my experience of people there is no real healing without real weeping. These days I try to value occasions for real sadness and cherish them as opportunities to dismantle the old boiler, soften my exterior self and be alongside others.

As an adult I cried only twice that I can remember, when I was saved and when I was called. Until Allister died I was still tight as a drum. When I wept for Rachel, before and after her death, tears returned and with them the gift of empathy to relate to others in trouble. More recently, since losing Elizabeth, I thought that my tear ducts were permanently dysfunctional. The Easter Sunday before starting this walk I quietly sobbed all through the service from beginning to end and during the first four to five hundred miles I frequently cried for the children until drained at last of the sadness they had caused. I now no longer feel weak when I weep. I know a different sort of strength. I still feel embarrassed, but not now ashamed. Tears still pool and they are drained with the right people and in the right place. But they keep me vulnerable, like Jesus before Lazarus' tomb, or before the crucifixion in the Garden. And I find I am not alone. Shared tears have often bridged the space between others and myself, a wordless form of hospitality.

Fit and fresh I attack the northern edge of Essex. I am in no mood for superlative buildings, like the great Gatehouse of St Osyth's Priory, the finest surviving Monastic building in Britain. I want Point Clear and the sandy edge of England. With a brief nod to Brightlingsea, now its live animal exports have discontinued, I keep up a cracking pace to the beach. On the way there are three little boys, obliviously happy, rolling round in the mud with absolutely nothing on. It just has to be all right. In no time I stumble on one of the choicest sites of British Naturism, and indeed there are some choice sights. Everywhere, pink boobs and bottoms litter the beach, tempting any full-blooded man to play a few practical jokes. Taking a strong hold of my basic instincts, I blunder on, a bloke with his bag and his boots. I have blithely travelled through umpteen nudist beaches of which there are twenty-nine officially so designated. To my mind there seems a lot of hesitancy and isolation. People are not bonded at all, rather drawn apart in tense bubbles of loneliness. There is no sign of folks being happier, though a couple with a frisbee seemed to be enjoying themselves.

I'm assured that naturists are a normal and gregarious people, who feel a welcome freedom when they extend their privacy to others, especially in their clubs up and down the country. They say they feel together from whatever background, all the same and equal. I am sure it is true that people who can be vulnerable with others are usually strong when just in their bodies and that people who are fragile may well need clothes to protect themselves from exposure or disclosure. Of course others can cherish and value their bodies differently, in their careful decisions to wrap them up attractively. Elizabeth went to a riotous pyjama party in New Zealand and there played a sort of strip poker. The shrieks of unaffected enthusiasm and the sheer unalloyed delight will ever be remembered. I entered on another occasion, inadvertently, into Elizabeth's bedroom. There she stood one night, emaciated, round-shouldered and breathing with difficulty, just as she was preparing for bed. "Oh!" I said, "I'm so sorry, Elizabeth." "That's all right," she said with a bright smile, "I always walk around like this at night. It lets God have a good look at my body."

Soon after Jaywick, which is having a face-lift, I skirt a cacophonous Clacton Pier, find low-tide sand and rejoin my companion, the sea. Boris Pasternak has said, "one can be bored by anything but the sea." I take a picture, her wavelets gliding towards my boots, so tranquil. Only once have I seen her temper and that was at Morte Point in Devon. I stand with Fred Cook, a retired builder, now eighty-three. He built several Type 22 pillboxes to defend the cliffs, should it be necessary. They are now washed into the sea, off a disappearing edge. He shows me his grandfather's headstone. He was responsible for saving nine hundred lives in the local lifeboat, one hundred credited to his own efforts, a good swimmer. We make the Frinton Churches' beach mission tent just in time to catch the final song, "May the mind of Christ my Saviour, live in me from day to day. By His love and power controlling, all I do and say." My eyes are moist with joy and gratitude.

"Wetlands of the world unite" is a stirring call for us to conserve the muddy flats and marshy areas of Britain. Thousands of resident and migrant birds simply depend on these moist lowlands being there year after year. Wild fowl and wild life species interact easily and reliably with their habitat, until threatened by drainage for agricultural or building purposes. So it is understandable that an English Nature Warden, demanding my credentials, should shake me awake this morning. Outrage, confusion and embarrassment surface through my sleeping brain at this unprovoked attack on a man's privacy. "Oi! You're not supposed to be here." I struggle to assemble a few intelligible words, but nothing comes. Apparently I am not only in a precious wetland site, Hanford Waters, not only on a Site of Special Scientific Interest and not only on an Essex Wild Life Trust designated area, but also by Bramble Island, sealed off and licensed as an explosives factory. The last time the place blew up, windows had cracked as far away as Frinton six miles to the south. Since 1875, it has produced chemicals for industrial, agricultural and military purposes. Now in the hands of Exchem Plc, it is a matter of law, health and safety, *that I be not there*. I am duly banished and find on leaving the area a plethora of signs in red and black, "DO NOT ENTER! DANGER! HAZARD AREA! YOU ARE APPROACHING A RESTRICTED ZONE." Personally, as an endangered species in the area, I ought to be garlanded, cosseted and carefully preserved.

Talking of rare species, the Tourist Information Officer called 'Ans' at Harwich has a thickish accent. "Oh!" she says proudly, "Harwich is the only town in England where you can get by without English." French, Dutch and Flemish immigrants fostered a flourishing trade up and down the east coast and settled in King's Lynn and Harwich. From Boston in the eighteenth century, to Dover at the end of the twentieth century, so the Edge has become thoroughly mixed. I am challenged. So who is English? Who is native and who is a foreigner? From the beginning, all my forebears came from the Continent: Celts, Angles, Saxons, Jutes, Picts, Normans, Huguenots, Jews and Poles. All they had to do in order to join this mongrel nation was just to come and stay, like Asian Ugandans ejected by Idi Amin. Babies born here today, as to a Czech, Slovak or Kosovan refugee, are English tomorrow; though 'Englishness' really needs two generations of growing up and absorbing the culture. It just has to be claimed and owned and acknowledged as the host culture. I am hospitable by nature and I feel welcome here in Harwich, but I hope these people are not English-speaking Dutch living in a foreign land but just Dutch-speaking English? The Rotterdam ferry takes my eye as she glides out to sea to Holland and Hamburg. I think to myself, the water does not make me different, but it does makes me very separate – and English.

I grew up a Yorkshireman and proud of it. Since then I have grown additionally many circles of an ever wider and richer identity. To my Englishness I have added Britishness, which includes the multi-ethnicity of the Commonwealth, and now to that I have also added a European perspective. I look at the map and feel European. Between 1983 and 1987 we left to live in New Zealand. It was a shock to find I was a '*Pakeha*' out there, like it or not, '*Paleface*', to the Maoris who cared not a fig whether I was Dutch, Italian, Spanish or English. I was a Western European and shared its common culture.

So at core I am a Yorkshire-born Englishman. Something just given. An Englishman over 60 years, I have come to believe in things like fair play, the BBC, Wimbledon and fish and chips. I am proud of the bulldog spirit and a certain stoicism when faced by the weather or a queue. Above all I feel it is right to be hospitable and generous to my neighbour. All I ask of my neighbour is that what has been given *him* by right of birth or arrival, his Englishness, he too must also claim and make his own. Add to that, over the last twenty years I have come to appreciate my European identity and, not least, the world wide church. I am Anglican and a Christian. These further circles of trans-national identity mean that I belong, I hope without undue hyperbole, to dioceses across the planet and beyond to Christ's Kingdom, in which we are 'all one in Christ Jesus ... in whom all things are coming together, things in Heaven and things in Earth.' I still rejoice in the unifying global influence of the English Language, still with pride wear the cross of St George on my stick, as well as the Union Jack on my rucksack and still, not least, want to sing, at top volume, *The Queen* and *Land of Hope and Glory* along with the heartiest at the Proms. In the centre of Harwich, I am somehow pleased to find a private house converted into a pub. Outside hangs its sign "THE BRITISH FLAG", complete with the Union Jack, its only other decoration.

Marooned above the high tide I see an extraordinary contraption, a naval treadmill crane, dating back to 1667. It is the only one left in England. Inside, a man on each of the two inner wheels can haul a boat up and out of the water. There is a snag, however, for no brake was ever fitted. I imagine the men's hamster-like frenzy going backwards. As if I need more experience with cranes, I take the sea wall out of Harwich. A mile further on I find myself entering a vast container storage complex. I am soon located on the radar, unceremoniously hitched up on this gigantic mobile monster and driven at one and a half miles per hour to the exit. I return the compliment written over the exit lintel "THANK YOU FOR USING HARWICH INTERNATIONAL PORT".

The exit from Essex lies through Mistley, with its malt aroma, its swans, its towers and its open secret, the Nuclear Bunker. The former county nuclear war headquarters gives me the shivers. I go down and feel the impact of this chilling reminder of the Cold War: How to survive! How to protect myself from blast, burn and radioactive dust. I feel the helplessness, the stupidity of it all and I recall the intense primal rage I experienced on emerging from the film scenario, *The Last Day*. It was shown in Tauranga, North Island, New

Zealand, itself a nuclear free zone. I came out and swore ferociously.

I leave the Tendring Peninsular of Essex with its sign written boldly in five languages, 'WELCOME!' I feel happy about that and cross the Stour to see, optimistically, what Suffolk might have in store. I find a treacherous tangle of mud and collapsing trees, the nadir of my eastern edge.

Chapter 12

Three Final Estuaries: Stour Orwell and Alde

TRUSTING TO GRACE AND GOODNESS

I BEGIN AND END THIS DAY WITH POTATOES. I LEAVE THE Cattawade Bridge, and start along the north bank of the Stour estuary. In front of me the *Grimme* combined harvester is living up to its name, slowly devouring a field of spuds. Whether it is pronounced Grim as in "grimace" or Grime as in soot, it spews into the machine at one end a stream of black filth and out at the other it offers clean white bulging bags ready for the market in London. In between, the transformation is achieved by nearly a dozen people cooped up inside and under orders, I presume, from Mr Grimme.

The map gives me no clue that the next two days will prove such a huge test. This part of East Anglia, it seems, just merges into the North Sea, avoiding the expense and inconvenience of having a coastline. It is a vast coastal fudge, in which the land and sea converge in a vindictive zone of chaos. The Stour edge in particular has dissolved, disappeared. Perversely the sea seems to have pulled everything down and left everything behind. Drunken twisted trees have slumped into the estuary and they force the walker either into the mud to sink, or into the branches to swing. Mile after mile the whitened skeletons of England's best oak, ash and alder shape a formidable graveyard all the way to Holbrook Bay. Dehydrated and pretty desperate, I turn inland for water and find an oasis of order and calm, The Royal Greenwich Hospital School.

This co-educational school was re-located here and is intended for the children of sailors, merchants and others – even volunteer lifeboatmen – anyone involved with the sea. Rich and poor, this classless ordered world of 800 largely residential children is a delight to find and, it seems a model of educational excellence. I find a house matron and am soon refreshed and back on course, much impressed by a really fine naval establishment. A path takes me into Shotley Gate past its Martello gasometer and with fading feet I struggle up into the village to the chip shop, where many Grimme bags now rest in peace. Ron and Anne give me just the sort of welcome I need, plus a five-pound note and I set off into the darkness. With my precious bag of fish and chips clamped under my sweatshirt, my pregnant form thus etched into the evening sky I skirt Cranes Hill and disappear behind a wood. The flaring lights of Harwich docks now illumine everything from across the water.

I lie contentedly within my sleeping bag, with the fish and chips comfortably within my waistline as good as any hot water bottle and feeling hugely grateful. As I slide into sleep I wonder why I cherish so much the kindly smile of Ms Harper, the matron and likewise the generosity of Ron and Anne behind their counter. I savour again their free and fleeting little offerings of grace. Neither had known the inhuman odds I had faced that day so their gestures were not sparked by my heroism, rewards for effort or sympathy for hardship. They were simply gifts of loving acceptance. They were gifts of goodness. They would fortify my spirit next day.

This was our joy on arrival in New Zealand, to receive similar tokens of goodwill, so that in effect we soon happily spilled over in ministry. Similarly on return, we were invited by David and Angela Burton to stay in The Cloverley Hall Conference Centre, near Whitchurch in Shropshire. A cleric without a parish has no home and we needed time to grieve, time to heal. It was clearly too soon to work in a parish, but not too soon to be loved. We were given the warmest room, after living in the sub-tropics. It was over the kitchen. We explored this banker's mansion, which later was for many years a school with its oak-panelled lounge, grand staircase, ornamental clock tower, steep roofs and high fluted Shropshire chimneys, all set among tall Californian hardwoods. Soon of course we became active, Heather in the kitchen with the greens, Sallyanne in the house sorting out new guests, and Graham in a series of painting efforts trying to improve the look of the house. And we enjoyed the tennis, the skating, the walks and the bike-rides. Back in England with just a few suitcases, (everything else in store at Southampton), we had little to offer but were privileged to receive of the Burtons' goodness, another spilling out of His love.

Today the sun is out. I have, I know, about thirty-two miles to go, the furthest of any day so far on my journey, all the way up and down the Orwell. This is the last major estuary, as the map tells me, a long finger variously described as 'Black Ooze' and 'Pond Ooze'. In no time the path is disappearing under my feet. The bank is degenerating and I am finding myself trapped once again. On my landward side, there are stretches of marsh and muddy water. The grass and reeds are growing higher and thicker by the mile, until I feel like the *African Queen*. Suddenly I burst into a clearing and startle a painter. This is Constable country and she is not pleased, but I take the chance thankfully to climb out and ascend to the watershed. It does me little good, as the path disappears again, and I am soon back to the water's edge. Clearly, mine are about the first human legs to be seen on this thin and sinewy path, as a baby partridge takes off just in front of me. He, or she, is scared out of its tiny wits and for half a mile just keeps a metre or two ahead, legs a constant blur. I have noticed that everything scatters on the trail and that birds universally flee to hide. I am sure that the Rev. Gilbert White is to be held responsible. He was the first to record avian creatures and would catch and kill in order to examine them. They got the message. Until quite recently, poor people ate them as well, so I suppose only the most fearful survived. Anyway, if I raise my camera they always duck and if I use my binoculars they usually hide the instant I get them into focus.

It is usually true that birds of a feather flock together on the ground and in the sky. Many times I saw spectacular feats of corporate aviation, as clouds of birds swooped together as one, dropping and veering instantaneously, as if connected by invisible threads. Messages evidently travel between them as some sort of group consciousness decides the direction and speed of the flock. Sitting having my lunch a few weeks ago, there was a cloud of starlings (I think) in a tree. Periodically they would drop down to scratch among the stubble. Then, mysteriously they would lift like a magic carpet to disappear back into the tree. Soon they would soundlessly flutter down again like heavy leaves rippling over the ground, until some alarm would send them up instantly once again into cover.

We individual humans despise such behaviour as unthinking conformity, because we so prize our freedom to act without the constraints of the crowd. Sadly, we seem not to think 'corporately' any more, except in corporations. Perhaps if we were to practise 'interdividualism', as someone has put it, we could recover a sense of being part of others, in family or society. Perhaps, instead of riding round in our metal bubbles and feeling safe and superior, we could wind down the windows of dogged independence and feel that yes, we do belong, we are loved and we can be led as well as lead. These thoughts emerge as I am talking with Richard, a local reporter who was feeling somewhat reflective after a brush with death. How easy to use the car to insulate ourselves so that we can watch other people rather than meet them.

I pick up a piece of driftwood, about three feet long, stout with stubby bits jutting out along its length. In my hand it seems to resemble a dolphin, or it could be a crocodile, perhaps a submarine. Depending which way I look at it, it becomes a kind of metaphor. Some love to plunge into life and swim with others, going with the currents and with the ebb and flow of experiences. Some of us stay round the edge and snap angrily at those who do like to 'go with the flow'.

Others perhaps like me, who really want to launch into the deep, still prefer to keep the submarinal skins of our upbringing, and watch in relative safety. I pick up my camera, 'just typical', and then put it away. I stuff my woody polymorph through the lid of my rucksack, for Sallyanne to take home later.

This day needs Herculean effort. There is only my chin to help me. I stick it out and soon my jaw is set in concrete. Most of us ask our bodies to carry what our minds refuse to face and so we displace on to some part of our anatomy the tension we feel about those things we cannot resolve. My teeth take the brunt. My dentist tells me that I grind my teeth at night. There was a time when my eating resounded to knuckle-crunching clunks. Sure enough I drop into the Pin Mill sweet shop and emerge in attack mode with a bag of toffee eclairs. Instantly I remove a long-standing gold molar crown. I throw the rest into a hedge (the sweets, I mean).

The Royal Harwich Yacht Club, unconsulted, is next to witness my fleeting steaming profile as I dissect its property. I pay for it – further up there is no way out. With great difficulty I strike out inland yet again, this time through a dense tangle of undergrowth, ferns higher than my head and blackberry brambles half an inch thick. Eventually I emerge to reach the brand new Orwell Bridge. I am indeed truly inspired by the crossing, except that regular yellow-anodised plates pinned to the parapet caution me to use the telephone number of local Samaritans before I jump. A beautiful park with some four hundred year old trees welcomes me down the eastern edge of the estuary. I keep up a good speed now that there is a proper path. But with my next box of stores waiting for me in Felixstowe, I am out of isotonic drink. Soon I can do little more than just plod on through the Trimley Marshes, taunted by the sharp unsympathetic piping of an oyster-catcher and the sheer indifference of egrets, until round the interminable port facilities I make the forecourt of Sainsbury's. I drop into the kindness of Alan and Joan Reeves and sink what is left of my teeth into Yorkshire pud, a roast and three veg. Next day at a hotel I rendezvous with our extra special daughter, Sallyanne, whom I had not seen for two months.

In 1975 there were two seriously ill children in the Vicarage and two medical friends of ours, Janet and Garth, were praying for something to happen to cheer the Jones family. And Sallyanne happened. On the day of her birth I was sitting eating sandwiches in the hospital ward. Heather and I were alone in a peaceful room, when swooch, out unexpectedly came our fourth. Still attached she opened her eyes, had a good look round and with a little help from Dad fastened on to Heather for her first feed. It was intended to be a Le Boyeur birthing under water. Instead it was just perfect. At the beginning we carried her in a little net shopping bag when out walking. At four, she stood cheekily for a photo-call in Grandma Frances' fur boots. At five, Heather is told by the teacher, "Sallyanne will be all right." Apparently at morning break on the first day at school she asked a girl for a crisp. On refusal the girl was picked up by the lapels and became instantly co-operative. Sallyanne's social skills have been modified since then, but she does stand her ground. It is just as well, as she was bullied for her accent on arrival in New Zealand.

Then, in Tauranga, Bay of Plenty, care for Elizabeth took precedence and Sallyanne had to survive on just fifteen minutes of Heather's undivided attention promised to her every day. I gave her a pile of wood shingles to kick. She learnt about crocodiles and tsunamis, about Maori ways and the bush, about sailing, skating and skiing, and finally about 'letting go'. Her most telling tribute to her sister was to go to the funeral parlour and without my help dress Elizabeth in her best clothes and Ghostbuster undies. With the undertaker she attractively shaped Lizzie's hair just right in the casket and then left her with *Trustworthy,* her favourite teddy. That, I think, is spunk.

On Monday morning the proprietor of Dorincourt is hassling us to be out by ten o' clock. We have boxes all over the room for a big sort out, as Sallyanne is administrator for

Walk 2000. The woman simply doesn't give up, chivvying us all the time, until, that is, Sallyanne goes out and says to her, "If I were to treat our customers like you are treating us we wouldn't have any left." Sallyanne, at nineteen years, is an Assistant Manager at Hooper's Department Store in Cheltenham. She moved with us into the town and started there as a temporary part-time shoe assistant. After a few months they advertised and interviewed for a job in retail management. She was appointed an assistant manager. The staff got behind her and only one person resigned in protest.

The ferry lets me off a thirty-mile journey up and down the Deben. My gold tooth is restored to its plinth and Sallyanne takes me to Orford Ness. I enjoy her driving. Calm, positive and considerate. *I* drive as on a mission, the hunter-gatherer who has to survive. No wonder, so I understand, men commit ninety-five per cent of motoring offences. We have teacakes under a green and white sunshade at the castle. It is very special. Orford Ness feels like an island, but is connected very tenuously to Aldeburgh, eight miles to the north. Its main attraction for years was secrecy. Strange pillars and pagodas stab the skyline. Radar defence systems, bombs and finally nuclear weapons all began life here. Now the National Trust has most of it and at the southern end the BBC have the rest for its World Service transmission. The last ferry is 'gone', I am told. The men seem secretive and uncooperative. I feel they are treating me as an agent of the KGB. The ferry is there, a monstrous grey tub, a WW2 landing craft, renamed *Genevieve* and it isn't very far. It isn't very late. They just want to go home. I climb on to some railings, which clearly announce "DANGER! UNSAFE STRUCTURE! KEEP OUT!" I grin defiantly, am photographed by Sallyanne and finally, dispatched, inspected and in good order, bound for the Scottish border, after a long and lingering hug.

I don't think my chin has quite settled back, because I am determined to cling to this indeterminate exasperating edge just as long as the East Anglian disease keeps smudging it. So when I see another notice advising me not to proceed in case I tread on a bird's nest, I ignore it. I feel justified in blasting on, seeing it is August and a bit late for avian nooky. 'Only one more form of life passing through,' I tell myself. I want to reach St Botolph's, stuck out on a promontory, but still at least six miles ahead. I round the 'Cape of Good Hope' in company with several sailing vessels, in fair weather and a good breeze, proceeding due west up the Alde estuary, ship's log 16.00 hours. By this time, on my port side, high reeds, bulrushes and nettles have flanked the river embankment and there is no escape. Slightly puzzled mariners are overtaking me on the starboard side. Basically my snivelling problem is short trousers. I reach Iken Church with my legs blotched, black and bleeding and generally stinging all over.

St Botolph was a pioneering missionary monk, who saw this high spot as a dry spot and desired to build a Minster here as his regional East Anglian centre for Christian witness. 'Icanhoh' was the village, now on the maps as Iken. It is for me a strange and lovely coincidence that I called my sign-writing business, "Iken Signs". At Cloverley Hall I laboured long and hard to renew all the signs, interior and exterior, and acquired some interest in the subject. After fifteen months of generous hospitality we moved to the local Vicar's retirement home in Ellesmere. Sallyanne continued at her school in Whitchurch and I set up a sign-writing shop in the garage. For a year I drove into Shrewsbury College of Science and Technology on a Monday and spent the day learning the crafts of sign writing, gilding and glass decoration. Gradually I gathered all the fascinating tools of the trade as time went by, like draggers and floggers and brushes labelled lark, crow, duck, goose and swan – with, of course, the essential mahl stick. Then other days, Tuesday to Saturday, I tried to build up a little business, bluffing and blundering my way through contracts that soon adorned the shops and restaurants, posts, houses and vehicles of the area. The name was a phonetic double take: 'I ken' (I see) and 'chen' the Hebrew for 'grace'. It helped a little financially and kept me out of mischief. But that is a long way from this thatched and ancient holy place on the Alde, Iken's Parish Church.

Talking about Holy Places, East Anglia is dotted all over with 2,000 such buildings, 900 in the Norfolk Diocese alone. They are as inseparable from the landscape as are spots on a polka-dot dress. In New Zealand Holy Places were 'tapu' and even vicarages were 'tapu' to the Maoris. One night after dark, I opened the door to a young man dripping with blood. He was a drug dealer and had been attacked and run out of the town centre in fear of his life. He stood in my kitchen with bleeding bare feet and a head wound, asking my help. Reluctantly he unloaded a knife, heroin and wads of bank notes on to my table. At least he was safe. So was I. I suppose one day my luck will run out, but then, I think to myself, 'Trustworthy' is the Old Testament name for God. Tonight on the Edge I dream about Elizabeth and sleep in an old school, warm and welcomed by friendly people, in the Blaxhall Youth Hostel. And I didn't need to deserve it. It was another spilling out of kindness.

Chapter 13

Iken to Cromer

LEARNING OVER AGAIN AND SURPRISE

I WOULD LIKE TO DECLARE THE NORTH SHORE OF THE STOUR a designated area of outstanding natural ugliness. Now, in contrast, come with me! Let me take you into Suffolk, as different from Essex as brogues are from wellington boots. 'It's official', the Suffolk coastline between Felixstowe and Lowestoft is designated one hundred miles of Outstanding Natural Beauty. Open heath-land behind low backed cliffs with quiet lagoons of reed-fringed marshes and sanctuaries of wild life, all mingle into long white sandy beaches. The feel of this county is discreet and distinctive. After the mud and drabness of Essex, ahead are the light and airy ice-cream colours of Southwold. My spirits rise and indeed, given the chance, I would swap my boots for a boat I see, called *Bright and Breezy*. I think a light touch and a bit of style are called for.

That, anyway, was what was wanted in the Cotswolds. Our move there in 1989 was definitely up-market. Priest-in-Charge of Bledington, Icomb and Westcote I lived in the Vicarage, almost new, thought to be worth then a quarter of a million pounds. My Lay Reader lived in Icomb Place, of Crusader fame. My first treasurer was No 1. at Cable and Wireless. My second treasurer was No 2. in the finance department of the BBC. Many commuted to Paddington daily from Kingham Station nearby. Many notables, I was also to discover, lived in the farms and cottages of the area, bereft of social standing but amply supplied with a quality and character that made them and my job very special. It seemed to me that the decisive issue was not 'what we've got, but what we do with what we've got.' Heather and I retrieved all our worldly goods from the store in Southampton Docks and from my father's at Lyme Regis. Dressed in my corduroy jacket, I started visiting the people in five villages and three churches. "That's better!" said Daisy, as she opened the door. "We like our man in a dark suit." I had been to the summer sale at Harrod's.

It seems appropriate that my next port of call, after the Youth Hostel, is the Maltings at the Snape Concert Hall complex, founded by Benjamin Britten for music and the arts. The Easter Islandish sculptures outside enhance the wonderful atmosphere. It is the 50th Aldeburgh Festival and everything looks its best. Except a sign nearby – the "Public Footpath" sign wreathed in blackberry brambles. Worse is to come, the next and worst sign of my entire journey. This sign would disgrace the entrance to Alcatraz after dark. The sun had nearly bleached out of existence the huge block capital letters "PRIVATE ROAD NO CYCLES!" At the top of a rusty iron pole the sign is just intact, roof capping, sides and base gone. Cracks that would dwarf those in the Wailing Wall have split the sign fatally and two enormous rusty bolt-heads are its most prominent feature. Except, that is, for a recent piece of white paper stuck to lower centre. Quoting from the 1971 Animal Act it announces in brazen Helvetica, "YOUR DOG COULD BE SHOT IF FOUND AMONG SHEEP". I feel like adding my own warning: "Sod the Dog. Beware of the County Council".

Sizewell Nuclear Power Stations, 'A' and 'B', hold a peculiar revulsion alongside the attractive local pub called *Vulcan*. Frankly the dome and two ugly square boxes do not sit well together, nor fit into this gentle area of south Suffolk. On the foreshore outside and far more absorbing is the discovery of a two foot high common ragwort in full yellow bloom. It is officially outlawed by the local authority being toxic to livestock, but here actually colonised and totally smothered by the Blue Adonis butterfly. Yet more fascinating still and only a little further along is *The House in the Clouds*. This structure near Thorpeness had been a water tower. Now it is a dream house, floating in the sky and seeming to follow me behind the trees.

In New Zealand, if a family wishes to move house it does exactly that. There a house, being of timber construction, can easily be jacked up onto a lorry and taken away. As long as the move is completed before six o'clock in the morning, it can just disappear from its garden and re-appear somewhere else. The Tauranga Baptist church just upped and offed one day. We saw it coming down the High Street and then it was gone. St Stephen's Cathedral, Auckland, simply walked across the road and sat down comfortably on the other side. I have a feeling that one day the most prestigious building in Aldeburgh, The Moot Hall, will have to be given a piggyback to somewhere else. Used for Town Council meetings since 1540, it stands today stranded on the beach shingle. Two rows of houses that once stood between it and the elements have long since disappeared into the sea. At Dunwich further up the coast, nine churches have disappeared since Saxon and Norman times. There the area Bishop lived among a town of fifty thousand people, half the size of London. Coffins still pop out of the cliffs and rabbits nibble round the sole remaining headstone, the only memorial to a once proud and prosperous port.

I have travelled nearly thirty miles today. The evening sun spreads a gold patina over everything in sight as I journey inland to cross the bridge at Walberswick. Soggy underfoot I cross the acres and acres of golf course in as near a straight line as possible. I creak into Southwold, empathising with *Crick Court* for elderly residents and come across *my name*. Fluttering on a bush is a blue card edged with reflective red tape shining in the sunlight. "WELCOME GRAHAM!" is its lovely message. It epitomises the charm and hospitality offered by Brenda and Maurice Wilde. They cannot do enough and are both so busy. The meal was a spectacular success, spread, prepared and offered with exquisite attention to detail. I left with wonderful memories.

On a wall in the Parish Church I am shown Southwold Jack. His axe-head falling square on a bell, he can send a clear and ringing message to announce the start of Morning Prayer or the arrival of the bride. I too have a gong fixed up in my hall. It is a trophy from the Himalayas, from a Nepalese mountain mule. It sends a deep and rich message through the house whenever guests arrive or a parcel arrives via the postman. When we lived in a Vicarage, the front door was never our own and a ring on the doorbell could just as easily herald problems as pleasures.

I had spent twenty-five years in large town-centre churches, so the rural benefice of Bledington seemed an easy enough assignment, well supported by well-heeled and well-intentioned laymen. What was a deceptively easy job, however, soon led into a steep learning curve and, after five years, to retirement. The headmistress and I shared our common experience on arrival of feeling de-skilled, like little children having to learn again how to walk. Nothing that I knew seemed to apply. The church for me had always been a warm and welcoming place, set in a cold and indifferent urban society. The church was there to offer acceptance and forgiveness. Beyond, society was suspicious and inclined to be judgmental. In Bledington I found the reverse. The building was cold, perched like a fridge on the highest point outside the village. The liturgy was formal and no one stayed to talk. The dear people just filed in and filed out. In contrast the village was warm-hearted and an accepting place, with a sense of humour, where I could tease and be teased. Instead of fellowship within and frostiness without, I found frostiness within the church and friendship outside in the village.

This strange reversal was partly to do with the building. A thousand years old, it had become a sacred place, too holy in which to have either a real laugh or a real row. I well remember my churchwarden and his wife, in a previous church, dodging round the baptismal font having a thorough ding-dong, while everyone else carried on drinking their coffee. There the church was 'home'. A second reason was to do with my predecessor, who over twenty-two years had been wedded to the classical Anglo-Catholic notion of the clergyman, daily praying in the church at five, as a symbol standing in for Christ. He was always dressed in black and avoided personal relationships. A deeply private man, approaching seventy, it seems he was unknown to anyone in the village as a human being, though as a chaplain to everyone he was a huge success. Then of course it was also to do with me. Fresh from short trousers and an open shirt in New Zealand, I was disinclined to emulate my predecessor and be 'in role'. After all, I had been asked to foster lay relationships. Called to a ministry of word and sacrament I favoured the first, teaching and preaching, and the parish preferred the latter.

It was hard. Though house groups and teamwork began to emerge in all three parishes, with the help of wardens and lay reader, it did rather knock my confidence. It was said that the insularity of these parishes began with the Black Death. They avoided contact with merchants travelling between Stow, Bourton and Chipping Norton, and so escaped the ravages of the plague. Three centuries later, they were still keeping themselves to themselves but could not so easily escape their newest plague – the Vicar.

In the Cotswold School, Bourton on the Water, Sallyanne found her place in the orchestra and played piano, flute and later saxophone. In theatre she played anything from Mary, the Mother of Jesus to Sue-Zuki the wild and hairy leader of a gang of greasers. In the Chipping Norton school where she took 'A' Levels she was the envy of the sixth form, riding off to jet ski with her rich boyfriend, and soon became Head Girl. But she did not know, with nine 'O' Levels, that the effect of attending eight schools over the years had left her education more leaky than the privatised mains water network.

In the past, Lowestoft spelt fish. Nowadays its drying frames are empty and stark on the shore. The Ness is acquiring alternative business. Curious, I stop by a shop doorway. Its two-inch sandstone doorstep has actually worn through. Mrs Iris Gibbs, a frail seventy-five-year-old widow, tells me it is the fourth worn through in a hundred and twenty years. Stocks of groceries are pitifully low. She breathes chestily. She is just carrying on because "there's nothing else to do" since her husband died four years ago. Then her face sharpens and her eyes glint. "I went to Scotland on holiday a few months ago" she confides, "my first since our honeymoon fifty years back." She leans forward with clear intent. "I had burglars. See those locks!" I notice all the windows have been barred and grilled with steel mesh. "Bird's Eye trade has gone and few come in these days. But I'm not giving up. I've been burgled four times in two months. I know who it is. He wants my property to develop next door. I know … and I'm not giving in." I made a mental note to have another doorstep delivered.

I stay with the Newmans and their rumbustious teenagers. Then in early bright sunshine John drops me off near the 'scores', narrow steep ancient lanes down to the Ness labelled Spurgeon, Went, Crown and Mariner. I spent a few moments inside Christ Church, the most easterly church in the British Isles. It had a rising sun on its notice board and the people still shine alongside the *Lighthouse Café* nearby.

The sea is up, and I mean boisterous and noisy. Wooden slatted breakwaters explode the surf into a million droplets. The air is clear and the sun is out. I take photos of everything, horses galloping along the sand and two old age pensioners, Don and Thea, heads down into a forceful breeze, daring the tide to beat them back to their car. "Don't let the ups get you down," they shout into the teeth of the gale. Many old tree-stumps and whitened curving branches stick out of the flat sandy expanse ahead. I stop discreetly behind a stripy windbreak, draped to keep out the airborne sand. There is a devoted mother patiently encouraging her handicapped child.

I long to stay and talk but the scene is too intimate. I move on. Soon I am talking to Chris and Tina, two evidently gentle and kind parents from the Midlands. They are out on the front at Gorleston-on-Sea with disabled twins James and Stephen, both six years old with a mental age of one and a half, and also Mark. He is fine, and so are they… I wish you could see their shining faces. Who's shining faces? The boys? The parents? Both! There is no even-handedness in our world and God is not tied to any one view of consistency, or simplistic views of comfort and the easy life. But these parents are blessed and a blessing.

Norfolk is what you make of it, perhaps an acquired taste, a challenge, bland and bleak and generally hard to get to. Or is it compelling, the home of misty-eyed 'birdies' and the wild-eyed seal fanatic, prepared to slog all the way to the end of Blakeney Point? There is much that baffles me about Britain's most eastern rump. I want to find out why a London vicar should choose to go to Cromer and more to the point why his widow chooses to stay there after he dies. Why I should lurch from jolly vulgarity in Great Yarmouth to African huts in Winterton, from North Sea gas amid spinach leaves to a momentous and mysterious encounter with an old woman, ensconced in a four-storey Victorian house, who will never, never give up.

Great Yarmouth, big and beefy, still sprawls untidily a mile down its dock facilities, sliced diagonally by the River Yare. A flimsy wooden ferry, which runs the gauntlet of mighty cargo ships steaming in and out, is on the blink commercially. From a massive statue of Britannia I turn my back on the port and walk into the blaring roller-coasting frolic of the fair-ground. Through town, I go by the ancient 'rows' to the old jail, down into dungeons and up into an Elizabethan house. I slump really tired into the back room of the Childrens Society Charity Shop, with a mug of tea and two antique treasures, Mary and Frances, who revive me. At five o' clock I am chucked out. A call to Heather from a BT kiosk helps a bit but the Palace Ballroom decked in pink so hurts my eyes that I find and climb up into the Coastwatch lookout on the beach and sit with Ernie and Reg, gazing contentedly out to sea. At least I am doing something useful.

I rub my eyes at Winterton. Nestling in the dunes are round white pillboxes thatched with African roofs. These conical huts are in the Hermanus Holiday Centre, much appreciated by their occupants. The chip shop seems the only sane place to go before disappearing into the Winterton Dunes Nature Reserve, the largest acid heath dune area in Northern Europe. I sleep well on a springy turf and awake to the anguished cries of a redshank. It is diving and banking to avoid the predatory intentions of a Great Black Backed gull. Twisting and wheeling and shrieking, the redshank finally escapes. No wonder these gulls are usually seen isolated and avoided, out on the edge of feeding flocks and I can certainly understand why some birds of a feather do have to stick together. Natterjack toads and two cobalt blue dragonflies vie for my attention a few yards away. The dragonflies are chasing each other like quivering bi-planes in a sort of aerial dogfight, except it was courtship. A toad was eyeing them expectantly. The toads feed off ordinata. The dragonflies in their turn feed off mosquitoes and midges, which make them carniverous, unlike butterflies that only ingest nectar.

Dragonflies have held an enduring fascination for me, quite apart from their sheer elegance and colour. They can take off like Harrier jets. They can cover sixteen yards in less than a second and can cruise at 40 miles an hour. To hover they create a vortex below each side of the body, as each pair of wings moves in opposite directions. Their most telling appeal for me however is their two-stage life. The first is a limited and bounded existence as a nymph, maybe for several years or only twelve months, crawling about in the comparative gloom and murk of a river bed, oblivious to the sunlit world above. Until, that is, its instincts take it up the stem of a plant out of water-world and into sunshine. In no time it shakes off its former skin, unfolds its wings and begins its second life in the vastly superior world above. Earth-bound and yet heaven-bound I am trying to live and dream beyond the comparative darkness of this world. I am trying to sense the light and colours of another world and those 'two hundred shades of orange' I was once told about. I do constantly look up, for surely I will travel there into the presence of my Father, my family and many friends. One day I shall fly, as my daughter Rachel, whose frail body likewise was visibly infused with that second life, and who, from within the confines of a hospital ward and before a beckoning eternity, slipped into a radiant young person before our eyes and then left us, to wonder at what we had seen.

This is high season and long empty beaches are punctuated periodically by explosions of colour. Windshields and bathing suits, hats, towels and buckets, all jostle round breaks in the low cliffs. At Happisburgh, spoken as it is written by many of the locals, the cliffs finally close in on me and I wade out to sea to skirt a dangerous section. I climb to the church where seven hundred men are buried, the victims of seventy wrecked ships, in 1789. The lighthouse is being painted like a squashed barber's pole.

Four miles later, high tide and high fences force me inland round the pipes and gadgetry of the Bacton North Sea Gas Terminal and I am intrigued to find fields of flourishing spinach stretching in all directions. The combination sets me thinking. An old friend joins me. From his arrival he exercises the privilege of any open-air walker, that of belching and breaking wind at regular intervals. Alternately seems reasonable. Simultaneously I did think was physiologically impossible. I too can so indulge with shameless satisfaction, when the need comes upon me, but Gilbert is in a class of his own with nuclear emanations.

Gilbert and I make it into Cromer, leaving behind a fetid cloud lingering on the cliffs. We remain good friends. He came to St Ives before pension entitlement and rose to the challenge of a new Council appointment, that of 'Town Centre Caretaker', on his knees removing chewing gum - with a smile and happy disposition.

It seems at the end of the day fairly safe to be on Cromer pier and have a quiet ice-cream. Soon mid-evening, I gaze up at a looming three-storey house. Ginny was a 'toughie' no-nonsense person. Typically, she had been the very first person to contribute by return of post, £250 no less, to the charity fund. My encounter with her would be daunting and full of mystery. Strong and independent, she had mothered and fathered four boys while her husband was busy all hours in the parishes at Rainham and Woking. Charles and Ginny then moved to Cromer Vicarage and before long she was a widow. Not a quitter by nature, she stayed. Now eighty and by herself, she leads me straight up to her first floor kitchen. Enquiries about my needs are abrupt and pert and kindly meant. "Help yourself!" she says. Nearby are a battered frying pan and a bulge-bottomed pressure cooker. They somehow unnerve me, redolent of a past tyranny. Welcome I am, I know, but somehow I cannot shut out the chilling stridency of her manner. In her presence I feel shrivelled and small. We have a reading from the Bible and go our separate ways to bed.

The next day brings a surprise moment into my Walk, another moment of learning again. My uncompromising host and I have been to church. She is seated on the settee for a photograph, when I glimpse another familiar face. The sun has caught her silver hair and in an instant I recognise the face of a woman I know. She is dead. She died three years ago. She is my mother, same height, same shape, same hands, the same silver hair. Even the eyelids are draped diagonally, giving the same sinister effect. Underneath, the same sort of ferocity evokes the same withering of my spirit. Rematerialised before me is the haunting presence of someone I know to have surrendered to a Dorset grave. I wince. Then comes the mystery of grace. I look again at the settee in Cromer, this time with some real acceptance of my forbidding mother, for in those shiny eyes before me I see a kindly joy. In this determined face, etched by hard work, there is moving a gentle spirit and in her hands lies an open Bible. Months later, I telephone her, with some vague misgivings. She has had a quadruple heart by-pass operation and I ask how she is. Just as I expect and quick as a flash, “I’m fine”, she says, “How are you?” I sigh and pick up my photograph of Ginny Searle-Barnes, with a sense of thanksgiving and genuine affection. I can see there the mum I never had. There also is the mum that now I can live with, and the person that now I can live without.

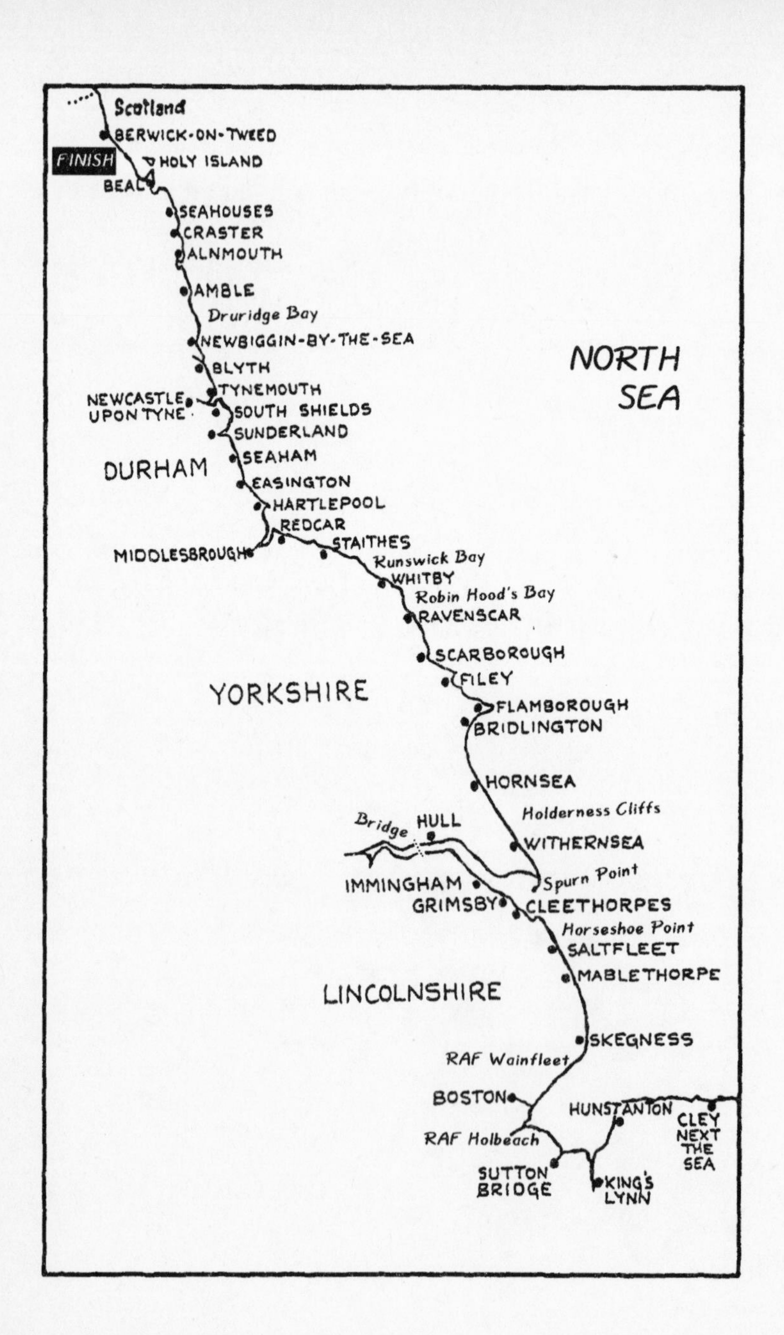
Scotland
BERWICK-ON-TWEED
FINISH
HOLY ISLAND
BEAL
SEAHOUSES
CRASTER
ALNMOUTH
AMBLE
Druridge Bay
NEWBIGGIN-BY-THE-SEA
BLYTH
TYNEMOUTH
NEWCASTLE UPON TYNE
SOUTH SHIELDS
SUNDERLAND
SEAHAM
DURHAM
EASINGTON
HARTLEPOOL
REDCAR
MIDDLESBROUGH
STAITHES
Kunswick Bay
WHITBY
Robin Hood's Bay
RAVENSCAR
SCARBOROUGH
FILEY
YORKSHIRE
FLAMBOROUGH
BRIDLINGTON
HORNSEA
Holderness Cliffs
Bridge
HULL
WITHERNSEA
Spurn Point
IMMINGHAM
GRIMSBY
CLEETHORPES
Horseshoe Point
SALTFLEET
MABLETHORPE
LINCOLNSHIRE
SKEGNESS
RAF Wainfleet
BOSTON
HUNSTANTON
CLEY NEXT THE SEA
RAF Holbeach
SUTTON BRIDGE
KING'S LYNN
NORTH SEA

THIRD LEG

Thirty (?) hopeful years
— retired and ready

Chapter 14

The Fenlands

TAKING TIME TO FACE THE FUTURE

I SET OFF ON SUNDAY AFTERNOON TO TRAVEL THE SHORT distance to Weybourne. At the East Runton Gap I drop down through rusty railings between pinnacles of chalk and scrunch across the flinty stones. A child has dropped a little yellow plastic egg. It rattles. The two halves contain a treasure, a pebble. I cannot throw it away and instead rejoice in its simplicity. My heart follows in a surge of gratitude for my parents and two sisters Cherry and Coral, my own children and wife, Heather, and not least for Ginny and her husband Charles. Forty years ago, Heather and her bike somersaulted over a hole in the road. Ginny and Charles had generously arranged for medical attention in London and for the cost of training in parish work at Dalton House, Bristol. A little further on I see someone who looks like Heather, walking among shiny-white pools of limestone on the beach, lit up in the evening sun. I capture the kindly understanding face of my wife and am so grateful for her accepting presence over thirty years. I am two-thirds through my journey and behind me are two thirty-year periods of my life. The words of our favourite hymn come to mind: "When all Thy mercies, O my God, my rising soul surveys, transported with the view I'm lost in wonder, love and praise."

Sallyanne is both ordinary and extra-ordinary, everything we could have asked for. She has emerged from sibling hardships to be a huge credit to her family. She has always been a delight and a great kid. Now she has grown into her own person with a lovely personality. Unlike the eagle parent who has to give the reluctant eaglet a firm push, a shove was not needed. Sallyanne had discovered her wings at Cloverley Hall and was using them to good effect at school. When she was sixteen I remember acknowledging that I could no longer protect her. She was hurtling down a steep alpine ski slope at forty miles per hour clearly out of control. Others on the slope were peeling off to let her through. Like a rogue bobsleigh, Sallyanne descended unable to stop and unwilling to fall. I caught up with her at the top of the next lift and told her very deliberately that she now had responsibility for her own life. Shyly, I slipped a little card into her ski-jacket pocket, "He cares for you".

A week before the Walk started we arranged a lively party for her 21st birthday. Over one hundred people turned up in their best clothes to grace her celebration at the Queen's Hotel. The difference between a star and a shooting star is the effect they have. One is steady. It is its own source of light and warmth. The other is attractive but leaves behind an icy trail of disturbed atmospherics. Sallyanne has many star qualities – in particular, she desires to leave the world a better place. Where better to start – than inner city Leeds as a social worker on a child protection team?

A few more miles and I strike inland to find The Street in Weybourne. It is easy – it's the only one. All others are going somewhere else, Sheringham Road, Holt Road and Beach Road. Rose Cottage lives up to its name, the delightful home of Frances Roby, who despite six grief experiences in the space of as many years still sticks out her jaunty chin and with her friends gives me a mighty welcome. Just as well because from here on life would not be so rosy.

After several years at Bledington I found that my judgement began to slip and that in counselling others *my* pain would sometimes emerge to over-ride the pain of those to whom I was listening. In services I found that my emotions were beginning to affect my preaching and in hymns and prayers I was finding it increasingly difficult to control tears. I took some time off and sought help. The diocesan consultant reminded me that for twenty-five years I had had, as he put it bluntly, 'a bloody bad time with the children' and diagnosed Post Traumatic Stress. Consulting the Bishop I was advised that just moving to my final parish would not change anything. Within twelve months I had retired on health grounds, and the house that Heather had previously spotted as a possibility for our pre-retirement plans became suddenly available again. Sallyanne, at eighteen, also wanted to find a job. We moved together into Cheltenham. My working life over, I could not help feeling let down and rather dumped.

Going west round the Norfolk rump I swapped the clean and crisp perimeters of the East Coast for an indeterminate world of sandbanks, a build-up of silt, that too was also being dumped, unwanted. Round the Wash, the Edge is simply out of focus and pushing steadily out into the sea, north and south between Gibraltar Point and Blakeney Point. Before the Ice Ages the Fenland was open water and the Thames may have run into the Wash, or as others say, into the Stour basin at Harwich. Then ice contracted the North Sea and created a freshwater lake into which the Thames and the Rhine both flowed at a joint confluence, roughly where the Dogger Bank is now. Sea levels rose again after the last Ice Age, and in Roman times one could punt out to sea from Cambridge. A dyke was built from Lincoln down to Cambridge to claim the land westwards. Since then successive generations have followed the falling sea level and reclaimed more and more land in a succession of dykes, high level drover roads and eastern sea walls. Now the levels are set to rise yet again.

Dan Green and I walk along the North Norfolk coastal path, which links Cley, Blakeney, Wells and Brancaster stranded on the old line of shore and quay. The open water can just be seen to the north. With Dan's parents, I am enthralled to venture out at dusk onto the flats, listening to the calls of countless wetland birds and on return to see the ghostly shape of a barn owl flit across our path as the light fades.

I treat myself to a rest inside the RSPB hide at Snettisham and watch little terns with yellow beaks and pink feet flitting about, darting and diving restlessly. They remind me of the dunnock, a sort of hedge sparrow that cannot sit still. If ever there was a bird with a nervous disorder it is the dunnock that flicks and twitches and flutters to no evident advantage, except perhaps its guileless pursuit of polygamy.

I am now travelling southwest towards Kings Lynn. On the path is Della, sprinkling the blackberry bushes with her tears over the divorce of her daughter. Off the path is William Sell taking customers up and down the beach on his amphibious WW2 DUCKS. Then the path itself disappears along with people, and the sky turns black. A horse and rider gallop for safety. The birds have already gone to ground. I can see lightning in the distance and I am ominously tall in this flattened seascape. I quickly unshoulder my pack and prepare for storm mode. I push my metal stick into the ground two or three metres away. My short trousers are stuffed with binoculars, tape-recorder, camera and anything metal and then, disconnected from their owner, they are wrapped round the stick. I am soon in my top and bottom waterproofs, spread-eagled on the ground. The storm breaks. The rain lashes and then finally splutters and splashes to a stop. The thunder is a bit scary but I enjoy watching the lightning and remember the little girl, who ran in to her mother and exclaimed, "Mummy! Mummy! God's just taken a picture of me."

Soon I am on my feet again to do momentary obeisance to Her Majesty the Queen, in residence a few miles away at Sandringham. I recall the day when I last dropped in on the Queen. I walked into her bedroom at Windsor Castle. I was collecting paintings off the walls to be taken to a museum, working for *Pitt and Scott Haulage Contractors.* I was driving a thirty-five foot furniture van – without a union card – for a holiday job, while studying at Northwood. I had to report to my fellow disbelieving ordinands that down each side of the vehicle was written: "IN SAFE HANDS".

I disappear into a deserted world of marsh and more mud. It is clear that the land is private, probably 'strictly private', but with no one to ask – there never is – I plough on. My legs are getting rubbery as hour follows hour of spiky grass and the wearisome crossing of dykes. I begin to wonder if I will ever see any recognisable landmark to know where I am. The horizon is empty. I am due at South Wooton and the light is fading. To my immense relief I see two specks: men in the distance. Twenty minutes later and within earshot I exclaim my pleasure at meeting them. As I approach, there is no reply. They stand silent astride the embankment. The younger and shorter steps forward and bars my passage. He gives me no greeting and no comfort, "This is private property. You shouldn't be here. What are you doing?" With no time for me to answer he continues, "Do you not know that you are disturbing the birds' nesting sites?" I presume he means game birds – but at this time of the year, late August? He and his father before him have been solemnly charged to repel all invaders. The other man, 'Bass' an English Nature Warden, takes a different line and leaving the youngster to his official script, offers to take me into South Wooton. We walk several fields to his car just as heavy raindrops return to sprinkle the roof, boot and bonnet. It is a fit conclusion to the day.

Liz and David Roycroft give me an extravagant welcome. I sink into a deep armchair, surrounded by little tables, each carefully arranged with all things nice, fruit and biscuits and a huge mug of tea. They could not have done more and, next day, take me round all the most spectacular buildings in King's Lynn, to finish beneath a most unusual domed façade of sixteenth century bricks, for a photo-call. Apparently the last witch to be burned alive in oil was said to have proved her innocence here. Her heart had jumped out on cue and transfixed itself to the lintel just above me. I am relieved and reprieved when I realise that King Henry the Eighth must take full responsibility having already changed the town's name from *Bishop's* Lynn. Soon on our way in the car, I am a bit sneaky. Asked to read the map, I take Liz and David a slightly longer way back to the Edge and save myself a couple of miles up the Great Ouse, heading once again for the wide-open spaces of the Wash.

I begin the Peter Scott Walk. It follows the first major arc between the Great River Ouse and the Rive Nene. Two-thirds of the way round and just before leaving Norfolk I am encouraged by an unabashed female walker. "You look lovely here with your tape-recorder on. Hope you have a good time, boy, when you go out of Norfolk and hope you've got your passport all stamped up when you go to Lincolnshire, and I hope everything goes well for you, boy. Cheerio! Now you keep yourself a troshing!" Then, in contrast, I meet an anxious woman. Her mother, at 89, still insists on cranking the motor of childhood. This dear lady just cannot disconnect from her mother's domination and disengage her end of the handle.

The whole empty horizon begins to colour, gradually tinting the whole sky with swathes of yellow, pink and gold, a mighty natural backcloth for some vast film set. I strain and shield my eyes and then out of the beauty emerges, like a scene from ET, a group of humans in light, leisure tee-shirts, sprinkling the path ahead with plain unpatterned colours of red, orange, blue and green, shimmering above grey skirts and several pairs of white shorts. How unusual and beautiful it is to see four adults and four children holding hands, united in family love. They pause, stand happily and smile for a photo. Half an hour later I reach the lighthouse where Peter Scott used to live. It is closed and in semi darkness, a pale pepper pot propped up by a few sheds and roofs. I walk past and find a light. A stout woman fills my containers and before I leave I am weighed. Basic kit is about 30lbs, loaded with food and drink, 42lbs. Clothed, with boots, I weigh 13 stone. With everything to cook and an evening meal and breakfast on my back, 16 stone. I cannot be less like ET.

Up early next morning, I travel nine miles to Sutton Bridge and back before pausing for breath. On each side of the Nene are interesting lighthouses. Both were built to mark the new outflow of the river one hundred and fifty years ago and for a while housed Customs and Excise men. The Normantons were converting the second, Guy's Head, on the north side. "Coffee is on the stove. Help yourself! I must keep going." Simon is due to start work on another nature film for Channel 4. Philippa is away shopping. He leaves me to play with his delightful young daughters, Bryony and Lorissa, who are charged with showing me round. Wearing my hat at crazy angles, Bryony led the way up and round a tangle of awkward curves, stairs and levels, full of innovation and full of odd bits and bobs from the days of candlepower. Most interesting to me is Simon's laid back willingness to *trust.* Later I learn, further down the track, that he had already been burgled three times and still he goes on to trust me a total stranger. Clearly trust is one of those few things that a burglar cannot take from us against our will. For Simon it is non-negotiable. It shows in his children as they gleefully roar round the house and garage enjoying themselves. It will surely bring a handsome dividend of quiet happiness in the future, perhaps the most valuable thing these parents could give their children.

For me trust has underpinned everything, trust that this whole project was right, was workable and, not least, safe enough. Many asked me whether I was going to be lonely, bored or scared or just too plain tired to carry on? My answer was to plan it. Think it through! Plan to succeed! Once I had peace that it was the right way to celebrate this special year, then it had to be properly organised, the schedule carefully timed and every item of kit weighed and examined before inclusion. It was actually a source of some comfort, rather than a cause for concern, that it all depended on me, on my legs, my determination and my sensible calculations along the way.

I concur with the thought of Bill Bryson referring to his book *A Walk in the Woods* covering the Appalachian Trail, which at 2,200 miles is virtually the same length as my Walk 2000: "If I ask you to think what is 2,200 miles, you'd immediately be thinking of car miles or aero-miles. But foot miles are just another different order of magnitude altogether. You don't realise what an undertaking it is, what a commitment it is, what a foolish enterprise it is until you get there and start doing it." (South Bank Show, April 2001, by permission of Carlton TV).

Basically, it is down to ME and THE EDGE. Within, I find myself juggling the demands of three huge issues: my Trust, my Body and my Integrity. My trust in God is primary. Whatever happens, I will try not to doubt His sovereignty or His presence. Basically, I believe God honours those who *try* even if they do not win. If failure in the Christian life is best defined as 'not trying' rather than 'not succeeding', then there is hope that we are not judged by what we do or fail to do, but by what we attempt.

Second, I have become deeply aware of my body and its needs. I don't have a five-speed gearbox. I have to rely on my legs just working properly for 2,000 miles. Three months training has made a big difference. However, each day I know I need to balance input and output and take in enough fluid and calories. I know that a 20% fall in fluid content means a 200% fall in efficiency, dehydration. So I allow for hot sunshine and always treat headaches as a message to drink. I have worked out that: TIME + ENERGY = DISTANCE. I have become aware that 18 to 20 miles a day is about my physiological limit. Anything over needs extra recovery time or I just cannot get out of bed. But I can make any distance as long as I have enough time left and enough complex carbohydrates in my system or rucksack to make up lost glycogen, energy. Still, I have no caddie. My body has to carry everything. I soon find that the more I carry the more calories, energy and time is required to achieve the allocated distance. I mentally juggle these issues all the time, especially when fully stocked at the beginning of the week.

The third inner struggle is with integrity. There is no point in moving the goal posts, or capitulating to convenience. My aim is to walk the Edge of England, the whole edge and nothing but the edge. If I dodge, duck and dive, then I only cheat myself. In the event there have been little bits missed out here and there, inadvertently, or ignorantly, sometimes through others thinking to do me a kindness. For instance, if I walk into a town, invariably my host will 'know just the right place' to drop me off – on the outskirts! At other times quite deliberately, I have to meet a commitment, and take a short cut. Also, I have to avoid parts that are actually inaccessible or banned by Act of Parliament. On the other hand there have been endless diversions inland, sometimes just to find my evening address. And for sheer waste of time, don't talk to me about curly creek walls that go back on themselves, or that leave you stranded out in the estuary for lack of signposts. There is no rule book. It's swings and roundabouts. I do my best. I just do not flinch from any discomfort and inconvenience, if it means I can keep to the Edge. That is my integrity.

It's me and the Edge then. We have to live with each other every day. I love the sea. That is no problem. I have a happy uncomplicated affection for the sea. The Edge is another matter. I can only describe it as a lust, a huge desire to wrestle and confront and triumph, like Jacob with his hidden challenger. For me, the Edge has become a fixed and slender line of daily truth.

If that sounds intense, nothing could be less so. I am enjoying every bit of this adventure and am deeply relaxed. Most of the time I am utterly absorbed in the kaleidoscope of ever-changing daily fascinations. My binoculars are always lodged ready behind my neck and I am always somewhere different. I constantly stop to read notices, listen to the birds, pick blackberries, take in a breath-taking moment, have an ice cream or capture something strange on film. I allow myself about twelve exposures each day, two rolls of film a week from fifty posted round the route. At other times I resolve that there be no delays and push on as hard as possible. That too is satisfying.

Actually, the most satisfaction comes from people. Apart from calls to Heather, Sallyanne and my Dad, overnight hosts, the media and many churches, there is a sort of daily quivering expectancy that people can change things suddenly and dramatically at any twist or turn of the path. Unforgettable encounters have already turned this walk into a pilgrimage of exchanged blessings. Meet Anne and Ray Missin of Wisbech on this beautiful day under a mackerel sky. They are picking samphire, which sells at a pound for pound locally or in London six pounds for a pound to the top restaurants. These succulent green shoots poke up through the salty mud. I dig around and then look up to see that picking things up is definitely not recommended. A huge sign warns me of unexploded shells. Soon I am investigating a helicopter landing pad and computerised observation tower. I am spotted and Bill Soames of Security at RAF Holbeach escorts me into his compound. Bill and Mike the manager treat me to a tour, a mug of tea and a parting gift of the One-Inch Ordinance Survey map for the Wash. Tonight I will need it.

Meet Kay! The day ends memorably at Shep White. Kay has been waiting on the sea wall. She is walking towards me, the breeze catching her hair and billowing her long skirt. She breaks into a gentle trot. She laughs and launches herself into a spontaneous bear hug, though we had never met. I love spontaneity. Caution so often sinks into cowardice. A spontaneous welcome is a giving of self. Giving is surely living. God so loved us that he gave us himself in his son. Kay takes me home to meet her friends. We have a party. The wine flows and Michael, clipped and cultured, volunteers to take me across the muddy outflow of the River Glen to slice off the final section of the Wash. It will save me a fifteen-mile journey up to Fosdyke Bridge and back. He is quite confident, too confident and I am tempted, keen to call his bluff. It is an exciting and dangerous venture. My map gives no hint of feasibility or any hope of rescue. We agree to meet. Next morning a rather subdued Michael has just rung – to call it off. He atones later by persuading the Church Council to send a handsome cheque to the Fund.

The nearest I ever got to asking for money was doing Bob a Job with the Scouts. Apart from the impertinence, to ask is usually counter-productive. People understandably hold on to money if only because it is not labelled. If it's in my hands then it's mine. If it's in yours, it's yours. But that's the problem. It is not actually worth anything until it is being passed on. There lies the challenge, for 50p is just a metal septagon unless it circulates.

I am spending £15 a day and earning £10 a mile, putting it baldly. Yet so far, money simply has never been an issue. It has not entered into my conversations, or even my thoughts. I collect it weekly from my next parcel and it is spent on treats, telephoning, meals, B&B, ferries and museums. £15 a day just oils the wheels. It does not begin to take away my neediness, nor my having to ask often for help. The money I am spending on this whole venture is a small fortune, but I don't see that. It is an outpouring of my thankfulness, for sixty years, for upbringing, health, family and this country. It is a chance to say "thank you" to God for my "creation, preservation and all the blessings of this life, but above all for His inestimable love in the redemption of the world through our Lord Jesus Christ" (Prayer Book). I am not 'paying my way'. Not at all! It is a sign of my trust in people and their trust in me, that we can exchange gifts of love as part of a common outpouring of gratitude. Thankfulness and generosity go together like knife and fork. They are the twin springs of the moral life and in between is empathy, having a feeling for others' needs as well as our own.

I am 'earning' £10 a mile if people rise to the target of £20,000. Again it is an outpouring. There is nothing else I need to do. It will happen. I just know it. People who overly hold on to their money hide pain. Their clenched spirit covers up insecurity and weakness. Money was never intended as a painkiller, but just a means of transferring benefit into others' lives and into our own. When it is kept and hoarded, it becomes addictive, a Class A drug and dangerous. As an object of our desire, as a goal in itself, *it* soon hold*s us*. It holds us in its thrall. So giving is actually good for *me.* It keeps me healthy and strengthens the bonds that link me with others. Mind you, I'm so stingy I even pick up rubber bands from the pavement.

Some of the best things that have happened to me have been when by myself. Today, in the Fenlands, I have walked all afternoon, the tallest thing for miles around. I am in that half-conscious state induced by monotony, when from my feet a great flapping instantly focuses my attention. Fumbling for binoculars, I see just in time the wings collapse and an owl drops out of sight further along the sea wall. Several times it has to relocate rather disinterestedly on my arrival. I never know next from where to expect its lazy launch. That is until now. Suddenly it is just standing there, a brown speckled short-eared owl on the edge of stubble. "With respect, Sir," it seems to say, "that's as far as I'm going." A study in concentration, he follows my legs to a stop. Breathless I gaze and he gazes back. He does not blink. His intense yellow eyes blaze into mine. We have, I muse, at least one thing in common, perhaps the other is the most interesting occurrence all day. We are mutually fascinated, a bloke and a rather butlerish bird. Both are content as neither regards the other as edible. Then time moves us on. I feel I'm an intruder. "Come on then! I haven't got all day," his eyes seem to say. "From here you travel on your own." I wink, but he is unimpressed. Those twin-communicating discs have one message, "Off my patch!" The spell is broken. He becomes a loved and lingering memory.

By the side of the Haven Canal I sleep under a full silvery-green moon. It gleams through the undergrowth and gently rises above the cow parsley. Now and again I hear the muffled beat of an engine and eerie shapes glide by, showing hardly a light. Up early, and it is still misty, I reach the Flood-control Bridge and am soon into the Morning Service at 'The Stump', Boston's parish church. The mighty tower used to be a navigational beacon rising nearly three hundred feet and visible thirty miles away from Lincoln. Its steps number 365 and with 52 windows, 12 pillars and 7 doors, the church is a veritable calendar in stone. Eileen on the bookstall specialises in warmth and would have given me mulled wine, except that Jenny Tonbridge, the Curate, has other ideas. She dines and wines me at home and we set off, with Heidi the dog, to a special stone memorial down-stream. From here the Pilgrim Fathers first sailed on their long journey to the States. Intercepted, they end their day in the town jail, objects of merriment to the people, but foundational and inspirational thereafter. I am reminded that transitions are difficult and demanding. Round this long detour back to the East Coast I have so much to learn.

Chapter 15

Boston to Immingham

MEMORABLE MEETINGS AND FEARFUL RISKS

I HAVE ALWAYS LOVED PEAKS – THE LAKE DISTRICT AND THE Peak District, Pen-y-Ghent, Ingleborough, and Whernside in Yorkshire, Snowdon in Wales, Annapurna in Nepal and Mount Taranaki (Mt Egmont) in New Zealand, which I climbed in 1985 with Mike Andrews of the British Expedition. This may well account for the fact that until a few weeks ago I have never set foot in Essex and would never have contemplated living in East Anglia. I would have felt hopelessly 'stuck' in an area of interminable dumping and deposition, of dykes and dredging and dreary flatness.

As a clergyman my ministry had peaked in New Zealand and after that the Cotswolds had been a valley experience. When I retired into Cheltenham I felt flat, and cheated. At the beginning I could not let go the dreams and strategies of parish life, with its lingering notions of role and value. I did not want to start dumping my baggage. Bit by bit, now, I am accepting that most of the questions I can answer are no longer being asked, and that most of the books I have acquired don't shake and stir people like they used to. I also realise that in truth, only as I release the past can I grasp hold of the future. I must learn again. So at last, years later, the house is right, my filing cabinet is re-organised and bookshelves slimmed down.

I am getting ready to leave the transition period and discover what the future holds.

First, one more day in the Wash would do me no harm. Leaving St Botolph's at Boston I am reading a large blue sign, which at first glance I rather dismiss. It is a Celtic blessing that exactly fits my need today to be more earthed: "Deep peace of the running wave to you. Deep peace of the flowing air to you. Deep peace of the quiet earth to you. Deep peace of the shining stars to you. Deep peace of the Son of peace to you. Thank you for visiting St Botolph's. Please have a safe journey home." Mmm! It's a long way.

I am entering a four-mile wide strip of dampness, deserted by humans, doused and dried at the whim of the sea, twenty miles down the Witham and up the coast to Wainfleet, where nothing relieves the monotony. I need to face myself. It re-occurs to me that if I hide behind the cobwebs of the past I cannot see through the windows into the future. To integrate my life, to root myself in the place where I am, I must withdraw blame and require of myself transparency, honesty and realism, to accept what cannot be changed. Creating scrapbooks has always helped in this regard, symbolically embracing and including everything. I completed four for Sallyanne at her twenty-first birthday and five covering our life since New Zealand. They help me to objectify, mourn and celebrate what has gone, and chuck out everything left over. There are no more unsorted boxes.

A few miles ahead and quite suddenly, peace and my ruminations cease. Without notice, out of the sky drops a rain of hot objects. It is not perhaps generally known that the east-coast fringe of this sceptred Isle has been virtually leased to NATO. Owing to the success of environmental lobbies of the Continent, target training now takes place at several venues, such as here at Friskney Flats: I suppose it is the French on Monday, the Dutch on Tuesday, the Germans Wednesday before lunch and the Americans when they feel like it. There are target ships out at sea and red and white constructions along the flats – and Jonah Jones has to choose to walk along the Edge. Time and again, falling out of the sky, are Tornadoes, Harriers and the distinctive F15, too fast to film and too deafening to hear. I pick up a metal cone, the tip of an Exocet missile, and make speed to reach safety.

Just when I think the darkness has me beat I spot a faint light. Through the grass I stumble heavy legged, towards a RAF compound. I ring the bell. It is 8.45pm and the night shift. After some hesitation and interrogation the computer-sealed gates are de-coded and generous Jim Wilson takes me in for the night. I am only allowed to stay on the condition that I leave before 6am when the shift changes. I sleep on upholstered chairs in the Boardroom and am horrified in the morning to find the windows dripping with condensation. Jim makes us both a hearty breakfast and later completed the Wainfleet RAF station log: "17TH AUGUST 20.00HRS. REV JONES ARRIVED ON SITE IN TIME FOR MATINS. CHARITY WALK FOR CHILDREN. AFTER A SHOWER AND A CUP OF TEA, HE SET OFF ON THE NEXT LEG OF HIS WALK FOLLOWING THE SEA BANK." The next two entries detail the arrival of a (male) missile, courtesy of Cassie at the hospital weighing seven pounds, and a live 1000 lb bomb which had been dropped inadvertently on Target 4, according to a suitably apologetic Major.

The RAF observation tower has an overhanging glass lookout section at the top. It occurs to me it is the obverse of Mistley and its underground bunker. Together they seem to illustrate our national defensive requirements for both top deck intelligence surveillance and secure cover 'down under' if and when we have to deal with the worst. I hope I am not stretching the metaphor too far when I suggest that the same is often true for people with personal survival in mind. Catastrophic events, especially in early life, sometimes trigger within a splitting into three levels of operating. If reality is too horrible to accept, a person may escape into their head and push the memory and their feelings about that event into their 'basement', out of sight and out of mind. The intelligence room, their brain, is used for observation, storage of information and propaganda, essential to successful plans. Often such a person likes to live high up and overlooking others, for that is where they feel safe to do their thinking. On the contrary, the basement of their life is a banned place, largely sealed, full of buried memories and devastating secrets.

The living quarters, sandwiched between, are fairly cramped and used mostly for presentation purposes. There, where they are in the public eye, the person can massage and manipulate their image and be very personable and persuasive. They will often be good at talking, at least for a limited period, until the strain or the cracks begin to show and then they have to go back up 'upstairs' to recover. This three decker set-up is conveniently built for blame so that the inevitable problems all belong to other people 'out there'. This split-life design helps the person cope with the perceived hostility of others outside. It is an essential device to maintain personal equanimity and mask unfaceable, unbearable inner weakness. It becomes the best way to survive in a difficult world, though at the cost of healthy emotions and meaningful relationships. It usually lasts a lifetime and woe betide anyone who wants to come inside and have a look round.

Stan Lane, an Oxford-educated social worker, steps off the train to rendezvous with me at Wainfleet Station. He is just the sort of chap I can admire. Largely undefended he can move around his life in a quiet unpretentious way. Stan is devoid of hubris. He is at home in the attic as in the cellars, able to speak realistically and with candour about life's ups and downs. Together we uncover this astonishing little village, Wainfleet. We stand where John Wesley stood on the market cross, and then for good measure visit the magnificent early moulded brick-built school. The School replicates the style of Magdalen College, Oxford; both inspired by William of Wainfleet, Bishop of Winchester. Now it serves as a museum, for life in school, life in the RAF and life in a Victorian garden. It is all being lovingly developed by Betty and Fred.

Via Gibraltar Point we set our sights on Skeggy, a favoured seaside target for Midlanders. Utterly unselfconscious, the breezy skipper, a laughing skipping statue of a fisherman, welcomes us into the town centre of Skegness. How good to see the back of mud and on the front four beautiful miles of sand! The best was next, the welcome at 65 Hoylake Drive, home to Joyce and Ray Porter. Within minutes of our arrival, we disappear beneath a flood of happy faces. Joyce is kindness itself and with her Methodist friends, who had taken Walk 2000 to heart, they have raised a phenomenal cheque. It is presented next morning, with Press in attendance, by her grand-daughter, Anne-Marie.

I meet Ena from Scotland, Val from the Manse and Ruby still alert and interested at ninety-four years of age. Ruby's house reared thirty-two children including the redoubtable Audrey Milner-Schofield (who cut off my socks in Nanstallen), here visiting her mother. Ruby remembers collecting water from the farm in two eight gallon buckets dangling from the handlebars of her bike. Electricity did not arrive until 1963, though the sub-station bordered her garden. It is hard to leave the warm Christian community and kindness of these people. They give up their beds and now empty the kitchen onto the breakfast table. Stan and I have twelve pieces of toast to start with and then another replica pile before we have finished, including the great British Breakfast in between. Their son is a member of the inshore lifeboat crew and Joyce always sends a hamper of tuna, ham and cheese sandwiches to welcome them on return. Goodness gushes through this home, inspired by Joyce and Audrey.

Stan has some thoughtful things to say about trust, risk and anonymity and I am missing his intuitive company. It is Mablethorpe and I need 'a caff', a real British café, run down, a bit seedy, with no view but a melamine table and on it a parched geranium. I'm feeling lonely for the first time and I'm feeling hungry because I am lonely. I don't think I could find it again. This place has no name except *Café*. It has everything else, white bread, margarine, rubbery eggs and fatty fries, which arrive on a Pyrex plate. There are just a few other folk. A real 'caff' should be mostly empty and the staff – well, uncommunicative. Just right and no fuss.

I steer clear of a raucous entertainment centre, sleep in the dunes and next day make good progress through Saltfleet, the end of The Fosse Way, to finish in the Donna Nook Nature Reserve. Then comes one of the most powerful and moving episodes of the whole walk. Land access for boats has long ceased since Saltfleet. Now there is another bombing range and beyond a featureless silent world of intertidal sand.

Charles, an agricultural adviser, his dog Ben and I, are the sole occupants of this desolate wasteland, just short of the mouth of the Humber. Donna Nook is named after a wrecked ship whose vessel and crew were swallowed by the treacherous currents and shifting sandbanks of this area. I trudge on. It seems endlessly inhospitable. The sea has disappeared. It is literally out of sight, four miles away, but returning and fast. It is an 'extra high spring tide tonight' I am told by a cluster of 'birdies', who are waiting to catch the thousands of waders pushed up under their binocular gaze. "It's too fast", I am told. "You can't outrun the sea. When the wind backs it up from the North, it can arrive at twenty or thirty miles per hour." It is chilling news. The problem at Horseshoe Point is a combination of deep gullies and a stream. The stream flows parallel to the shore and the gullies run deep out to sea, interconnected by scrubby creeklets forking left and right on the way. The water rushes up behind and then seawards again, outflanking the unwary. It is too deep, too wide and too fast. And spongy quicksand is everywhere to suck down the unwary. It is really frightening.

I keep to firm ground and breast a slight rise. My eyes follow a fence towards the sea, some chestnut paling. I investigate. At the end are faded flowers and tattered tributes to "Ian" and "Nathan". In May, a few months earlier after I left Cheltenham, television news reported three lads drowned at Horseshoe Point. I glance down not knowing about this and to my astonishment water is streaming by and has already flooded the end of the fence. In no time, the whole area is under water. My eyes are running too as I read: "Forever in our hearts, always remembered, loved and missed so very much, Mummy, Daddy, Nana and Grandad," an unbearable litany of love unrequited.

I nod to my 'birdie' companions and look away. It is getting late. I walk for another hour with neither sign nor sight of life. The world is deserted. I see a path and in desperation presume there will be something at the other end. A mile inland, a security light announces my arrival. I am generously stocked with milk, water and a couple of eggs. By now it is pitch dark and in the blackness I can only blunder from gate to gate around the farm property. Nothing seems right and I seek guidance. Do I go back to the sea or go on? It is either grass with crap and cattle, or high, dense fields of wheat. I press on, perhaps half a mile down a narrow strip of tarmac. I can feel if I cannot see my way. And then a light twinkles in the blackness. A labourer's brick cottage emerges on my left. It has no front door, just a lean-to kitchen on the side. I walk hesitantly round the back, tripping over children's toys. The door opens and a towering man steps out of the porch. Several children tumble out from behind him and in the light I can see, arms akimbo, a stiff unsmiling woman inside. He scratches his head continuously. He cannot think of a place for my tent. Embarrassed, with only just room to turn around, I retreat, wishing him well and wish the same for his wife.

Twenty minutes later as I grope along the road, headlights suddenly swamp my private little world. A car pulls up. "Jump in!" says Chris from the cottage, "I remember now. I'll take you there." A short drive through the village and he pulls up on the far bank of Tetney Lock. He leaves his lights on while the tent is erected and a meal prepared. And Chris tells me his story. How in May, at Horseshoe Point he lost his lad. He is the father of Scott. He is the parent missing from the tributes, whose son's name he cannot bear to have tied to those railings. In a flat and empty voice he tells me how they found the bikes but not the lads. "They never found his body. I'm out every morning, walking the flats, looking for him, but he is never there. The missus, she won't talk. She doesn't want any interfering busybodies from the Social. We'll be all right. We'll get through." I begin to realise why he was unable to think of this little flat stretch of grass by Tetney Lock. He needed to be taken out of that house and away, where he can talk, here with one person who can perhaps just understand. It comes forcibly home to me. I am managing this walk, but, as I said to Stan, it is also being stage-managed for me.

Statistics tell us that twelve months after the loss of a child, seventy-five per cent of parents are considering separation. A year later Chris's wife left him and took some of the children. Grandparents are trying to fill the empty space, but the loss of Scott is having widespread repercussions and will, for better or worse, affect succeeding generations. Did my visit make any difference? Did Chris take heart after feeling suicidal? No one could carry his load. I could only just bear to listen. Did he find acceptance and come to know that he too was loved? If love and grief are inseparable could he understand God coming to look for His own lost created child, mankind? Could he dare to believe that God even sent his own eternal Son to find us and bring us home?

Who taught Chris's wife to have iron control over her emotions? Was that her family's traditional reaction? It could well have slowed down the children's adjustment and choked off a healthy and reasonable response from both parents. Emotions ventilate and invigorate. If we block one then we block them all. If anger and sadness cannot surface, neither can joy and forgiveness. Perhaps we need to see that whatever comes in the first few months of grief should simply be respected. Tears and tantrums, shouting and wordless silence are all appropriate for members of a grieving family. Erupting gas and volcanic anger is better out than in. Instant and early reactions are neither 'good' nor 'bad', neither 'right' nor 'wrong', just ways of coping. All in time will subside into a degree of acceptance both of the tragedy and of the other participants involved. Otherwise inhibited from expressing themselves, parents in particular may begin to grieve separately and run the risk of simply missing each other. They will not understand nor feel understood and may soon lose the desire to relate. Honest emotion, as it comes, is an important part of the swirling currents of healthy, if struggling, family life.

I have a theory that there are 'the wishers' and there are 'the connectors', those who are often found wishing that things were different about the past or the future, and those who just 'connect' with what is there, right there in front of them. They grapple with each day, each person and each eventuality as it arrives. I was soon to realise it is not as easy as it sounds. Walking down the side of the Tetney canal I am thinking of Chris. I am thinking of all the strange things that have come my way since Boston. It has been flat as a pancake and yet an emotional roller coaster from start to finish. I want to get back to the sea and, somehow distracted, I fail to identify the correct fringe sea wall. I find myself becoming stranded at the end of a dwindling bank of muddy scrub jutting way out into the bay, cut off from destination Cleethorpes and aware of the tide on its way. I do wish I had been concentrating but there is nothing to be done except 'connect'. The shiny slippery unstable mud feels like Weston all over again. My bare feet are better at gripping without boots. I chance it. How I hate mud.

I march across the zero meridian line on Cleethorpes promenade and am narrowly missed by a weaving Noddy train. I snap three little girls, shuffling their bottoms for pride of place on the sea wall and then climb up behind them to walk the wall. "Is the tide going up or down?" I ask stupidly, thinking of water round chestnut palings. "No!" says one, "It's going out." The Grimsby harbour perimeter fence proves an easy challenge and restores my self-esteem. I spent some time chatting to the Harbour Master and experience a force nine gale in the National Heritage fishing centre. The Dock Tower is a twelve-story Victorian folly transplanted from Sienna in Italy. It marks the beginning of the Humber estuary.

Now 'folly' is just about the best word some would use to describe the way I find my accommodation tonight.

Assessment of risk, someone said in the ancient classics, is about the degree of gravity and the degree of probability. However grave or uncertain, if all of a particular risk falls on me, and me only, then I can take some chances that I would not take were I, say, in charge of the children. In any case, at no time and in no place are any of us ever going to be completely free of danger. Playing safe in life is never safe enough. About nine hundred people die every year getting out of bed. I understand about ninety people die every year *in* bed because their headboard falls on them. The only totally safe place in this world is in the cemetary.

The main risk at South Killingholme, near Immingham, is that of incurring official disapproval, something anyway that I kind of relish when it happens. There are, if you like, three sorts of temperament: rule-makers, rule-keepers and rule-breakers and if there has to be a choice, I would rather be the last. At College I became Jonah the prophet, accustomed at the evening meal to facing down the Establishment, but I don't quite bargain for the sheer ton weight of official disapproval I experience at Britain's foremost port for handling petrochemical products. The wall clearly is built to keep the sea out and not for ferrying people along its length. As I leave Grimsby behind, I have been aware of increasing industrial activity, large storage tanks and steaming aluminium chimneys. I simply stick, as per plan, to the Edge in the hope of reaching a nature reserve on the other side. The sky is overcast and the day almost spent. I can see a double metal gate, looming ahead, with high fencing on each side. As I come closer a concrete ramp leads me up to a sign, which indicates: "Strictly No Admittance!" and everything is plastered with barbed wire. I remember that the last footpath turned off a long way behind and in any case, like a mantra in my head, I say to myself 'I am not for going back.' Behind these double-breasted gates are three-foot diameter pipes, travelling half a mile out to sea, serving tanker terminals that can handle their explosive cargoes. I peer over the wall. The sea has again surged up high, right to the wall. There is no beach and no way of going under the pipes. There is nothing else for it. I have to climb over. I decide that if I can only break in they would be obliged to get me out.

The first problem is the barbed wire. I have to travel out seawards to get round it, right down to the low tide mark. So I find myself suspended over the water, in full kit, stick dangling from my wrist, inching along in the gathering gloom. Repeatedly hooked, plucked and pierced, my knees are beginning to shake when I reach the end. At last I am free to climb and with all the strength of departed youth, I heave myself up and over the pipes and on to the roadway above. Security lights soon pick me out. The cameras do not. The Immingham Seamans Mission bus is returning crewmen to a tanker. An arm grabs me, bag and all, and delivers me unceremoniously to the guardhouse. The bus disappears too quickly and I am under investigation. Perhaps I am tired and less than amenable to interrogation, but the Security Officer is not easily convinced. Eventually with scowls and dire warnings and the recitation of company rules, details are recorded and the aforementioned bus summoned to return. It is then, to my embarrassment, I get nearest to incarceration or incineration. The security officer is working in front of me on his impressive display of monitors. It is a perfect photo opportunity but I forget one vital matter. The flash! Electronic cameras are outlawed in a petrochemical complex. Rarely have I seen a man move so fast. His face is puce. His wrath is palpable. His words unprintable. But I did not ignite the eastern seaboard of Lincolnshire. "Just six foot of grass," I say to the driver, "anywhere will do."

David McCarney is made of rather different stuff. "You're coming with me, home!" In no time I am introduced to lovely people, Pauline and David, a devoted Catholic couple, who do everything they can to help. Pauline prepares my room and kit for the next day. David, a trained chef, serves a mixed grill that deserves three star Michelin rating. It is a joy to hear about their three children and their dedication to the Immingham Seafarers Centre.

Despite Hamlet's declaration, I *had* hesitated and I was not lost, thankfully. But was I right to risk my safety? Was I prudent to risk the safety of others? That bit of the Edge was dangerous, even without me being there. Company safety was compromised and a bit of a hullabaloo did follow. Since then a huge explosion and a two hundred foot fireball have rather illustrated the point and required, as I write, an instant mile wide exclusion zone round the Conoco plant.

It is not easy to separate faith and foolishness. Faith is often spelt 'RISK'. To become a Christian is itself a huge risk. To live Christianly is to take more risks. To serve Christ as He deserves is to throw the dice of life decisively away from self-interest, knowing that when you have four aces against you, mysteriously, there is somehow the fifth that usually trumps all others. There are those who think me a fool, risking my health and safety. But then millions live beyond foolishness, as in sub-Saharan Africa. Is everything we have so valuable that nothing can be chanced, not even our reputation? Surely the greatest hazard in life is to risk nothing. Someone has said that the person who risks nothing does nothing and has nothing, only his chains. He who *can* risk is truly free.

Chapter 16

Humber Bridge to Filey Brigg

RETURNING TO ROOTS AND A MIXED RECEPTION

I AM A YORKSHIREMAN AND THE PROSPECT OF GOING HOME brings a quiet gladness to my heart. For a while the area north and south of the Estuary was 'Humberside' and separate from the East, West and North Ridings. It included Northeast Lincolnshire. Now, after a decade or so of schizophrenia, the north and south banks have agreed to part company. Like 'Great Grimsby', it sounds better to hear this bit is being run by 'The North Lincolnshire District Council'. I am on a section of the Nev Cole Way and the path is strewn with purple bell-shaped flowers, in contrast to the decaying hulks of abandoned vessels stuck in the mud on my right. I think of pilgrimage. It is partly about going home and partly about being at home all the time. My desire is to be tuned in constantly to the Walk's 'magnetic' field. I need rest and trust in my spirit, to accept with simplicity the bounty of others. Thank you, Lord, for David and Pauline. I need to take risks. It is all right to live beyond the edge of things safe and predictable. I also need anonymity, and regret that I pulled rank with that security guard. Vicar indeed! I'm just a bloke, with a bag, a beard and dirty boots.

I am really enjoying the wild mighty thrust of the Humber, a triumphant estuary that drains one third of England and effortlessly drops its daily cargo of rich, brown silt, as a table cloth on which thousands of birds find their breakfast, dinner and tea. I walk through New Holland dock and peer into a bulging grain silo, swamped by the golden harvest. Outside is one of those old-fashioned road signs with a black puffer train and smoke to indicate a crossing. Barton may claim distinguished links with Harrison of longitude watch fame, with Sir Isaac Pitman of shorthand and with Chad Varah of Samaritans, but I am aiming for the one thing I can see on the horizon, The Bridge. An inland detour prepares me for the long run up to this tremendous spectacle of civil engineering. As if to stress its vaunting modernity, on the left and right are ancient brick properties, tile and rope works. From between springs the first of two concrete piers, each with twin hollow legs that soar to five hundred feet. From the top of these, from ropes as thick as my boot, is suspended a single slender arc, a dual carriageway two miles long. One long mile is the central span and at each end there is another half a mile to the north and south. It is stunning. It takes me forty-five minutes to walk this dizzy highway into Yorkshire.

"Hear all, see all, say nowt," sums up the canny Yorkshire traditional approach to life. "Keep tha sen to tha sen," is a more guarded version. Things are changing. Since 1996 there has been a regional assembly and a Campaign for Yorkshire to have its own parliament, so that the people of Yorkshire and the Humber can determine their own domestic affairs, "should it be their settled will to do so." Freddie Trueman thinks the idea is 'a bit bloody silly' and recommends we do what we always do and just keep our mouths shut.

This year is the one hundredth anniversary of Kingston-upon-Hull's Royal Charter. The town is full of energy. It once supported two thousand men in the whaling industry and today has roughly that number employed in the discount trading business alone. Wilberforce, Brian Rix and Maureen Lipman have all spoken up in their different ways. Lionel and Wendy North, two lecturer friends of Stan Lane, provide a gentle, restorative overnight stay, and pay for a hop to Paull by taxi. I should explain. There is a BP petrochemical complex in the way and the town jail, rather too conveniently, is situated nearby.

From the north side, at Sunk Island, I count one hundred and forty-nine industrial chimneys, no less, strung along the south bank with Great Grimsby's Tower in the farthest distance. I go on to count another forty-eight cranes and gantries and innumerable electric skeletons striding in all directions the other side of the Humber. As darkness falls, a tinsel-thin strip of glittering light ribbons the coast from east to west, punctuated here and there with fiery exhaust emissions. In the morning it is all a hazy smudge and instead, the sun has lit the proscenium, my foreshore. Front stage are bright green lichens and moss, sprinkled over olive coloured humps of grass with buttercups expressing nature's simple beauty.

In Yorkshire I can usually count on plain unvarnished truth. People call a spade a spade with their friends and neighbours. Yet in many families there are those who do play 'let's pretend' with their offspring in the mistaken idea that children must be shielded from the truth, that they cannot be asked to cope with the raw facts of life. My experience tells me that children actually cope very well, and even better than adults. More to the point, they know instinctively when their seniors are playing games. Heather and I have had a long-adopted policy of telling our children only truth, as and when it was necessary. What is more, they knew that we would never deceive them and would not shirk, when the time came, from giving them the facts. Excruciating though this was at times, our children rested content and reassured in the knowledge that they would never be patronised, tricked or caught off guard. They rose to that trust and have proved rooted, adaptable and resilient in the face of hardship. It has meant that we all lived life to the full. John and his wife Naomi, a sensitive and caring young woman from our first parish in Chesterfield, knows us from the inside of a vicarage. We picnic together on Spurn Point, with their daughter Corinne and talk truth with each other. Without explanation, we know the spiritual rock from which our children have been hewn.

I set out to walk to the end of Spurn Point and back, about ten miles. Any winter this slender wispy proboscis could be breached. It is changing all the time. Efforts to defend it are now frozen and residents know they are on borrowed time. A lifeboat crew is on standby for the estuary and the men supplement their income from garden gnomes. Most of the historic features, like the railway and lighthouses, seem to be unmaintained. The jetty is looked after and an Information Hut by the Bell Inn is in good order with a café and loos. But I came away feeling 'it is the oddest place in England,' an appendix awaiting removal. I sleep near an RSPB hide and before setting out next morning, I poke my head in. Counting birds ranks high on the scale of obsession. I quietly close the door.

Being a man of insatiable curiosity, I am hard to bore. But Holderness does just that. Nearly fifty miles of brown boulder clay, falling from fifty foot brown cliffs, tumbling over fifty yards of brown beach just turns the sea into gravy. Some mud I have seen is glorious and glistening, interesting and challenging, juicy, slimy, sinister and at least in some areas playful. But until beige is back in fashion this beach is boring, particularly the stretch between Hornsea and Mappleton. The cliffs buckle under boredom. They just sag and slip and slump all over the foreshore. In three drizzling days I try to inter-act with Britain's most boring beach. I photograph children jumping off tank traps and take a picture of concrete remains about to plunge down from the edge, perched at a crazy angle. To contrive a little excitement I pitch my tent twenty inches from the edge, just to see the sea and maybe the sunrise. I wake to see nothing for almost eight hours. It rains continuously from 3a.m. to 3p.m. I climb out mid-afternoon stiff and hungry. I yawn. Twenty-three villages have come and gone into the North Sea, so there is no help here. I make some 'brunch' of porridge and raisins and reach Withernsea.

I find a large helping of fish and chips and, wearing short trousers, slip into Pleasureland. I sit at a child-sized yellow plastic table, on a child-sized red plastic seat, sipping tea from a white plastic beaker. "WITHERNSEA IS THE PLACE TO BE" it says on a hoarding. I walk along in the dark, prayerfully wondering where, if anywhere, I should spend the night. I choose a guesthouse with a smart PVC porch, *Vista Mar.* Rod shows me my room and that is that. No hint of any social life. I go to bed wondering and thinking. At breakfast I sit on a collapsible wooden chair. I stare at the strawberries on the wallpaper, about a foot in front of my face and finish my coffee. Is it time for me to go? And then Viv shares her heartache. Both of her daughters had recently each lost one of their children. But breakfast is busy. I pay my bill and then decide to post home some stones off the beach. In my pockets are an intriguing collection of sea-smoothed stones, carried here in glacial times from all over the North of England, Scotland and Scandinavia. With Rod's help and a padded envelope, we manage to seal the parcel and I set out for the Post Office. Now the Post Office in Withernsea is part of a self-service cafeteria, which itself is part of a self-service supermarket, which predictably belongs to a chain, and the whole thing *en bloc* is closed. Closed on a Monday! Then, stupid, I discover it is Bank Holiday. Nothing else for it, I have to return to Rod and Viv Hirst and request they post it for me later. They are sitting and enjoying coffee together. I warm to them and we sit for a while – and talk.

My garage is stuffed with stones, and every imaginable piece of geological bric-a-brac from lava found in Iceland to red granite in Australia, fossil fern from Sinai to a sample scoop of Chesil Beach. In my front garden there is a path and two steps of Derbyshire sandstone, a wall and rockery of Yorkshire limestone and an excavated Victorian pavement of engineering bricks. The design incorporates history and truth. All truth is parallel and because I tend to think analogically, the meaning of one world is easily moved into synchrony with that of another. With geological time well represented on the Walk I can now begin to build a rock sculpture in the back garden. It will be a symbolic landscape brought to life with water. We shall see if the sculpture can be made to work. I am hoping that water will feed in at one end and wine emerge at the other.

Hornsea is brisk and bright in the morning sun. It has been re-designed with a classy feel. I could feel at home in the Floral Hall, The Bowls Club or the Rainbow Leisure Centre. So too sparkles Bridlington. The multi-million refit of the promenade – with a spanking new marina development – is its millennium present to itself. Shopping is good except that I am not buying anything beyond a wee small can of Camping Gaz. Despite strenuous efforts I am told there is none "for about fifty miles". I suddenly feel bored. I decide to phone, foolishly as it turns out, a distant member of my family.

Nothing like family, I muse, and then remember it is at least fifty years ago when we first met. I have another attack of fifty phobia, and not without reason. There had been bad blood in the previous generation. Although we had only ever met twice, I just know this is going to take more than charm. Mentally I list a few basic needs that can justify a quick visit: Dubbin for my boots, Bostick for my rucksack and a handful of plastic bags. Good psychology, I think to myself. I dial the number and the receiver purrs with an old fashioned buzzing, too long for my liking. Then my aunt answers and hands the phone to her husband, Uncle Ted. "Graham here! Just wishing you well ..." In about ten seconds flat, it is dead. I am shocked, flushed with rage and hurt. I am not welcome and I am family for goodness sake! "Don't bother us," I had been told abruptly. "We want to be left alone." Now I'm all for telling the truth to one another, but well, I mean to say ... My hand is trembling as I replace the receiver. I sit in a coffee shop, feeling quite desolate for half an hour. I learn later the history of pain and rejection caused by *my* family's behaviour. What is more, there is something I do not know. He is dying of cancer.

I mentally scan the faces of my family and my parents' family for clues to understanding. Victorian faces were grim enough anyway. I can only see the eyes of my own parents, eyes that dominated me, my Dad when he was angry and my mother when controlling. At fifty yards, my mother could shrivel us to a crisp, my sister and me. Across a room we would be helpless in the grip of her glare. Now I know, deep in my spirit, that I was a twinkle before I was born and an apple after I was born, in the eye of both my earthly and heavenly fathers. I find a surge of renewing joy. I have found in Scripture that God's servants from Noah and Abraham, David and Samson, right through to Mary the mother of Jesus, all "found grace in the eyes of the Lord". I discover that this phrase is an Arabism. Like the many nautical allusions in our English language, this is a desert allusion preserved in the Hebrew. It was given to teach Abraham that God had chosen him *by grace* and loved him and totally accepted him *just as he was* through his faith. The vehicle through which God chose to express this was the camel, already a walking mall of maternal provision. At night in the desert a camel calf would often be slain and its skin stuffed and put back under its mother's nose, to keep her milking. The look of the mother as she gazes on her lifeless child and the echoing sound of the mother mourning for her lost offspring were customarily described in one simple word, 'CHEN', pronounced gutturally. That one word, five or six thousand years later, still embedded in our Old and New Testaments, describes what is to be found 'in the eyes of the Lord', the heart-broken concern of a parent for his lost child, you and I. That word in English is 'GRACE'.

Long before Abraham "found favour in the eyes of the Lord", we learn that God's gift of that same free grace was visually conveyed to Noah through the rainbow. As I approach a few houses in North Landing of Flamborough Head there is no welcoming response to my usual requests for hot water and cold water and two slices of bread. But as I pick my way over Dane's Dyke, there appears a little rainbow over the sea. I am encouraged. I take a picture and remember George Matheson's famous line: "I trace the rainbow through the rain," except that he intended and originally wrote it to say, "I *claim* the rainbow through the rain". After all, anyone can trace it. It takes faith to claim it. I also pot-shot the lighthouse against a yellow sky and drop into the *Headland Café,* open late. There everything comes right. "Sure we'll top you up," said Pete, "and here, have a banana!" That is enough to pull me out of the blues and twenty minutes later I cross the links and settle down on the edge, where the path offers a safe pouch for my body. I was between the fifth tee and only eighteen inches from a four hundred foot sheer drop into the sea.

In this day, I have felt discouraged and disappointed, rejected and elated, angry and hurt, sad and surprised, disgusted, thankful and joyful. I am glad that I have feelings and that today my brain and body have reacted and inter-reacted reasonably well. These emotions have been connectors that circulate round my system enabling me to think, feel and respond appropriately. To me, my feelings are friends, close friends. I rely on them to inform, stimulate and motivate me. They funnel my attention so I can be sentient and sensitive. Sometimes like water they trickle and sometimes they surge. At other times they resemble slow moving magma that drags stuff from the surface into the interior to re-surface later changed and capable of making change for the better. I bought a circular piece of dark marble from Battlebridge in Essex. It was for a little table in our living room. It reminds me that my emotions are not for indulgence but to indicate and facilitate change.

I used to be hard on myself over emotions like jealousy, fear, despair, lust, loneliness and pride. I now see these emotions, indeed *all emotions*, as morally neutral, neither positive nor negative,good nor bad, just essential parts of my humanity, essential equipment to connect with and react to my world. I have counted nearly forty shades of feeling, with which we humans interact with life.

Actually, the initial element of an emotional response is purely physiological. It is a function of the amygdala and the frontal lobes of the brain and beyond instant control. So if God has placed this capability in me, His likeness in me, then no emotion is to be banned or labelled 'bad'. In that sense they are all supremely God's gifts, to be revered and not reviled. All of them are 'natural' aspects of *His* nature and wonderfully intended to equip and enhance *my* nature. I can smile to myself and say, 'it's OK to be miserable!' I include as my basic 'natural' emotions: fear in my need to survive, anger in my need to protest, love and jealousy in my need to belong, delight and disgust in my need to discriminate, and pride and grief in my need to acquire. All, of course, are coloured by self-interest and therefore easily over-indulged and under-examined. They often get the better of me. And in practice I do find it takes time to get a grip. But there lies the crunch. What I then *choose to do* with my emotions *is* very crucial. Like blame or an apology they begin to affect others. From now on they will affect my attitudes and inform my actions, how I behave responsibly and honourably towards other people as I meet with them.

Perhaps the only two 'unnatural' emotions are shame and guilt, about what we are and what we have done. I believe, these were never part of God's original intended endowment for humankind. Nevertheless, most of my life I have felt a half-conscious shame over my body, though for most purposes an excellent machine. It was never acknowledged at home and so I felt it was never acceptable to others. Likewise, for years I had tyrannical guilt over my children, the flip side of parental responsibility, but it was *felt* guilt not real guilt. Real guilt is about our sin and is to lead us to our Saviour.

I have concluded that 'what I am', 'what I've done' and 'what I have' are not three sticks with which to beat myself. As a Christian: what I am is accepted unconditionally and totally by my Heavenly Father at the Cross of His Son; what I've done, along with all the debts and ties and memories, is being constantly cleansed away by the Holy Spirit now in charge of my conscience; and what I have now in Christ is His life and His love embedded in mine, and, yes, a call to love the things He loves and to hate the things He hates, like secrecy, pretence and hypocrisy, the challenging themes of His famous

Sermon. One more thing: I think He wants me to be far more passionate and compassionate about His earthly offspring mankind and the state His world is in. Lord help me to be real, and be like you, to feel like you. Just give me a little more time …

In the morning I catch a glimpse of the gannet focussed in action. At the Bempton Cliffs the RSPB guards a large colony that clusters on the vertical chalk of the famous Flamborough headland. I see their handsome buff to yellow plumage and striking five-to six-foot wings, tipped black at the ends. With no external nostrils they dive for mackerel from 100 feet and cleave the water at 60mph. I see a black kite flying in huge undulations out at sea. But everything disappears under persistent rain.

Head down, most of the way to Hunmanby and Filey, the only diversion is Joe Caruso's cottage. An ex-miner turned magician, Joe performed all over the world until retirement at North Landing. He has customised his house and garden with everything quirky, anything that came to hand, the novel, the nude and the naff. There's Flash Gordon's No 2, a full-size, flaxen-haired blow-up in a bathing suit. There's Laurel and Hardy in the window and, lining the coastal path on both sides, are jokes, something to guarantee a smile on anyone's face. A woman said, "I want my husband buried twelve feet under: because deep down he was a good man." A man went to the library for a book on suicide: the librarian said, "we used to have a lot but those who borrow them don't bring them back." Another man, 109 years of age, is interviewed: "To what do you attribute your old age?" "The main thing was", he said, "I cancelled my trip on the Titanic." A drunk on the Titanic said, "I ordered ice, but this is ridiculous." "Everyone dies – that's life!" and finally, "A smile is the finest facelift in the world. Smile and you live longer." I screw up my forty little muscles in the driving rain and plough on round Smuggler's Cove.

Sylvia, an old Yorkshire-speaking friend from sign-writing days, rescues me from the torrential weather. A pragmatist, she has ready for me her chosen thought for the day: 'the less clothing you wear, the harder you walk, the warmer you get and the quicker you dry out'. Next step is Filey, unpretentious and familiar like an old pair of slippers, pressing all my nostalgic buttons. The Ravine and massive sea wall made of two- and three-foot chunks of gritstone lead on to the beach. There, after a youthful swim, I was ritually sand-papered by a sand-laden towel in the hands of an over-zealous mother, before the weary walk back to the hotel. Amid the colourful sailing dinghies a fishing coble is being rescued from the sea. A tractor drives into the waves, hooks the vessel and its catch and drags them to safety. From Staithes down to Bridlington, along the inhospitable Yorkshire coast, these famous boats stand up to the North Sea. Thirty to forty feet long, the coble is still sailed and beached 'bow on' into the shingle, with two sledge-like runners instead of the conventional keel and, being light at the back, the raging surf lifts it high and pushes it out of the water. Then there are people at leisure watching others throwing stones into the sea and erecting windshields. There are kiosks shouldering each other for room on the 'prom'. Each doorway billows with balloons, flutters with flags and is cluttered to the eyebrows with buckets, spades and tea towels. And there are other people just content to sit with an ice cream. After that, the Filey Brigg is a must.

Chapter 17

Scarborough to Staithes

HERITAGE COAST: A TOUGH JOURNEY THROUGH JOY

SCARBOROUGH SEEMS TO ME A THRESHOLD TOWN. TO THE south, it is sad. The mock Tudor *Holbeck Hall Hotel* and millions of tons of headland recently slumped unceremoniously into the North Sea. Round it are seventy dead trees stranded above the water table, silent, pale and leafless. The south marina swimming pool is empty, closed and cracked. Even the cliff lift looks tired and ready to give up the struggle. To the north, in contrast, is the glory of the Yorkshire Heritage Coast and the Cleveland Way. On its doorstep and on the edge of the town is "Thisldo", a guesthouse run by Hilda and Percy Clark. They are both over eighty and been married for nearly sixty years. They welcome me into their beautifully appointed home. They evidently enjoy their guests and care with limitless attention to detail. I look into their faces and search for the secret of their joy. It may be found in their paraplegic son, Melvyn. He and they have somehow transformed this tragedy or maybe have been transformed *by* this tragedy. I can only judge by the family's trademark, a people-affirming, life-affirming panoramic smile that is genuine. I am surprised by joy.

I am myself on a threshold and eagerly await the future. AD 2000 only sharpens my desire to move on. I want to clamber out of the cobwebs of the past and push open the window of my future. Then I remind myself we had joy through pain but it was real pain and the pain has not left. It has just changed as time has taught us now to deal with it. I could spray-paint the past in rose-tinted colours. I could pronounce blithe those things that were a blight and canonise the catastrophic as God's will. It would be in vain, for cystic fibrosis is a scourge and our children died young, Allister a baby, Rachel eight and Elizabeth thirteen. Nowadays, cystic children become adults and I imagine that soon the disease will become a thing of the past. Still, however dreadful the disease and however dire it feels to be without grandchildren, these three children have been God's especial gifts to us. And we measure their lives not by the number of years but by the impact of those years, the effect they have left behind on others and on us, a trailing edge of glory, tinged with grief.

Were the parents given to the children for the children's benefit or were the children given to the parents for the parent's benefit? Who knows these things? Given from the heart of God to the heart of any family, children in themselves are missionaries and carry a powerful personal message. Through Elizabeth I learnt so much, especially in the last year of caring. She once said, "Adults *need* to cry. We're all made the same, whatever age we are." Coming out of the hospital after five weeks of intravenous treatment, she was crossing the hospital lawn after a refreshing downpour. She said, "Isn't it lovely and clean. Not clinical medical clean but *God's* clean, refreshing not artificial. Listen! All the flowers are going 'zup-zup'. Can you hear them slurping, Daddy?" She became my teacher and I, in a way, her pupil. What is more, all our children have carried that same trademark of joy, the smile, a smile that in Rachel's case was to spread all over the final hours of her earthly life as she was transformed ready for the next.

As temporary caretakers our guardianship is now over. All parents are no more than trustees. We have only to complete three essential tasks, tasks that burst nearly every emotional blood vessel, but tasks for our children that have to be done and each done well: *to have them, love them and let them go.* True devotedness serves, enjoys and then releases the loved one, for no human relationship lasts forever. All come and all must go; and now our cystic children likewise must slip into the past.

Actually it's the future. Like as so often on a country walk children will come up from behind, overtake and disappear on the path in front, Allister, Rachel and Elizabeth have all heard the call to move on ahead. Though left behind is a cavernous yearning, ahead, inseparable from the joyful prospect of meeting them again, is the smile we shall recognise and the intimacy of love that will follow. It is the light from behind, the clarity of knowing, the pull of acceptance, the surge of emergent health and the eager clasp of recognition that will follow the words of the Master, "Well done ... enter into my joy."

Meanwhile Heather and I move on up the path. We need to move on and find joy in the gift and giving of the years to come. With such thoughts I dismiss the oppressive Grand Hotel and the run-down boats on Peasholme Park. I want to travel upwards and onwards along the Edge, the joyful, alluring rising edge of the North Yorkshire Moors.

At last I am climbing the cliffs and remember the words of Dr Elisabeth Kubler-Ross: "Should you shield the canyons from the windstorms, you would never see the beauty of their carvings." Her final annual lecture, arranged by the Tauranga Grief Centre where I worked in New Zealand, was dedicated to our Elizabeth, just after she died. Were we to shield ourselves from hardships, we would never see the beauty of their carvings.

At 12.40 pm on August 29th all the birds of the region, near and far, on land and sea, suddenly lift off in one instant. A huge explosion rips through the air and appears to tear the horizon apart. Shock waves distort the atmosphere and ripple the trees. The Army has just disposed of a bomb in the next bay. I am courteously allowed to proceed. I duck under contorted horizontal tree branches at Hayburn Wyke and dish out some blister pads to four teenage girls. Straight from A levels, they are determined to impress me and their boy-friends with their superior courage in the face of pain. A long climb and I reach a high plateau.

Perched up, Ravenscar is a chilling place and indeed grim like its name. No shelter, few walls, just a gaunt grid outline of empty roads with one or two houses to mock the intentions of a Victorian speculative builder. Would-be investors were not impressed, alternately soaked by the Cleveland Roak off the sea or blasted by the wind off the moor. Today it fails to sport even one through road to anywhere.

Nearby is Britain's first chemical manufacturing works making alum, a yellow crystal vital in textile and leather production. I can imagine the smoke creeping out from under thirty-foot piles of burning shale and the ash slurry being filtered and then mixed with urine. This ammonia catalyst was obligingly collected from the doorways of Yorkshire and the streets of London. It is said the empty urine containers excelled in conveying extra tangy cheese back to the Capital.

I am ready for bed at Boggle Hole, but the YHA is full. I drag my legs up the hill beyond and round the coast. The edge gets steeper and steeper and there is no way up or down the cliffs. With light fading fast, I find a bush that looks strong enough to hold me and peg myself in for the night. Not bad for a pad, I think, suspended between cows above and white horses below.

Up and down the Yorkshire coast countless vessels have foundered and their crews been lost. Over fifty off Flamborough Head alone. I find myself astonished and humbled at the courage of men who fish the seas at risk of their lives. But surpassing all, however, has to be the courage of lifeboatmen manning a rowing boat in the teeth of a north-easterly gale straight out into the North Sea.

On one night in February 1861, three hundred and fifty-five ships were lost to the North Sea off the coast of England. At Whitby alone, eleven were beached and five were lost. The lifeboat was successfully launched four times but on the last occasion thirteen crewmen drowned. The sole survivor was the youngest, Henry Freeman. He had been given a new cork jacket. Until then cork had only been used to line the gunnels of a boat, allowing room for ten oarsmen and several spare oars. The records show Freeman was subsequently involved in much daring and drama. On the eighteenth of January, twenty years later, the brig *Visitor* ran ashore in Robin Hood's Bay. No other boat could help. A message was sent to fetch the Whitby lifeboat. It was deep winter. The vessel was hauled through seven-foot drifts of snow, over six miles to the Bay. 200 men with eighteen heaving horses were needed to clear a path and climb 500 feet. Others prepared the way to receive them and guide the vessel, with only inches to spare, down the narrow street to the harbour. On the second attempt, all of the crew were saved. The coxswain that day was Henry Freeman.

In the morning I am soon away on the old railway path to Whitby and am joined by Rita and a friend. Rita has been left with daughter Bettina, after her husband died of cancer. Very positively she says, "Life is like a book and God writes the last chapter." Life is a story. She is right. We write the detail and He sees to the plot. There might be comic and tragic bits and a few blind alleys, but it is not empty of meaning. It is supremely a drama and part of a divine drama where nothing is totally random and nothing need be wasted. Everything can be and is being woven into the ultimate denouement, and like any good story satisfaction comes by the end. The plot will be understood. We shall see and be content.

Only a fortnight to go, I am sad the Walk will soon be over. I record on tape my desires: to be more human, more available, more thankful, more prayerful and more hospitable – and I would add, more realistic. I record the attitudes of a pilgrim on his journey: a focused patience to walk one step at a time; an earthy self-discipline; a faith to receive and return blessings along the way; and the conviction that God is ever present, stage-managing the drama according to His purposes.

I help Jim Laroche recover from tumbling off his bike. We walk together to Hawsker Trailways and I set course for the edge and the Hawsker Bull, a fog horn audible over ten miles. I pass the ruined Priory and find St Mary's, Whitby. This extraordinary church has no electricity and depends on central sky lighting above its three-deck pulpit. Whitby is an authentic old fishing town, buzzing with life. After fish and chips in the *Sands Restaurant*, where the hat is passed round by the staff, I just want to stand with Captain Cook and follow his gaze over the harbour and out to sea.

My eyes refocus on the Bay of Plenty, 'down under'. Heather and I lived there in the North Island, New Zealand from Christmas 1983 to '87. We knew Poverty Bay and Cape Kidnappers, where the locals scrapped with the crew of *Endeavour*. I visualise the Maori church where I worked, and the loving people in Tauranga. I remember the Cook Strait from the air and imagine his hundred foot three-masted brig, battling with ice and heaving with wild winds, as he explored the perimeters of Antarctica. I admire his curiosity and the meticulous approach he had to cartography and research. I admire his calm courage and sense of adventure in the face of huge risk taking. I admire his leadership.

Cook returned to marry Elizabeth and have children, and I think of the privilege of taking ours to New Zealand and back on the luxury cruise ship, *Canberra*. In Cook's day the men had little privacy, a hammock and pickled cabbage, which they were forced to eat or be flogged. Then I think of the strange timing of an encounter I had with his ship, a modern replica of the *Endeavour*. I discovered her moored one morning in Newcastle, NSW. I was in Australia for my sister's doctorate and out training for Walk 2000. All was still, about 6a.m. I crept on board, explored and left, without alerting the crew. They had just started a celebratory trip round the world and two years later would tie up in Whitby harbour, just as I was leaving Cheltenham on this Walk. So here I am, 250 years after Captain James Cook had set out on his first journey and one hundred days after setting out on mine, standing brown and a bit battered before his commanding bronze statue, thinking that I had better be off on a northerly bearing quick, in case he orders a flogging for unpardonable delay.

I am staying in Whitby with the Rev. Jack Cooper, a retired vicar and now an ebullient customer-friendly guard on the North Yorkshire Moors Steam Railway. Over a splendid meal on Saturday night he reminds me that he and Pam came to see us just before Rachel died in the local hospital, August 1977. A few days later she stepped over the Edge and we were permitted to look beyond and through her to see the reality and prospect of 'joy unspeakable'.

The long narrow road to Kettleness stops at the cliff edge. From there on, it is a wonderful view: a view of the sea and of the ships that pass gradually out of sight. My family is not lost, but just out of sight beyond my horizon. I turn round and see a hundred yards of grass and then an extraordinary building, a station on a railway that has disappeared. "It's let aart," the man says. "The Boy Scouts keep cummin like." I can see the painted flagpole and the well-kept coastguard storage shed and I begin to see the thirty active adults who live here, as well as the goats grazing where the track should be.

Runswick Bay has 'the runs'. Each year the Ice Age boulder clay, or till, slides a boat's length towards the harbour. The County Council chucked two hundred tons of concrete on it five years ago and it just continued downhill, at twice the pace. Now all that has gone and instead five hundred pins are being inserted to keep the village where it has always been. There I met Janet and later Jim, who were acquainted. I said to a rather harassed Jim, "Life is one darned thing after another." "Yes!" he said adapting Mark Twain, "Love is two darn things after another."

Entering Staithes down a steep hill, the cottages shove and shoulder themselves into the valley. They huddle on top of one another and crouch in the deep gorge as if to escape the bitter winds from above. Staithes has gone to bed. I cross the little iron bridge and up the other side coax bread and water from the last but one property. For a night-cap I set myself to climb Boulby Hill, which at 626 feet crowns the eastern seaboard. It is boggy and bleak and soon black as night. With the flat of my hand I feel for prickles and sheep's poo and then sleep in the lee of the trig' point. Stiff and perished at breakfast, I pack and step back to photograph this inhospitable site with three steaming potash chimneys in the background, and grind my toothbrush deep into the mud. After the regulation pause, I take stock. At least it is downhill.

In perfect weather I have followed a magnificent Heritage Coastline and crossed many prominent geological dislocations. The Whitby harbour and gorge is itself a fault line and the land to the north drops forty feet. The whole of 'Whitby' has been buried and uplifted four times, oscillating from one to six thousand feet. From my limited perspective on personal history, nothing can take away the up-and-down memories of family life, the joy of having and loving children and not least, the pain of losing them. Halfway through our family journey we experienced a huge discontinuity in our expectations, leading up to a roller coaster of hope and dread. Could Rachel somehow survive, somehow be helped, somehow healed? Promises from above and special prayers, services and anointings punctuated the inexorable decline in her condition. Several times she experienced the relief of pain and symptoms. She said she felt so much better and ate a hearty meal. How we wanted her to stay a little longer on this earth. Hope does not die easily, for pains of childbirth are nothing compared to the pains of death in the heart of a mother and father. Nothing could assuage the agony that slowly gripped our gut. Daily the paediatric consultant, Janet Goodall, grappled with the facts as she found them and later wrote up some of her moving observations in the *British Medical Journal*.

Asked why he believed that Jesus rose from the dead, a Christian replied, "Because I was speaking to him only a few minutes ago." Rachel knew the Lord and that was our abiding comfort. One day I heard a conversation and called up the stairs to her bedroom, “Rachel, are you all right?” “Oh yes!” she said, “I was just talking to Jesus.” Christianity, simply, is a relationship. Speaking about her chest pains that she had had all her life, she once said, “I’m sure that God must have a plan in all this.” Thinking about us, she said, “It is better for boys and girls to die, than Mums and Dads. Because if Mums and Dads die there’s no one to look after the boys and girls. But if the boys and girls die the Mums and Dads don’t need anyone to look after them.” Her faith shone into our sorrow.

Rachel was still managing to walk ever so slowly to church, when in early July 1977 she was admitted to hospital for intravenous treatment. Jack and Pam made three specific prayer requests: that Rachel would die without distress, happy. Second, that *we* would know that to be the case; and third, that we would both be there at her death. So began the familiar stage-managing of events, the placing of special people, the timing of moments of meeting and the mystery that would weave together an extra-ordinary life-changing drama, the facts of which I will relate from detailed notes that were taken at the time and verified by the sister in charge.

On the morning of August 5th, Dr Goodall had returned from holiday in Scotland. A cancelled clinic meant she could be with us in the latter part of these events. Heather and I decided early morning that we would travel together to be with Rachel. At about 11.30am we could see through the round glass panel windows of the two swing doors a battle for life. By mid-day the struggle was over. The team of doctors left. Plugs were disconnected, tubes taken away and machines switched off. No more special feeds, no more physiotherapy. No more oxygen masks. We were left to sit beside our daughter. Her lifeless form was still. This then was it. We sat in silence, shrouded in thought and numb with shock. There was nothing to do and nothing more to say.

Twenty to twenty-five minutes passed, her body still inert, when suddenly her eyes flickered open, not as they had been, like slits, for weeks, but wide and wider by the minute. Like saucers they ogled in amazement. Her head began to swivel from side to side on the pillow as she gazed in growing astonishment at what she alone could see. Her face by now was a picture and she began to speak. Her chest had collapsed so she could only use her lips. "Why?" she said, over and again, "Why did you not see?" Each word was shaped separately, urgently and repetitively, at least half a dozen times to ensure we understood. Whatever was it? We thought, "What's wrong, what didn't we see?" At last she made it plain what she wanted to say. "WHY DID YOU NOT SEE THEM SINGING?" Angels, men, women, a massed choir? – for our Rachel? She could not understand why we were not sharing what was so real to her. It dawned on us gradually that a veil now lay between us and our daughter. Time was running out. Rachel was travelling. She had started her final journey through joy.

Just after one o'clock came her first smile. She was sitting up now, still rapt with all she could see. She began to move down the bed towards someone. She beamed a dignified little smile. I noticed that she was no longer hunched over. Her back was straight. The nurses put her back on some pillows. For about fifteen minutes she would periodically tip forward as if to do something and the nurses would gently place her back. Then defeating their best efforts, Rachel slid on her bottom down the bed, swung her legs off on my side and without help, stood up. She smiled a huge beaming smile that seemed to cover her whole head, a smile full of happiness. We put our arms round each other and loved and laughed and cried and prayed and rejoiced together. The nurses suddenly lost their nerve and fled the ward, all but the Sister in charge. Was she healed? Do we get her clothes and take her home? Time and again came these huge smiles of joy on tides of evident pleasure. But one thing was different. She was not looking at me at all *but through me,* appreciating an unfolding world of which I was not yet part.

After quite a long period on her feet, Rachel seemed to sag a little. I put her back on the bed. This time she wriggled over to Heather's side and climbed on to her lap. "Hullo!" she whispered twice and gave Heather the biggest possible smile, full of contentment, joy, serenity and sheer bliss. Clearly she wanted to thank us. 'I'm OK now,' she seemed to say; and asked Heather, "Are you coming with me?"

She sat on the end of the bed. It was about 1.40 p.m. She gazed straight through the birthday cards on the wall, and was responding to all that was going on in the world beyond. Periodically she raised her arms, as if to acknowledge those who came to welcome her – including, perhaps, her brother? At one moment particularly, it was as if a tangible beam of love was enveloping her. Her joy was obvious. I asked her, "Who was that, Rachel?" She turned slightly, as if I ought to know, "Jesus," she said.

Heather returned from a quick visit to the toilet. We sat on either side of the bed and were now both feeling distinctly inferior. Rachel had changed. Gone completely were the deathly pallor and the lines of fear and panic of a child. Instead she seemed to have grown in stature, more like a young woman. Her chest was out, her shoulders back. Her cheeks had returned and were rosy and smooth. Her skin seemed to glisten – indeed, her whole frame was animated by interactions invisible to our sight.

Scarcely daring to believe all that we had seen, about three months later I went to see the sister-in-charge to obtain an independent account of our daughter's passing. Fully expecting to have our own memories punctured by clinically hard facts, she related what we had remembered and more besides of those heart-breaking, heart-stopping events. She concluded her observations by saying that as it appeared to her, at the end, "Rachel was absorbed in the happiest game of her life". And that was her death.

How can death be a terror, if all it does is to usher us into the Father's presence? Said Jesus, "Because I live, you will live also." When we fall asleep in this world, we are wide-awake in the next. We may plough through problems here but will dance through death at the climax. I used to go and see Rachel last thing each night and hold her hand and pray. The previous night I had sat down beside the humidifying tent that enveloped her bed and this time her thin, little arm came out and gripped mine. She said, "Daddy, I love Jesus so much I could put my arms right round him and hug him. When I die I would like to take him a present." Next day she took him herself. After about two hours and thirty amazing minutes, the doctor gave her failing body into the crook of my leg. She tucked her head thankfully into my armpit and was gone, in a moment. A quiet joy filled that place.

Chapter 18

Skinningrove to Lynemouth

DOWN TO EARTH: CHARACTERS AND KINDNESS IN THE NORTH-EAST

THE BRITISH MEDICAL JOURNAL, 3.3.79, SUMMARISED THE END of Rachel's life. She was "semi-conscious. Suddenly, she struggled out of bed, smiled happily, and hugged each parent in turn, before dying quietly in her father's arms ... who said, 'This was not passing from life into death, but passing from death into life.'" Elizabeth loved to hear Rachel's story and it helped her manage the end of her own life nearly ten years later.

As for me, I discovered that, uniquely, deeper than sorrow is joy, always ready to bubble through. I found that joy and grief belong together in the same well and that anything to do with children is shot through inextricably with intense pleasure and pain. Pain there is in letting them go on to independent life, but if we do not release them we risk losing them anyway. The more offspring we have the more heartbreak we can have. If we have one, we may mourn the absence of many. If we have none, we may feel the childless life later, especially after miscarriages. In most families, everyday pleasure is important and we save up money to treat ourselves later. Perhaps we should likewise budget for pain and try to accept loss and let-down, even rip-off and betrayal as important, predictable, 'given' aspects of life, not unlike the weather. I came down from this mountaintop experience still learning.

Dropping down from Rock Cliff at Boulby, I enter another world, the industrial landscape of the north-east: Tyne, Wear and Tees. It would end with a family of seven in a van and begin with an empty pigeon shed. Brian locks up his few lobster creels and we walk together into Skinningrove, into a steep-sided rather gloomy valley. Steel above and mines below, it used to thrive. Now the harbour is in ruins, the schools have gone, clubs have closed and iron contamination oozes out of the river. There had been little evidence of pride, until recently. The village is fighting back. Houses are being rebuilt, pavements re-laid, banks replanted and the empty old school buildings are being used to inspire and train the young people, most of whom are unemployed. The Carnival, Bonfire and Link-up projects are putting heart back into the High Street, where Brian Magor suitably lives at Number 1.

He sits me down in his living room surrounded by well-displayed trophies on the wall, on the telly and the mantle-shelf. This year he is president of the Snooker Association. He was five years in steel and two years down the potash mine, until his two mates were killed. Today he fishes out of a friend's boat from Saltburn, despite being washed ashore and half-drowned when his own boat sank. Their home has been burgled, precious things taken and even his pigeons stolen. What a man! Now his time and love is lavished on his family of six. I meet Samantha studying IT and Michael who was born down the toilet. He surfaced with a lovely smile and has kept it ever since.

As I was climbing out of the village, under the old railway-bridge, two enormous green and yellow Emperor dragonflies fly in tandem overhead. In one heady episode their life is climaxing in a riveting romp. Locked in mid-air copulation they will not for anyone let go. Round and round they cavort, like two stricken Sikorsky helicopters, till finally they ditch exhausted on the path in front of me. No amount of prodding persuades them to fly until suddenly, they do. Below me lies Skinningrove – once ditched and which now has at last taken off again.

High up on the path I find three dramatic metal sculptures, made at British Steel celebrating the complex interactions of hard working people with their world. The Cleveland Potash Company is also trying to help local people and it plans to re-instate a railway from Boulby to Skinningrove. I leave the path to investigate an old Guible fan, an enormous twelve-foot disc that was once used to ventilate the ironstone mines, 3,000 feet below. The potash and salt workers still descend the height of Pen-y-Ghent. They then travel a further five miles from the factory to reach the facing panels under the sea, and soon will be due to travel south under the Moors.

As if the day has not been interesting enough, I walk through Brough House Farm to find an oil-fired machine shooting out flames to dry the grain. Neville Henderson has steadily built up the farm over 30 years. He is a massive man, built like a shed door. So is his large heart as he and Christine insist I take a £20 note. A peregrine falcon swoops to honour the moment with its own aerial fly-past.

I leave the Cleveland Way behind and set my sights on Marske, where Captain Cook's father was buried. He died unaware that his son had been killed just three weeks before on a Hawaiian beach. Melvyn Clark is a tonic in his special room for paraplegics at Marske Hall, travelling like Tarzan on his aerial swing way, independently, to the loo and back. How glad I am to stride the remaining miles to Redcar inside my own two legs and boots.

I have one thing in mind – to see the British Steel Works complex, now under Corus, previously Dorman Long, *at night*. It spreads over six square miles, south of the Tees Estuary. It is already dusk and the show is on. I gape at the restless man-made monster that lies sprawled before me exuding steam and stench. It is fed continuously with limestone from the Lakes, iron ore from Australia and coal from South Africa. Floodlit and flaming, it belches and farts, rumbles and crunches, but never pauses. Great cavernous vats and contorted concrete vents spew bad breath. It has its own territory and it has its own meteorology, billowing steamy smoke high into the sky. I decide not to squeeze past and travel the Teesdale Trail. I am late and catch a train into Middlesborough to meet my host at the fire station.

The Rev. Brian Rice, chaplain, introduces me to a number of hunky guys, each with a broad and genuine smile and a vicious handshake. They had just installed showers for the firemen and each of them without fail follows his remarks with an invitation, "Have a shower?" After about the fourth occasion the penny drops. We grab a sandwich and following Brian I soon find myself one of a sea of heads pouring into Hartlepool football stadium. Brian leads a short commemorative silence for a former player who has died. In the Directors' Box I have canapés and drinks, more lusty conversations and end up in the sponsors' lounge. There I am ceremoniously draped with every fan's most coveted trophy, the embroidered football scarf, which I should have passed on to Brian after his forty years of ordained life. His has been an amazing maverick ministry and mine an amazing day. I don't like to admit that this is my first soccer match ever. I am a rugby fan and soccer has always gone with tennis and poetry – slightly wimpish.

At 7 a.m. next morning I wave goodbye to Val and Brian, and find myself exploring the huge blue Transporter Bridge, a giant metallic insect straddling the Tees on its spindly legs, cradling traffic North and South. Clamped in by security fences I fail on my first attempt to find the estuary flats. Gone are the sands and the empty spaces I expect from the map. In their place is a mesh of pylons and pipelines linking gasworks, an oil terminal and even a nuclear power station. Beyond, and surprisingly, "The Snooks" have been well preserved as a nature reserve, and grey seals bask by the roadside. After six miles I am desperate for breakfast. Eggs and bacon, baked beans, sausage and fried bread with coffee taste so good at Seaton Carew, all the better for being served by a smiling chubby-face. She had a mop of curly fair hair and eyes that sparkled behind twinkly glasses. The waitress makes me glad I am back on the Edge of England. She is the sort of person, like my daughter Sallyanne, of whom I can say, "When I'm with you I like myself better."

By mid-day I walk into Hartlepool's Historic Quay and marina. I decide on my 'tough and bluff' policy, and gain free admission as a Long Distance Walker. It is magic, the smells, sights and sounds of an authentic old-time seaport. I listen enthralled to the story of George and Harry press-ganged into the Navy. I hear the officers choosing their weapons, and watch unfold the sea-battle that follows. I examine the earliest of children's games and climb on to a fishing coble's deck. I tour the Napoleonic frigate, *H.M.S. Trincomalee* and the *PS Wingfield Castle* that plied across the Humber. Then the management changes its mind about me and I am politely asked to leave by the Chief Security Officer. It is always best to go to the chief in the first place.

Next, I think, is the closest I get to impotent rage. Come stand with me. It is almost too silly to tell. My map is too small, Hartlepool is too large and there is no sign of the sun. Under a leaden sky, I am in a maze of terraced housing and lost. I presume simply to ask for, "The Coast, please!" I set off confidently to follow local advice. I check with an old woman, then a housewife and finally a teenager, each time covering a fair distance, but always in a completely different direction. It is like a fast-forward tape of a woman entering a supermarket, collecting from everywhere the things she needs and returning to the place where she first came in. Does no one know where they live? "The COAST PLEASE!" I ask in strangled Geordie. "Am I the butt for your entertainment?" I wonder, as I pass the same set of traffic lights for the third time. Then truth dawns. Hartlepool town fills a vast south-travelling lobe of land. On it one may travel to the sea towards any point of the compass. Worse still, the only route North is blocked by a twenty-foot railway embankment and instead of finding the coast I am advised to go inland W*est* and then by miles of dual carriageway North to Hart Station. I find the footbridge and eventually the path to the only friend I have left. Still there, the sea. I rest and dream ...

... The pre-Jurassic period is hot. I am in an immense steaming jungle of carbon-rich vegetation and strange plants. The 'County of Durham' swelters not far north of the Equator. Early dinosaurs roam and rule this land. Then comes inundation by Tethys, a warm tropical sea enabling the skeletons of multi-trillion vertebrates to form the limestones of the Permian Age. Then (on fast forward) deltaic deposits from south-flowing rivers create shales and mudstones. Hot deserts come and go as the British Isles moves into its present position. Finally, tree-less tundra takes over. The bitter winds and glaciers of the Ice Ages cover and denude the landscape and, from the ice, meltwaters cut ravines such as Castle Dene – where now, feeling a bit chilly, I am gradually coming back to life.

So were laid the economic foundations of the industrial Northeast, coal, limestone and iron ore. Here George Stephenson built his first railway to carry coal across Durham and strange to say, in my first curacy, I used to stand before his memorial tombstone each Sunday morning, taking communion. It was his home church, Holy Trinity in Chesterfield.

Further along there is no way up the unstable, horizontal remains of industrial slag. It is scary. I have taken advice and manage to beat the tide – only just, and am a bit wet. I reach a welcome breach in the cliffs. I climb up towards Easington and ignorantly into a nightmare. On the cliff edge I meet Tom walking his dog. Rusty buckets have only just disappeared from the waste disposal conveyor on the cliffs behind me. This is Easington Colliery, the scene in 1951 of a horrible community disaster.

Tom is toothless, pinched, short and limping. He cannot see well but waves his stick into empty space, at a flattened silent, grey and abandoned expanse of land. There, as a lad, he had heard the dreaded siren summoning help to the colliery gates. At 4.30am, on 29th May 1951 he was out of the front door in short trousers and no socks. He climbed to the top of a stack of waste and looked over. He watched the families gather in stunned and terrified silence. Slowly, over three days, he saw eighty-one miners and two rescuers brought to the surface, burnt, blackened and dead. The explosion caught two overlapping shifts of men and blew the guts out of the community. That day in his early teens, something died in Tom. Apparently he never went below and hardly ever did a decent day's work for over thirty years. Someone says, "He's a waster. He beats his wife and drinks his Benefit. His hobby's a metal detector and he'll scrounge whatever he can." Tom generously takes me to a cemetery where all are remembered on a hill, beside a rail-tub of coal and a cutter. He says little. I wonder briefly why he does not invite me back home.

Meet Tony, "Tor-eny" as he says. Evidently he has a Durham miner's skill and grit and a young family. To me, it looks as if the Council has done a good job improving the lighting, amenities and terrace façades and I say so. Tony has no time for anyone. "It's a ghost town," he says in broad Geordie. "They've killed it, man. Used to be proud of it. Now kids vandalise it, the bairns need it." With that he jumps into his Ford Mondeo and is off. Who, I ask myself, is he angry with?

Then I find Mary. She had lost her father John and her brother Billy in the disaster, the only family to lose two of its menfolk. Billy at 28 was called in specially to join his fifty-seven year old father on the fore-shift at 3.30am. Her older brother George also had died at sea in the War. Mary stands square in the living room, at peace and at home now with grief. Her son is fitting a new PVC window upstairs and she is helping him. Outside, the front yard is planted up, a pleasure to see – tidy, clean and cared for. How true, 'that it is not what happens to us but how we respond to what happens to us that really matters,' as someone has said. Mary speaks simply and sincerely, "Almighty God has given me a cross and I'll bear it. Just give me twelve more years." I do not delay further to ask her meaning but look over the wall as I leave, at the heap of chaos and neglect next door. Mighty strange or is it? That is where Tom lives.

Tom, Tony and Mary have all experienced grief differently, a grief that was uniquely their own, deep and very personal, as did Heather and I, and Sallyanne. Grief isolates. Indeed, no one else *can* know how I feel. A stricken individual needs time to lament, to protest, to keen and to bleed, as only he can do. A person will do this instinctively, as he or she has been taught to handle loss from the very earliest of years. If that means affirming and expressing feelings with others, like sobbing and hugging, that certainly will help. Otherwise, he or she may have to find different ways of externalising grief, like compulsive talking or activity for, as I have found, silence and inertia do not take a grieving person very far.

However isolating it feels to experience grief, it is in fact rarely solitary. A small group, a family, a church or a community can bear and share grief *together*. At many different levels "no man is an island" and here lies the value of ritual, symbol and anniversaries. They help us bear and share grief together, expressing things that are almost too deep for words. Eighty-three trees were planted in a special park the other side of Easington. They are growing and expanding into each other. Grief is a rich source of compost for those who want to grow not only strong roots but also branches that reach out and touch others.

Can I presume to know how I would respond to such a cataclysm? Before I leave I return to the desolate scar on which had once stood one of Europe's most productive collieries. To my surprise, lorries are carrying loads of infill. I speak to the man in charge of directing the vehicles. For a few moments we are alone and it is quiet. Then, suddenly, his intercom splutters into life. A voice crackles, "Mike, do you want more smack?" Mike doesn't answer but carries on talking. "Will another thousand do you?" Mike, embarrassed, growls, "Not now!" and switches it off. Another lorry comes and a furtive exchange takes place. A new scourge is filling the cynicism born in this blasted patch.

By now I am way behind and eventually sit shivering in the dark on the steps of Seaham Parish Church. Veronica, a distant cousin, collects me from Gosforth and drops me back next day, a distance she travels four times to help me. John is Managing Director to four companies. He wants his managers to attempt more even if they fail more. "Just remember," he says, "anyone can make an honest mistake, but there's no such thing as an honest cover-up." His exuberance is tangible. In the morning the family shows a refreshing 'hands on' approach and leaves in a flurry of well-wishing. It is not easy to forget my encounters the previous day and within half a mile there stands a reminder on the cliff top, a spectacular sculpture in stainless steel of a coal-cutting machine.

Clearly no one is expected to arrive in Sunderland via its southern coast. It is derelict and dangerous with metal protruding everywhere. Even the railway has retreated inland and I am left high on a deserted embankment of grit-stone blocks, capped with patches of brick, rubble and concrete. I stub and jolt my way to the end and jump six to eight feet down onto a pile of scrap metal. I scrabble further down and into a stream of dusty high-wheeled lorries heading for the port security gates and there receive a kindly ticking off. This is Wearmouth. It gets better, I think, with new dockside developments in ice-cream colours. Port cranes rear up on high thick back legs to applaud the towering mighty Bridge itself. A Brunelian structure, it flings its mighty weight into the task of stapling together the north and south banks of Sunderland-on-the-Wear.

Monkwearmouth honours the Saxon Church of St Peter and the monastery of the Venerable Bede. Bede first advanced the notion of "England" as a united nation, "an island in the ocean". He became the most learned European man of his time and was described as "a new sun in the West to illumine the whole world". I leave behind Sunderland University and climb over the glass roof of the National Glass Centre nearby. In that moment a huge rainbow spans the entire maritime horizon by 180 degrees. There are only seven or eight rainbow colours visible to the human eye, only a very slender sample of multicoloured reality. One old lady, who returned from a near death experience, described with shining eyes how she could see at least two hundred shades of orange. I feel a bit like God looking down through the thick glass, watching the men and women at work below. My thoughts are no longer of the pit of coal but of the pot of gold, the inheritance promised the Christian, kept unfading in heaven, where now live more members of my family than there are in Cheltenham.

Uncluttered level grass headlands are a feature of the coast between Wear and Tyne. In the distance some fulmars and puffins still linger on Marsden Rock. A solo cormorant patrols the inshore rollers and, round a cliff-top bench, goldfinches and linnets are hoovering up picnic crumbs. There, "In loving memory," is carved "Jack Souter and his Mam, Dad and Sisters." Ahead is the Souter Lighthouse and by it Mike Simpson, the warden, working on another replica bench for the cliff-top.

On the beach is magnesium limestone, quarried since Roman times. In the 1780s an old miner, Jack the Blaster, worked these cliffs and tended the limekilns, living in a cave with his family. In 1820 his 'home' was developed into a pub and now Nick and Sue Garvey have thrown themselves into *The Grotto,* a top quality three-decker restaurant and rendezvous for those who want something different. As I ascended the lift shaft to the surface, I stare at the beauty of sunlit stacks and cliffs on Marsden Point; the famous arch had just recently fallen. I echo the words inscribed near the entrance, "FEAR GOD AND GIVE HIM THE GLORY".

No more delays. I set a blistering pace round the South Shields promenade, past *The Rattler,* three railway carriages wrapped round a clock tower, and Dolly Peel, a bronze statue of a local fish-wife, heroine-cum-brandy smuggler, who epitomises the independent spirit of the Geordie. I am welcomed off the ferry and spend a lovely evening with Luke and Jo, both doctors and their two delightful children in Tynemouth.

I stop by some families and join in looking for crabs among the seaweed. I photograph an empty playground against a backdrop of Blyth's nine whirring wonders. Strung out the length of the East Pier, mighty wind turbines pierce straight down through seven metres of bedrock. Along with two giant size versions offshore, these provide enough power for nearly four thousand households. The coastline of Northumberland is going to be different, but not quite yet.

Blythe's long curving jetty completes a strategic deep-water harbour for freight ferries and the import of vast quantities of bauxite. This ore feeds into huge silos for the Alcan smelters, which, with the flux cryolite, yields precious aluminium for a thousand uses, from aircraft and satellite technology to cans and kitchen foil. Just north, the Cambois Power Station will soon reach the end of its life and Cambois, short of cryogenics, will surely follow. The village now is one little ribbon of terraced housing, including a church and a Miners' Welfare centre. Colin and Jock are stand-ins for a bygone era and the corner shop has only room to stock chocolate. A tub of coal is all that marks the yawning windswept space beyond, sitting sad on six feet of rail with colts-foot for company. Over a hundred years, 1,141 men worked here to produce 28,000 tons of coal a year. Mines in this shrunken landscape once injected life into the great industrial arteries of the North-East. Now signs of life concentrate on Lynemouth to the north, where open cast mining is sufficient to keep Alcan in business and bread on the table for over six hundred families. The company is passionate about supporting local people, their schools and farming and even has time to give me a ten-pound note.

For a couple of hours I have peace and quiet. I dip down to the fishermen's huts at the Wansbeck outflow. The only boat has its motor in pieces. I sigh and have to detour inland and back to get to the Newbiggin Bay. Its impressive sweep, lit up by the evening sun, takes the eye to St Bartholomew's, whose graveyard is vandalised by the sea, where bones are washed up on the tide. Black bollards have red painted puffin heads crafted on them. But coal dominates this day.

I have seen several coal outcrops in the cliffs and gypsies collecting black bits off the beach. Now I just want to reach Lynemouth before hitchhiking inland to Stannington for my weekend stopover. The light is failing as I stride over a golf course and north along the beach. In front a huge unshapely black mound has possessed the beach. The tide is up and the edge has gone. I take a time exposure of this ghastly spoliation and turn inland, determined to face its perpetrator. I discover a hole in the Company perimeter fence and find myself in a tangle of endless black tips and labyrinthine conveyor belts. By now everything is black – above, below and sideways. I can barely see my feet and soon lose all sense of direction. I persevere for perhaps a mile, constantly blocked and baffled by this weird world of looming shapes, until I see a faint light in the distance. It is the guardhouse. No worries! I am bathed, disarmingly, in goodwill, offered tea and helped onto the road.

I raise my rucksack, with its reflective strip stuck round the base, and wave it at several sets of headlights. A battered mobile caravan pulls up and I am squashed into the front passenger seat, already occupied by son and mum alongside 'Mick', dad and driver. From the rear jostle at least another five or six heads eager to get a better view of their latest visitor. Mum, pale and evidently under strain, introduces me to them all, kindly, one by one. Three have serious health problems, two life threatening, and the others, slightly awed, are obviously a very mischievous bunch. Apparently they all live in this vehicle under the Newcastle Bridge, waiting to be housed by the Council. There is never hope of a smooth bedtime routine. So their standard practice is to take themselves off for a very long drive, until all are exhausted and ready to head for 'home' in Newcastle. They have every excuse to pass me by but these generous and loving parents find time to take me all the way to the Stannington village petrol station. My eyes are misty as mum still tense, dad still joking and everyone waving, they roar off, probably untaxed and uninsured, into the night, their night and nightmare.

Cosy in bed, I recognise the Parable of the Good Samaritan in a different light. The man robbed and mugged was probably rich. The Samaritan was probably poor, certainly an outcast and despised socially. He probably needed help himself but found time to be 'good'. Mick stopped to help and give of his precious resources and I was privileged to receive of his goodness. I think of Diana of Wales, a bit of an outcast who identified with outcasts. A victim who refused to play that card, who chose to give of herself to Aids patients, land-mine amputees, dying children, battered wives and homeless families. As lover of the loveless and champion of the underclass, she struck a chord in so many people, on the day the world stood still.

Chapter 19

The Northumbrian Coastline

THE SECRET KINGDOM — OPEN TO CALLERS

I AM HALFWAY DOWN THE STAIRS, GOING TO BREAKFAST. It is Sunday morning, August 31st, 1997, in Whitby. Jack Cooper's upturned face appears through the banisters, "Diana is dead," he says, "Princess Di is dead. Car accident in Paris." Everything in me stops. It seems inconceivable. Dumb and numb I gaze blankly at the TV screen only half believing the sketchy reports. There must be a mistake, somewhere, somehow.

I am away late and walk only half concentrating. By Tuesday and Wednesday I can see little bundles of flowers appearing by church doors, outside council offices, on market crosses and in front of war memorials. Candles appear here and there in windows, with favourite photos stuck to the glass. Upset and realising the nation's grief, I begin to feel increasingly cut off. By Thursday I know what I need when I find myself ahead of schedule. I ring Robin and Marion. "Yes, that's fine! Come on Friday instead of Saturday." At about 9p.m. I am picked up from the Stannington petrol station. A light meal and Horlicks and I am ready for bed. Then I learn that the Luscombes will be out all next day and, yes, it will be all right to have the telly on and watch the funeral, a wonderful chance to be involved. It seems perfect.

Clearly something in Diana has touched me, as others across the nation, and each flower each candle I see is a very personal response. Each offering is an unspoken connection: 'Diana, you held the broken-hearted, I want to hold you. You felt grief and sorrow and hurt and you cared. I care too. You were scorned and humiliated, you were wounded and now you have been killed. I will miss you.' In hamlet, village and town the floral tributes continue to grow and spread down any suitable flight of steps. Inside, queues form for people to write down their thoughts that link their names with a lost 'Queen' and friend.

In the Luscombes' lounge on Saturday morning I weep for myself, for the years, for the Princess, for her children and for my own children. Without embarrassment, hot scorching tears are rolling down my face as I see the hearse disappear under a continuous hailstorm of flowers, 'the People's wreath'. Here is someone who knew the language of love, who thought with the heart and spoke with the eyes, now no more.

I know something bad has happened in this tragedy, yet here I see a national outpouring of goodness. It seems cleansing, natural – and nothing official, planned or prepared by the clergy. It may well prove to be the affirmation of a new emotional self-confidence right across the country. I make a resolve within to be more giving of my honest self. I have long since known of the Secret Kingdom, the Messianic Kingdom Jesus had to conceal at the beginning of his ministry, a Kingdom of meekness and powerlessness that continues within his followers, one of openness and honesty and self-giving. I long since have realised that the use of rank or clout, the pretension of lofty principles, the claims of unfailing service all fail to reach hurting people like a simple honest admission of frailty. I feel that Diana somehow threw off the shackles of status and the entrapments of wealth. She put *herself* at the disposal of the dispossessed. Now she has overcome by being defeated and would somehow live on despite her death. Can things ever be quite the same? Perhaps

Diana's death has encouraged us into a new way of being human.

This morning a beautiful sky beckons me to the coast, to Cresswell. 'The industrial North East' with Alcan and its bleak black beach is behind me. I step north through a Narnian wardrobe of freshness into a secret kingdom, into a pristine landscape, six miles of Druridge Bay, sixteen miles of National Trust property and sixty miles to the border, the whole coastline an Area of Outstanding Natural Beauty. The ancient Kingdom of Northumbria seems to have a secret, because English Heritage does keep going on about fascinating history and fifteen castles and forgets to mention the vast sculpted bays of sand as good as any in the Caribbean. The sea is a trifle chilly, but the beauty and breadth of this sandscape, between sheltered light green dunes at the high tide mark and vivid green platforms of seaweed at the low tide mark, hallow a place only to take photographs and only to leave footprints. All morning I only meet a man, a woman and a dog and, at mid-day, a redundant personnel officer carrying a plastic bag of coal. They become specks before disappearing.

At Amble the open market spills handbags, shirts, games and belts all over the quayside. I sit in the Chandler and enjoy fish and chips along with two well-coiffed ladies sipping tea. Outside, Kevin beefs about the shrinking fish business. Amble has only eighteen trawlers and fifteen cobles. Outside the twelve-mile limit Danish factory ships are scooping up everything in small mesh nets, illegal in the UK. On the other hand, if he lands more than MAFF allows, it has to be dyed blue and wasted, good quality cod. He then tells me he is building his own boat for £80,000 and looking to buy 'a track record' (the right to fish) that could cost £100,000. I make sympathetic noises and try not to look at the marina full of expensive boats. I see the Teleflorist sign and send a bouquet to Heather.

Via Warkworth castle I soon retrieve my solitude at Alnmouth Bay. The Aln is uncrossable. The river changed course in one dramatic night and bequeathed a wildlife sanctuary. Today it is dotted with dotterel and ringed with plover, lapwing and sanderling all in a feeding frenzy for colder times to come. I hesitate at Waterside Farm. At first it looks deserted. Wendy has a 'Yes' face, dark hair and an easy smile. She loves cycling, swimming and tennis with her elder daughter Sarah and helps Emma, who is into Bugsy Malone, with lessons on flute and piano. I warmed to her and her energetic father-in-law, kindred spirits who always say 'Yes' unless there's good reason to say 'No'. I leave with some bread and milk and hot water in my flask, and profuse thanks.

St Cuthbert, in the sixth century, had much less than that to keep himself alive, apparently just a few onions. He lived as a hermit on a small island, after ten years as Prior on Holy Island. The Alnmouth Synod had elected him bishop, but only after the King rowed out to persuade him did he concede and become Bishop of Lindisfarne. The Vikings plundered Alnmouth, the Picts burnt it down and the Plague ravaged its people. John Wesley judged it "famous for wickedness" and Hitler thought it worth a stick of bombs. But all is not told. This evening proves unforgettable. I climb up on to an undulating golf course aiming for the cliff edge. The sun slips from sight and unfolding before me, as if I was centre stage, is a riveting celestial sequence of Imax proportions, sheer glory. The whole sky, a fan of cirro-cumulus, begins to ignite as if lit by a moving bonfire. From end to end pink is turning to crimson and then flaming vermilion red. Set above a distant skyline of pine trees, heaven is on fire, a furnace of roaring colour. Awed and hushed by the experience I linger for photographs. At the fifth tee the sight and the light are nearly gone. I make a meal inside a little golf hut, slip into my bivi-tent, set my watch for an early departure and close my eyes to dwell again on the orange world above, to experience again what my friend had told me about, those two hundred shades of orange.

It seems a shame that my camera has malfunctioned for this latter third of my Walk. Nearly all the pictures I take prove to be out of focus. And yet this section is 'my future' and I am happy with the notion that I am not allowed to see too clearly those things yet in store for me. At least two good things I take along with me. One, my stiff upper lip, because I feel as tough and as strong as ever. The other a tremble in my lower lip, which I no longer need to hide. It is all right to be hurt. I shall not mind too much if I am used and will try to accept as gone those things that I lose, including those things I never have had, but have dreamed about. I hope with time will come a new confidence to live without self-pity or resentment. Tomorrow I'm tested.

Cobles are still made at Boulmer. Several on the grass had a Viking look with high prows and quite low midships. Rumbling Kern is especially beautiful, where the sea gurgles up internal gullies. High on the cliff I stick to the literal edge and come across Howick Bathing House. Astride the path, seated on a blue bucket, is a man in an orange jumper and a white hat sketching the cottage. He takes me in to meet his wife and their friends. Charles is an eminent plastic surgeon in Florida, specialising in the facial reconstruction of soldiers injured in Vietnam. He loves the house, blasted by the wind, patronised by politicians and now visited in his eyes by Phineas Fogg. Allowing for Yankee extravagance, I do indeed have a weather-beaten luxuriance and that probably inspires the largest mug of tea so far on the walk. Later he sends the painted sketch to Sallyanne with whimsical references to my arrival and departure, "clothed with radiant physical and moral force" and a letter to me, which begins, "Your Reverence". I thought he was 'taking the micky', but he continues in ever more Chaucerian hyperbole about my noble and doughty purpose and encloses photos of my disappearance over the hill, beneath Northumbrian storm clouds, "neither daunted nor deterred, a veritable paradigm of the pilgrim " on my final fifty miles. "Come and see us!" signs Charles Edward Moore M.D., Florida. It is a heart-warming, dotty and delightful episode.

Craster and the Kipper Trail are next. I imagine old wooden huts with smoke filtering out through cracks. In fact the four well-built local stone smoking rooms of Robson and

Co. are 140 years old. Plump, oily herrings are selected, salted and impaled on tenterhooks, which are hung like bats from the roof, 4,000 at a time. It takes sixteen hours to cure the fish and five or six rekindlings of the oaken fires to ensure satisfaction. Alan Robson's face shines with a happy pride. He is a real craftsman with his tools. Everything is in its place. He played football until fifty-four and has long since been President of the local club. He is also the Harbourmaster and takes dues from leisure and fishing vessels to maintain the massive twin piers. The seaward extremities of the harbour used to sport a powerful crane, hopper and engine house to export road-chips quarried from the whinstone outcrop nearby. So you could say he started the first successful fish and chip business. Most of the kippers go to Waitrose stores, and some of course come to me.

Northumbrian clouds have indeed threatened all day and suddenly the lightning cracks like a whip. The storm breaks in dense sheets of rain. I shelter in an old harbour limekiln and talk with an inshore lobster fisherman. He works non-stop round the tides, except in the winter. He patrols ten thirty-pot 'fleets' and returns with about thirty crustaceans at a time. He complains that octopuses eat the bait and seals eat the lobsters, so he gets what is left at £3.50p each. I slip into *Sea Breeze*, the Beadnell General Store and buy a Magnum choc-ice to lift my spirits, which is just as well, as that night I face disastrous accommodation and will finish up 'a right charlie'.

Sometimes I get it wrong. I plan to visit the Farne Islands. It does seem important to get the right B&B if I am staying two nights. I pass several possibilities that do not seem right and after taking advice, walk the entire length of Seahouses chasing three other suggestions, none of which I can even find. On the way, I stop off and enjoy really the very best of British fish and chips at Lewis' restaurant. I backtrack to a guest house that has not been recommended. The room is primitive. The bed is bowed and there is absolutely no concession to comfort. The price, which I accept, is more than I have paid anywhere on the whole trip.

Next morning, it becomes obvious the proprietor, doubling as waiter while his wife cooks, simply has not grasped the basics. I resolve that another night just has to be at a reduced rate, in other words, a rate for two. I am alone in the dining room and raise the subject with Alan. But he is adamant. I point out, in as pleasant a manner as I can muster, that I have had some experience and the room is the least congenial and the most expensive of my entire journey thus far. "No!" he says. "Two nights means twice the rate." By this time I have made a number of discoveries. First, I have found a leathery skin under the egg. Second, the bacon is too tough to cut. Third, one of the sausages sports tissue wrapped round it and, finally, there is a four-inch hair hanging out of the marmalade dish. At any rate, I reckon I am on the home straight and imply these are gold-star grounds for a negotiated two-night deal. "Are you criticising me?" he shouts. "That's fair. Yes I am!" Before I can suggest that criticism from a client is possibly as valuable as his money, seeing as most people say nothing and do not return, he simply roars at me, "Well, you can b***** off right now," in classical Geordie tones. Just then his wife comes in embarrassed and concerned. Undeterred he gives his final ultimatum. "Go on!" he yells, "Get out!" I put on my boots, hoist my gear and make as if to leave. "Oi!" he says, "Here's your bill." Taunting him, I reply "I thought you said I was to b***** off?" He threatens to call the police so I decide not to push my luck and pay up. This is only his second season, after leaving Newcastle, trying his hand at holiday catering.

I have no idea whether the enduring value of that encounter is intended for me or for him. Perhaps I do not need to know. Certainly my intuition has not served me well on this occasion. I am left with a huge ambivalence about my behaviour and attitudes. The Farne Island trip is a splendid distraction and only takes a morning. In and out of a really excellent Heritage centre for marine life and fishing, I am soon heading in the direction of Budle Bay.

Violent behaviour is written into the wild and wilful history of Northumbria. It was the most powerful kingdom in Britain with its twin capitals at Bamburgh and York. It stretched from the East Coast to the Irish Sea and from the Firth of Forth to Humberside. It claimed the capital of England and was the home of a succession of kings and queens in a period that followed the departure of the Romans and presaged the arrival of the Normans. It had to fight the Picts, the Scots and the Vikings, all intent on opportunistic conquest. It had to face the pirate fleets of the Angles from 'Denmark' and then the Saxon raiders from 'Germany'. Worst of all, having allied themselves with the latter, the Britons then fell out among themselves. So began battle and bloodshed, mayhem and murder, torture and treachery on a monumental scale and so much of it was centred round Bamburgh.

On the whole Northumbria is a gentle Carboniferous limestone coast. Through it, however, volcanic igneous basalt stands proud in the great Whin Sill. It forms the coast at Craster and the cliffs at Dunstanburgh. The castle there built in Norman times gives me the creeps. Now a ruin, its gatehouse, a Norman keep, jabs the skyline like two broken molars. I am glad to leave.

The Whin Sill at Bamburgh disappears out at sea in a tangle of twenty-eight tiny treeless islands, the largest of which, Inner Farne, was home at the end for St Cuthbert and still is home to hundreds of breeding puffins, guillemots and razorbills. I can see the famed Longstone Lighthouse, a dramatic setting for courage and rescue on the stormy night of 7th September 1838. The steamship *Forfarshire* lost its engines and broke in two on Big Harcar Island. Forty-three were drowned and eighteen clung to wreckage until saved, largely by the efforts of the Lighthouse keeper and his doughty daughter. In the darkness of a terrific storm and through terrible seas they rowed a twenty-foot coble from the lighthouse to rescue the survivors on the rocks. Grace Darling was a heroine at twenty-two. Slight and frail she was honoured throughout the land. Three years later she had died of tuberculosis. The boat is the centrepiece of a cottage and a collection of artefacts to her memory in Bamburgh. The church nearby is a wonderful place to remember all the Celtic saints and people of this turbulent time in our history.

Above the frailty and feminine simplicity of Grace Darling in her humble cottage tower the gigantic proportions of Bamburgh Castle. It sits high, on one hundred and fifty feet of red basalt, dominating the view for miles around, a counter-poise of masculine pride and greed. I find it intimidating and before moving on I try to cram it all into one photograph. Making adjustments amid sand dunes I carefully place my binoculars in a clump of marram grass.

A few miles further on I am soon in Budle Bay. I knock on the door of an unpretentious, rather run-down cottage for water and a little bread. The door opens just enough to release an inelegant rebuttal from a rather upper-crusty Mrs Cruddis. Round the back, Flora and Trevor welcome me into their caravan and next door I meet Jim, Ken and Joan, magnificent, generous people. I have left them only a while, when I remember, yes, the precious binoculars. I pitch in a field over-looking the bay, so grateful later to have retrieved my glasses unharmed, after a further four miles on my day. I have not lost one item of kit in nearly two thousand miles. (My camera was returned). But, oh, my legs! Tomorrow, DV, I would reach the border.

"Deo volente" is easy to say, but twice in one day, "God willing", I have been rebuffed. I need to pause and take stock. Sure! I was tired out last night and only too ready to find fault this morning. But what was I supposed to do? Relish the hair in the marmalade or use it to floss my teeth, then smile through them and pay up? I was being over-charged *and* for that matter, Mrs Cruddis, I don't like doors shut on me. Maybe I'm getting fed up and a bit blasé with only a few days to go. I think injured pride is my real problem.

Frankly, I am easily hurt and more sensitive than I used to be. Counting up to ten might have just given me crucial time to realise that Alan could not *make* me feel hurt. If I'm hurt that's *my* problem and *my* reaction and it's probably my memories that are getting in the way. In which case I could have paused and said to myself, "He's hurt too". I could have got up and gone over to him and said, "I'm sorry to criticise." In a clash both parties have a handle and both need a chance to disengage their end. In kindly language I might have said, quietly and with gentleness, "You do seem hurt and upset, Alan, I'm so sorry. I'm sure Elizabeth has done her best with the breakfast", and perhaps a door into his world might have swung open. I would have heard his story and what it has been like settling into a new way of life. I might have solved the puzzle behind his intemperate outburst. I tell myself again, "solve the puzzle first, then sort the problem and then perhaps you can salvage the relationship". If I had trusted and relaxed, He would have worked it all out for good. Surely that's the Secret. Maybe it was meant for our learning. Besides, I did not need two nights in Seahouses.

So I press on, forgetting those things that are 'behind', except that they trail behind me for a while until I forgive myself in the warm sunshine of His Love. Like the kinked wire and electric buzzer of the fairground challenge, pain forces me to return to the centre of my Hope and Strength and I feel a surge of optimism. I sense the key to this enterprise has been at least forty loyal people who have prayed for me all the way round. I have been the manager of this ambling odyssey. Yet throughout, He seems to have been in charge. Again and again and again, I have synchronised with someone in the right place at the right time, as indeed on cue, it was soon, amazingly, yet to happen again.

I am travelling round Budle Bay with the decision that as soon as I am about level with the Castle on Holy Island, I will turn inland and hitch-hike to the Border. I will then walk back to the Island, ten miles down the coast, from the north so as not to travel that distance twice. At Easington railway crossing, the A1 comes temptingly close. I can see the traffic. Instead I stick to the Edge, determined to cut no corners. I reach Elwick and beyond and gradually the distant Castle comes level with me on my right and the road conveniently curves gently away to the left. “Just right!” I say and quicken my pace. But who’s that in the middle distance, someone just standing there, legs apart and motionless? “I recognised the purposeful stride of someone for whom walking had become a way of life,” he later wrote to me. It was Arthur Wood surveying paths and constructing a map for The Ramblers’ Association local branch. “I recognised that habit of looking away to the horizon,” he continued in his letter, “and I was interested to find out where you had come from.” Little did he know that, continually glancing up at the castle, I was judging the moment to quit and catch a lift! Well, there it was, laid on and waiting for me.

Chapter 20

The Scottish Border to Lindisfarne

AT LAST – OVER THE EDGE …

TO BE HONEST, AFTER FIVE MONTHS WALKING THE EDGE of England, I cannot wait to get off. I do not mean escape, come back to safety, back to the centre, back to my comfort zones. No! Not at all! I mean, step off the edge the other side. Turn right instead of left, drop over, leave for good, pop my clogs or better my boots. My last day on planet earth will be the greatest day of my life. I shall not be alone. I shall be met and mobbed. I shall be blissfully happy. I shall be fit and totally healthy in a body capped by a full head of hair. I shall know myself accepted, loved and full of joy. I shall be free and yet held spellbound, captivated by the desire to honour, worship and serve the source of my life and happiness.

If caught in a disaster, in the course of my journey, I knew I would never be 'lost', only found. In a pickle, I knew I could never 'perish', just bloom. If it all suddenly ended, I knew that I was not 'finished' but just beginning to experience what the Bible describes as "the inheritance that can never perish, spoil or fade, *kept in heaven* for you" (1 Peter 1:4). That is the Promise and it seems presumption not to believe it. If that is true then the *real* thing is yet to be. Here we can only experiment with life, using limited resources in an unsatisfactory anteroom bounded by space and time. Here we can only blunder about, doing our best with tools we have, heroically no doubt but with clear terrestrial limits to the damage we can do and the progress we can achieve. I have heard it said, "life is for living, it's not a rehearsal!" But perhaps it *is,* just that, exactly that, a place to make our mistakes and acquire our wisdom, so that we shall not mess it all up for others when we move into the real thing. Soon enough the call will come for us to move from the outhouse to the main building. There we shall learn to travel in many dimensions with nothing but the confines of love, to work in many creative ways within only the constraints of service, and to worship happily, naturally and thankfully, in the embrace of His joyful acceptance.

Over these last five months, I have recognised parallel truth, that the landscape of this world with its cliffs and holes, its mountains and valleys, is indeed a metaphor for our passage through and into the next. Furthermore, I am beginning to see that I have only been watching the trailer and now the curtains to the main picture are about to open. My excitement is rising. The paradigm is soon to be over. I have to face the miles of shifting sand across to the "holy island" called Lindisfarne, the transition from the mainland to the Island, or rather from the island to the Mainland through the decompression chamber called death, a junction not a terminus on the way. I know that this Way is back-lit by glory and that the contours and colours of this old world quickly surrender to shadow as I will discover myself known, loved and taken onwards. The transition beckons. Like the dragon-fly nymph, I will soon look up expectantly and transformed I will "*... fly*", as David Adams the Vicar of Lindisfarne wrote for me in the flyleaf of his book.

First, I come to the end of England and catch a glimpse of Scotland. Imagine my excitement as I approach the Border, after 2,000 miles. I can feel the prickles down the back of my neck and spine as Arthur Wood pulls up in a lay-by. A large rectangular sandstone plinth says 'SCOTLAND'. I know, now, what it is like to feel English. I have planted my feet all round the edge. I have paced it and measured it with my legs. I have scrambled and slipped and slept on it. I have seen it, felt it and smelt it. I have a metal shield of St George on my stick and a shy little Union Jack stuck to my sack. I feel glad. My daughter Elizabeth was involved making the largest Union Jack ever. It took thirty people to hold it in the wind, about thirty feet high and sixty feet wide. It broke into the *Guinness Book of Records*. My Englishness is a gift to be proud of. Today I claim it and own it and appreciate it. It is not xenophobic but inclusive. It is essentially fair, hospitable and generous at the margins. It spreads itself easily and exports itself to far corners but here for me it defines itself, on the Edge.

I stand tall and we swap photos. Arthur treats me to the best in Berwick and eventually drops me off in Burnmouth, six miles inside tartan land. I celebrate at '*the First Inn in Scotland*', with wine and smoked haddock. In a discreet nook all to myself, I lean back in my chair and think back over the day. It is such an extraordinary and fitting privilege to have met Arthur. What a gracious moment out of the blue, to be welcomed and feted by a regional chairman of the Ramblers Association! Delicious serendipity, it has to be the hand of the Master. Call it what you will, for me it is just one of sixty or seventy moments of encounter with mystery. It has become a familiar, though never predictable, aspect of this celebratory walk; something that no amount of human engineering could ever have achieved. I look back with awe. I started out on the very same date as the Archbishop's pilgrimage across the United Kingdom. I arrived in Lyme Regis on the very day of my birthday. I jumped off the Solent Ferry just as the "*Canberra*" was leaving on its last-but-one voyage before the wrecking and breaking on a Pakistan beach. I knocked on the doors of a grieving father, Chris and double-grieving grandparents, Rod and Viv. I was in Jack's house, of all houses, when Princess Diana died and I found myself a whole day ahead a week later, to spend Saturday with the telly in an empty home in Stannington. Today of all days Arthur is placed in just the right spot. Tonight of all nights I arrive in Scotland and tomorrow the Scottish people vote for Devolution. The Walk has been a mosaic of meaningful and amazing moments, occasions when blessings were given and received with startling precision. What alternative is there to guidance by prayer and grace? Arbitrariness?

My presence in the bar triggers a slightly intemperate debate with a drunken Scot, but I feel welcome. Jack and Hilda Johnson nearby with their granddaughter are genuine and open people. He has dug a hole in his lounge floor to get to his lobster creels in the cellar, so great is his fascination for fishing. Until, one night, a local lad stole all his fishing gear and today he still refuses to name the culprit. Large-heartedness and generosity are to him more important.

Inclusive too is my name. It starts with a Scottish clan 'Graham' and ends of course in Wales. Sandwiched between is a common English name, Fred, actually Saxon-European in origin. Today the Scots are voting for Devolution and the polling booth policeman offers to escort me over the Border. I murmur something about ethnic cleansing and choose instead to walk beside the railway track heading for King's Cross. A path emerges and a sign, discarded in the grass, says: "Haste ye back to Scotland".

Berwick-upon-Tweed is the most complete walled city in Europe. I can understand its massive Elizabethan ramparts. It has changed sides, north and south of the border, thirteen times in its history. A major commercial centre for the Lowlands, it became an impoverished fortress and today has only 12,000 people in the borough. For three hundred years it proclaimed itself 'a neutral and independent state, in' (but not within) the 'Kingdom of England'. Indeed, it negotiated a treaty with Tsarist Russia. I am feeling conciliatory and in no mood for feuding and rieving, so I do the obvious thing. I buy a bag of their famous pies and cakes and head for *The Sanctuary,* housed in the old military stables.

Before entering a special flotation room I am photographed, front back and sides, to see how my frame has been changed by the Walk. Some family snapshots over the years have become very important to us, not just as *aides mémoire,* but as capsules of truth, without which memories would long since have left us stranded. Our pictures are collated in nearly forty scrapbooks of living history, that act as touchstones for talking, triggers for healing and means with which to go back, to let go and to move on. Sallyanne tells me that if the house were on fire, these would be the only things she would try to save. They serve as an *entrée* into essential threads of meaning that help her to know who she is. I understand that in moments of near death or experiences of utmost extremity, sometimes our whole life is allowed to flash before us, as in instant video replay, to help us see ourselves whole and evaluate what is still left to come. For me now the show is nearly over. My last night has come. I feel at peace.

I sink my tired body into the Sanctuary's special bath and feel all round the nurturing presence of Christ, in whom 'I live and move and have my being'. It is a salt flotation bath, the ultimate in disconnection. The room is soundproof and very dimly lit. Soft music gently suffuses the atmosphere and the salt water, more dense than the Dead Sea, keeps me only half submerged. The water at skin temperature is unnoticed. The tank neutralises the effects of gravity and gives my head a holiday. There is nothing the brain needs to do. There is no reason to reason. I drift off, joyful and serene.

The weather is bright, too bright. There is a mixed forecast. I choose the oldest of Berwick's four bridges and follow the Tweed estuary to Spittal. At last I reach the sea, now on my left hand. I am so glad. I remember windsurfing into the sunset, across the harbour at Tauranga, NZ. I remember we dropped Elizabeth's ashes into the water at Mount Maunganui and they swirled round Sallyanne's legs. Today I am going to face and brave the sea, if I get there in time to cross the sands. My destination is the holiest of islands, Lindisfarne, separated from the mainland twice diurnally by the incoming tide and offering just a few hours this afternoon in which to pass over safely.

My journey is nearly over and my story complete. The Irish man said to the traveller seeking guidance, "If I were you I wouldn't start from here." Truly, we have no choice where we are born and little more when or where we are going to die. Does it matter that much? The world is as transitional as the womb, for death is no terminus. It is a junction on the way into a wider and even more wonderful world. For me it is as if my first three children skipped a bit, jumped ahead and left me to walk the long way round. So I am keen to finish this stretch and catch them up. It has been an odyssey of adventure and hazard, of exhilaration, tiredness and sometimes frustration. There have been maritime moments of madness and encounters so crystal clear they seemed touched with the miraculous. Now I yearn to complete this part of the trail and, like Odysseus, more and more I am seeking the love of my heart and the solace of home.

Sallyanne pulled a face when her bedroom pictures came down and her world collapsed into packing cases for New Zealand. Until, that is, she came to realise that 'home' is where you are loved, indeed, that home *is* love, that *his love is our home* and like the snail we take it with us wherever we go. Elizabeth took ET as her favourite soft toy. She saw the film several times for the love of home is its enduring passion. Except, for us humans, we do not 'go home'. We are taken home. It is homecoming. Celebration is in the air and already three telegrams await my arrival on Holy Island.

A few days before my father's farewell at 98, we had communion together with Bristol Cream sherry. Sixty minutes before his homecall, sitting up and alert in bed, we opened a bottle of champagne. My father's eyes lit up and his face glowed with excitement. Tom listened to the scriptures about the welcome in store for believers, about the feasting and fellowship yet to be. Tom heard our prayers and slightly tearful toast to good health at last, to happiness, healing and wholeness in travelling on. He knew with whom he travelled and sipped the Asti Spumante with eagerness and delight, anticipating all that was awaiting him, his crippled, physical self at last to be left behind and his true body, mind and spirit gloriously intact. Across his face would soon be the stupefaction and incredulity that was written all over the face of

Rachel, at the gift of a renewed life, the experience that straightened her shoulders and brought colour back into her cheeks.

After a short sharp shower in Spittal, the path ahead is beginning to peter out. Initially, there are wildly folded strata, now the edge is just crumbling. I must leave it soon. I am walking the margins and find myself strangely comfortable, an edge person among a dwindling few human beings still walking the edge. Perhaps if I could have my youth back my Father would now counsel me, unlike my earthly father, 'Graham, will you please go on to the Edge, stay there and never leave it.' Does He ask me yet to help others go there and be there among people who have been pushed out, knocked out or who have pulled out, among those who have dropped out, fallen out, or just plain preferred-to-be-out rather than in? Because margins do not last. People do fall over and sometimes they jump. Better by far, margins are to be thresholds for new starts altogether. The Christian's call is to help people onwards and sometimes over, from the end of one world into the beginning of another.

Sure enough, the grass, the dunes, and a hard-packed six-mile sandy introduction are leading me inexorably into an unstable region of shifting ends and tidal new beginnings. Nearby is the first of the ancient poles. These high slender stalks set out across the Bay to infinity, about one hundred and thirty, spaced at twenty-eight yard intervals to keep the traveller away from quicksand. The distance is about four miles. It will take me at least an hour and a half to complete the danger zone, two hours to the Marygate Community where the staff will be waiting. The sea is advancing. The strict times are posted, clear in bold black print. The window of safety is stark and unyielding. It beckons and warns. It is now gone. I must go.

I have not noticed until now, the oystercatchers are strangely quiet. A swan stands immobilised in a pool. Overhead the sky has turned dark and ominous. I negotiate the end of a long line of concrete tank traps, and pause. The sky is now intensely black. I hurriedly change and pull on my waterproofs like a shroud. Everywhere seems eerie. I tie on my hood over my hat and hope it will hold. At last I'm ready, and in one step I am over the Edge and on my final journey, and in that instant the storm breaks.

It is the fiercest of my entire pilgrimage. Walls of water suddenly drop from the sky and gone is my confidence, indeed any visual reference points. It is wipe out. I am plucked and buffeted from behind. Raw gusts of wind propel me into the maelstrom. Poles just appear out of the confusion to help me forward in the nick of time. I try to look round but cannot in the tumult. One pole at a time is all I have. They come like friends out of the chaos. I try to touch them but the water is too deep at their base. I am wading, splashing and trusting, as time moves on and the eager sea moves in. I know my Father owns the world on both sides of this transition. I know my home is in His love and yet even here, as these wooden sentinels affirm my progress, I am unnerved. I have never been here before. I know where I have been and I know roughly where I am going, but here I am utterly alone. Yet it is all right. I am hoping and embracing the unknown and am drawn on.

And now things are changing. The sand is more firm. I see ahead clumps of samphire and some marshy grass. The storm subsides and I can see in the distance the misty outlines of the Holy Place of my dreams. Already I sense the glow of arrival and soon hands will be outstretched towards me, David, Ray, Gillian and Frances … Allister, Rachel, Elizabeth and Tom. I am Home and at home – among God's people.

Through my life, through my coastline journey and through this trial of passing over, two things have kept me going: I have known where I was going and I have known Who would be there to greet me.